392.5

WHEN YOU MARRY

WHEN YOU MARRY

Evelyn Millis Duvall, PH.D.

Reuben Hill, PH.D.

with chapters in collaboration with

Sylvanus M. Duvall, PH.D.

REVISED FOR OLDER TEENS

ASSOCIATION PRESS   NEW YORK

Cartoons drawn by

WYNCIE KING and HUGH DEVINE

THIS edition of *When You Marry* is specifically adapted for modern teen-agers. Since its original edition it has enjoyed seventeen years of successful experience among college age young people at the threshold of marriage. Now, in recognition of the maturity of today's high school-agers, it has been shaped to fit their needs and interests.

Ninth and tenth graders are now, in many ways, as mature as graduating seniors were twenty years ago, according to studies of adolescent development over the years. In experience, interests, dreams and plans, today's teen-agers are far more grown up than many adults realize. Boys are asking questions their own fathers never put into words. Girls are grappling with life's most difficult problems while they are still in school. In many a community, concerns about love, sex, courtship, and marriage loom large in the minds of teachers, counselors, parents, and other adults who work with young people.

Unfortunately, studies show that these are the questions that most young people cannot talk over freely with their parents. Yet these are areas of central importance for the individual's well-being, and for the future of the family, central unit of our society. So, the Golden Anniversary White House Conference on Children and Youth recommended without question that family life education in schools, churches, and community agencies be strengthened to prepare today's youth for the homes of tomorrow. This book is designed to help fulfill such a purpose.

As in the editions that have preceded this, *When You Marry* pioneers in forthright functionality. By *functional education* we mean the education that begins with the interests, needs, and known readiness of the student, geared to assist him in finding answers to his questions. As his interests grow, so does the breadth of coverage, in ever-widening circles. Functional education is clearly distinguished from the traditional academic approach which customarily starts with the historical backgrounds of the problem and the theoretical concepts employed, only incidentally getting around to the student's current interests and questions — and usually late in the course sequence if at all.

Our philosophy, expressed in the content and the format of previous editions of *When You Marry*, is that love, marriage, and family life do not need to be dull. We gear into the motivations that lie latent in the universal interest in men and women, their loves and problems, their interactions and plans in dating, courting, getting married, and raising a family. From the lift of the kick-off cartoon and its human interest questions, through every chapter, written to be readable, with frequent illustrations, graphic presentations, and subtitles, the design is *reader-centered*. Check tests are located to help the reader check his comprehension of the material as he goes along. Teachers report that new units of work are effectively introduced by the stimulus of such a self-test device and/or an appropriate illustration. Each cartoon depicts a problem situation that the student may view more objectively for having caught it visually. Flashed on a screen or copied on a blackboard, cartoons become live material for discussion.

Research, surveys, and education in marriage and family life have grown tremendously in the past two decades. A wealth of new data, new concepts, and new insights now undergird generalizations about personal, marriage, and family relationships. Not all the facts are in, but teen-agers today can tap helpful resources in social science research as they explore such questions as, "What is expected of me on a date?," "How can I know when I am really in love?," and "Will mine be a happy marriage?"

By this time our debt to others who have blazed the trails that we follow and who have encouraged us in our pioneering is too great to spell out in detail. We appreciate more than we can enumerate the thousands of colleagues, friends, and students who have encouraged, assisted, and prodded us through the years. Their criticisms arising out of their experience in using the earlier editions have played a major part in the focussing of this edition of *When You Marry*.

We reaffirm our faith in the collaborative process. It is truly creative for those rugged enough to take it. This new edition is much the richer for the mature contributions of both of our growing families that in the intervals between the various revisions have completed several stages of the family life cycle.

When You Marry represents the active participation of two whole families, who jointly dedicate this book to growing families everywhere.

Evelyn Millis Duvall
Reuben Hill

$\mathcal{F}$OREWORD TO THE FIRST EDITION

THIS book, exemplifying the functional approach to teaching marriage and family living, is timely. American youth by the hundreds of thousands are concerned as never before with problems of adjustment. The hasty marriages of wartime, disturbing wartime experiences, and separation of husbands and wives have created problems of personal and marital readjustment which are taxing all our resources of knowledge, research, and skill in education and counseling. Equally important are the problems arising from the great number of marriages, as hostilities cease, of couples already engaged and of others who have postponed marriage.

While there are several excellent books already available on preparation for marriage, this new volume combines several distinctive features which make it particularly helpful. First, it presents the findings of recent research in several pertinent disciplines as they have practical application to the many adjustments to marriage and family living. Each chapter begins with the questions young people raise in the area to be discussed, and the material that follows is organized in the light of these concrete problems rather than in the traditional fashion. Any valid research finding, regardless of the specific scientific field of its origin, is applied to that particular problem in personal-family adjustment which it is most helpful in solving.

Second, the readable and lively style of the book makes it usable not only for students of the family but also for all young people personally interested in getting married. Illustrations as visual aids are especially helpful in clarifying the material discussed and in focusing attention on major concepts. Numerous tests throughout the book are designed to assist the reader in self-checking his progress in comprehension. All in all, the book is admirably designed as an integral course in a program of general education; for use in discussion classes in colleges, schools, churches, settlements, and young people's associations; or as part of a community program of education for marriage and family living.

Third, the book is exceptional in its wide coverage of interrelated fields and in their synthesis into a new educational approach. This quality derives from the interweaving of the backgrounds of experience of the authors and from the unique beginnings of the book in the combined thinking of many educators.

This volume has an interesting and significant history. Its conception occurred in the spring of 1943 when a committee of the American Council on Education was charged with developing a design for general education to meet the interests and the needs of men and women in the armed services.[1] This committee defined general education as "the type of education which the majority of our people must have if they are to be good citizens, parents, and workers,"[2] and it included in the fourteen courses proposed as a basic offering in general education one on Marriage and Family Adjustments.

All fourteen courses were planned to be functional in the triple sense that they were devised to meet felt needs of the individual in preparing him for life, that they had a social emphasis in enabling him to discharge the privileges and obligations of citizenship in a democracy, and that they stressed integration of different fields of knowledge in application to significant life situations.

The Subcommittee on Marriage and Family Adjustments appointed to outline the course in this area consisted of Mrs. Duvall, Dr. Hill, Dr. Oliver Ohmann, then of Western Reserve University, and the writer as chairman. The functional approach undertaken by our committee may be illustrated by quoting from the published report of the statement of objectives of the proposed course on Marriage and Family Adjustments: [3]

General education should lead the individual as a citizen in a free society to think through the problems and to gain the basic orientation that will better enable him to make a satisfactory family and marital adjustment. In order to accomplish this purpose, the student should acquire the following:

A. *Knowledge and understanding of*

    1 The ways in which the American family differs from families in other countries and in earlier times

[1] A *Design for General Education for Members of the Armed Forces,* A Report of the Committee on a Design for General Education (Washington, D. C., American Council on Education, 1944).

[2] Quoted in the report from Earl J. McGrath, "General Education in the Postwar Period," *The Annals of the American Academy of Political and Social Science,* Vol. 231 (1944), p. 74.

[3] A *Design for General Education for Members of the Armed Forces,* pp. 36–38.

2 The trends in American society affecting the structure and functions of the family and the role of women and children in our society

3 The personality make-up of the individual as it affects his relationships to friends and to members of the family

4 The ways in which experiences in family life determine the personality development of the child

5 The effects of the war on love, courtship, marriage, and family life

6 The factors making for success in marriage

7 The development of relationships of friendship and affection: dating, courtship, engagement, and marriage

8 Major family crises and conflicts, and ways of meeting them

9 The biological aspects of reproduction and of prenatal and postnatal care

10 Problems involved in earning and spending the family income

11 Available resources for premarital, postmarital, and family counseling and education

B. *Skills and abilities*

1 Skill in meeting and cultivating members of the opposite sex in wholesome relationships

2 Skill in resolving conflicts, hostilities, rejections, and overattachments

3 Habits of discussion and cooperative planning in family situations

4 Ability to relate oneself and family to the broader relationships of social life, and to become identified with larger causes

5 Ability to discharge parental responsibilities in child rearing

6 Skill in planning ways of meeting the problem of in-laws and other relatives

7 Skill in household management, including the budgeting and spending of the family income

C. *Attitudes and appreciations*

1 Realization and happiness in marriage and family life as a significant value, the achievement of which may be aided by preparation

2 Appreciation of companionship as an essential element in the success of a marriage

3 Recognition of democracy as a way of life to be realized in the family in relations of husband and wife and of parents and children

4 Appreciation of family members as persons with needs and interests of their own

5 Awareness of the importance of the prevention, early recognition, and treatment of marital discord and of behavior problems of children

6 Appreciation of the role of religion in personal and family living

The authors of this book, who had already served as two of the members of the committee that prepared the outline of the course, were asked to prepare a workbook to be used in conjunction with a textbook as the basis of a prospective course in the United States Armed Forces Institute. Although a course in Marriage and the Family has not yet been included in the program of the Institute, the authors were encouraged, by indications of widespread interest in a course with the same objectives for all young people preparing for marriage, to write the present volume.

The authors of *When You Marry* are unusually well qualified by their training and experience to prepare a volume meeting the present pressing needs and concerns of young people. Evelyn Millis Duvall has a thorough background in biology, and has completed her residence requirements for the doctor's degree in the field of human development, which is an integrated program of study including pertinent courses in anthropology, biology, economics, nutrition, psychiatry, psychology, and sociology. As director for eight years of the Association for Family Living she gained an understanding of the problems of young people of all social classes, and of ways of working with them in the discussion of their questions. Dr. Reuben Hill had his graduate training in sociology. Organizer and director for four years of the interdepartmental courses in marriage at the University of Wisconsin, with further experience in the University of South Dakota, Iowa State College, and numerous informal collegiate situations, he has intimate knowledge of the problems of college youth and experience and skill in methods of teaching adapted to their interests.

The authors have brought together their combined training and experience in a collaboration that, through collective thinking, has produced what may be considered a new integration both of material and of point of view. The book possesses a vital down-to-earth quality and, at the same time, scientific soundness and thoroughness that would not otherwise be possible.

Ernest W. Burgess

UNIVERSITY OF CHICAGO

Contents

CONTENTS

ANTICIPATING MARRIAGE

CHAPTER ONE

He didn't learn that out of a book!

WHAT YOU BRING TO MARRIAGE

What makes you YOU?

How can children born and raised in the same family be so different?

Can you hope to reform the person you marry?

How does the past influence the present in your life?

*W*HEN YOU COME TO MARRIAGE, WHAT DO YOU BRING? A NEW wardrobe? A nest egg in the bank? Some furniture you've inherited? A dependent relative or two? A good job and the prospect of advancement? Whatever your tangible assets or liabilities are, there is something even more important: that is *you* as a *personality*, the way you act toward people and the attitudes which you bring to marriage.

The kind of marriage you make depends upon the kind of person you are. If you are a happy, well-adjusted person, the chances are your marriage will be a happy one. If you have made adjustments so far with more satisfaction than distress, you are likely to make your marriage and family adjustments satisfactorily. If you are discontented and bitter about your lot in life, you will have to change before you can expect to live happily ever after.

There was a time when people thought that unhappiness in marriage resulted primarily from a poor choice of a marriage partner, from some mysterious incompatibility in sex adjustment, from money troubles, or in-laws, or religious mix-ups, or some other chance circumstance. Sex is important. Whom you marry also makes a difference. Money troubles and in-law interference and religious differences all are part of the picture. We'll look them all over soon. Right now let's get at the most important consideration, the personality bases for marriage.

What Is Personality?

Personality is not just an endowment which some people have and others lack. You are not born with a good or a bad personality. The attractive sparkle or the unfortunate habits which make you stand out from others are not a coincidence or a gift of the gods. The many aspects of every personality are not accidental, but have causes and often elaborate histories. What makes you *you* depends upon years of responding to life's situations. Your personality is made up of many things: the kind of body you started with, the type of home you were born into, the sort of people you have associated with, the way you have been brought up and the things you have learned, and most important of all, how you have felt and acted about them. Your personality is the sum total of the characteristic ways of feeling, responding, and behaving which determine your place in society.

What You Started With. Although you were not born with a ready-made personality, many of the potentials of your personality were already established at birth. You were born with a certain kind of body: it was fat or thin, strong or weak, active or quiet, responsive or relatively insensitive. Your personality is affected greatly by such factors as energy output, drive, push, and indefatigability. There is a physical basis to personality.

People are born with a capacity for responding to situations with varying degrees of mental alertness. Environment can do little for idiots and similar defectives, but even the poorest surroundings cannot black out the brilliance of a genius. Even though the great majority of us fall somewhere between these two extremes, our capacities are usually so much greater than our use of them that we can get little scientific encouragement for attributing our personal failures to a low IQ. Recent studies have indicated that these native talents of ours are greatly influenced by the stimuli for growth they receive and by our active willingness to cultivate them.

You were born a boy or a girl. This fact has far more than a biological significance. Whether you are going to grow up to be a man or a woman, a husband or a wife, a father or a mother, does not mean nearly as much as does your early acceptance of yourself for what you are. An American girl of today no longer needs to apologize for her sex. In certain societies, however, being born a girl would have meant the end

of her right then and there. Even now, the fifth girl born in a family
of girls longing for a boy cannot be guaranteed the welcome and the
feeling of importance and personal security that a long-sought girl baby
in another family might have. Being born a girl in a family where
mother finds womanhood satisfying, or a boy in a family where father
relishes being a man, adds to the biological heritage of sex the important element of sex acceptance that is so vital for good personal and
marriage adjustment.

Oldest, Youngest, or in Between. You were born into your family with
a special place all your own. No other brother or sister came into and
grew up in the same family constellation that you entered. If you were
the oldest you had a unique place in your parents' life for a period of
time. When younger brothers or sisters came along you were faced
with your first powerful threat of deprivation. You had to share your
parents and your home with the newcomers. Were you the youngest
in a large family? Then yours was inevitably the place of the baby of
the family, with all the others ahead of you in age and size and power
and protectiveness. If you were somewhere between the oldest and the
youngest, yours was the problem of stretching ahead to the older ones,
while you hung back at times to play with those younger than you.
Only children, although not as spoiled as popular opinion so often gen-
eralizes them to be, live in an entirely different family set-up from the
youngster who shares his home life with brothers or sisters. Children
who arrive long after the parents' marriage come into a far more stable
but rigid family than do those who come while parents are still getting
acquainted and getting used to the idea of being married. Where and
when you came into your family gave you a unique place with its own
assets and liabilities.

Your Status in the Community. You were born with a place in the community. By being a member of your family, you shared their status in
the neighborhood, the community, and the world. As a child in a
minister's home in the Middle West, or of a tenant farmer's family in
Georgia, or of an old-line Boston family, you took on the distinctive
marks of their particular way of living and became a citizen of their
world. Being born across the tracks or on the hill, being born a Negro
or a white, an Oriental or an Indian, coming from parents whose home-
land is far away or from folk whose forebears migrated to this country

several generations ago, makes a difference in the status of the individual within the community.

SOME SOCIAL CLASS DIFFERENCES

Working class people drop out of school earlier [1]
Middle class people get more education [1]

Working class people go to work sooner [2]
Middle class people start work later at more highly skilled levels [2]

Working class people wean babies at later ages [2]
Middle class people wean babies earlier [2]

Working class people toilet train babies later [2]
Middle class people toilet train babies earlier [2]

Working class people expect their children to be neat, clean, and "manner-able" (traditional conception) [3]
Middle class people more frequently want their children to grow at own rate, to learn, to be happy (developmental conception) [3]

Working class people believe mother's job is to wash, cook, clean, and keep house [3]
Middle class people more often say that a good mother should put emphasis on development of children and self [3]

Working class people have fewer troubles but weather them less well [4]
Middle class people have more troubles but weather them better [4]

Working class people are more promiscuous before marriage [5]
Middle class people have less premarital sex intercourse [5]

Working class people are more direct in sex response [5]
Middle class people have less direct sex response, more petting [5]

[1] W. Lloyd Warner, Robert J. Havighurst, and Martin Loeb, *Who Shall Be Educated?* (New York: Harper, 1944).

[2] W. Allison Davis and Robert J. Havighurst, *Father of the Man* (Boston: Houghton Mifflin, 1947).

[3] Evelyn Millis Duvall, "Conceptions of Parenthood," *American Journal of Sociology* (November, 1946), LII, No. 3, pp. 193–203.

[4] Earl Lomon Koos, "Class Differences in Family Reactions to Crises," *Marriage and Family Living* (Summer, 1950), XII, No. 3, pp. 77–78.

[5] Alfred C. Kinsey, Wardell B. Pomeroy, and Clyde E. Martin, *Sexual Behavior in the Human Male* (Philadelphia: Saunders, 1948), Chap. 10.

With Better Home, School, Medical Care,
Johnny Could Have Been Jimmy

From *The Races of Mankind* by Ruth Benedict and Gene Weltfish (Public Affairs Committee, Inc.)

Research studies such as those reported in sum on page 6 have been numerous in the twentieth century. They show clearly that each of us has a given status in the community that we recognize and that those who know us place us in; and that furthermore, much of what we do and think and feel and want and become is determined in part by the social class to which we belong.

Many of us become aware early in childhood of distinctions in status and try to better our situation. The wife who nags her husband to make something of himself, the husband who insists upon his wife getting into a smart social set, the couple sacrificing to get ahead, all are driven to be better off than they are. Often the reason for selecting a certain marriage partner may be little more than that he or she is a means of stepping up the social ladder, as those who joke about marrying the boss's daughter so well recognize. The drive to climb the social ladder is a motivating force and is often the basis of ambition and the source of conflict.

Becoming Human. We learn the fundamentals of social living through interaction with other people. We learn from them how to get and eat food, how to get around, to use tools and machines, to respond to people and act appropriately in many situations. These learnings would not be possible, of course, without the essential biological equipment which it takes to be human. Consider the house cat — he lives for years in close association with people, yet he grows old and dies — still a cat. Even though a fond mistress dubs him one of the family, he is forever limited by the fact that his own parents were feline and is thereby classed forever in the cat family regardless of his residence.

Many of our assets as persons come to us as members of the human family. We walk upright; our hands have amazing dexterity; our eyes and the flexibility of our bodies make it possible for us to know what is going on; we have voices that are the last word in communication and ears that are built for good reception; we have good heads on our shoulders and a long childhood in which to learn the complexities of human behavior. All these and more are ours, simply because we were born with human potentialities.

But it takes more than biological inheritance to make us truly human. Studies of children reared away from human society reveal that we obtain a great many of our characteristics from associating with other human beings. Gesell [6] has told us of a baby girl who strayed from her mother early in her infancy and lived for years in a friendly wolf den. When she was brought back to human society, she could not walk upright or talk or laugh or express affection or carry on any of the human activities which we take for granted in human children. She howled and prowled like a wolf in the stillness of the night and until her death acted more like a wolf than a child.

Another study [7] indicates that isolation from human companionship results in marked backwardness and deprives the child of the opportunities of learning those roles and habits which we think of as making up personality: the ways of responding to situations, the habits and feelings which make human personality unique. Such evidence supports the established theory of personality development, that personality develops mainly through contact and communication with other persons.[8]

You bring to marriage the particular set of habits and customs of your home-town folk. A child of the Tennessee mountains learns the ways of the hills and brings those patterns to marriage. The city child

        [6] Arnold Gesell, "Biography of a Wolf-Child," *Harper's Magazine* (January, 1941).
        [7] Kingsley Davis, "Extreme Social Isolation in a Child," *American Journal of Sociology*, Vol. 45, pp. 554–565.
        [8] This concept of personality development has been developed through the first five decades of the twentieth century by a number of students, notably, C. H. Cooley, *Human Nature and the Social Order* (1902), *Social Organization* (1909); John Dewey, *Human Nature and Conduct* (1922), *Experience and Nature* (1925); George H. Mead, *Mind, Self, and Society* (1934); and Ellsworth Faris, *The Nature of Human Nature* (1937).

learns another set of folkways and operates in conformity to them. By and large the freer the communication with the greater number of people, the more elaborate is the personality development and the more complex the marriage relationship.

CHECK YOURSELF   There are correct and incorrect ways of using the term "personality." Check each of the following statements as true or false according to the description of personality used by the authors in this chapter.

_____ 1 Personality is a kind of inherited charm.

_____ 2 Anyone who wants to can be a fascinating personality.

_____ 3 Some people are born with personality.

_____ 4 Your personality is the sum total of the characteristic ways of behaving, feeling, and responding that determine your place in society.

_____ 5 Everyone is born with the same chance for developing a lovely personality.

_____ 6 Brothers and sisters should rightly have the same kind of personality since they are born into the same family.

_____ 7 If you had been born a member of the other sex you would still have had your same personality.

_____ 8 In the last analysis every personality is self-made.

_____ 9 Personality grows out of family living and rubbing elbows with people outside the family.

_____ 10 All you have to do is take a course in charm to become the kind of personality you would like to be.

★ KEY   True: 4, 9   False: 1, 2, 3, 5, 6, 7, 8, 10 ★

Who Am I?

As soon as a child learns the difference between "I" and "others," he begins to explore the question, "Who am I?" [9] This adventure into the self continues throughout the lifetime of the person, coloring many of his actions and determining much of his personality. When the child is still very small he learns that he feels different in different situations, and that people expect him to behave and to be different as the occasion demands. He may be messy with his sand but not with his pudding. He may hit a ball but not his baby sister. He may urinate but only in prescribed places. Although there is some agreement among

[9] For more extensive treatments of the rise of the self, see Kimball Young, _Personality and Problems of Adjustment_ (New York: Appleton-Century-Crofts, 1952), and Erik Erikson, _Childhood and Society_ (New York: Norton, 1950).

his family about such things, in other areas he finds a considerable variety of treatment. He may be mother's darling baby and be expected to be sweet, cuddly, and affectionate when he is with her. His father may expect him to be a little man, keeping a stiff upper lip when he is hurt, not being soft or mushy but showing a sturdy self-control. To his older sister he may be a pest who will very probably be naughty, get into her things, and play the role of general nuisance. To his Sunday school teacher he may be the little angel who passes the hymn books and sings on key. The children next door may run when they see him coming because he is so rough when he plays with them. To each of these people he is a different person. All of these roles are part of his rapidly developing personality. This multiplicity begins early in his development, and its elaboration as he grows older makes for the familiar contradictions of personality. These earlier impersonations, assumed in the child's first experience with people in the family, set the general outlines of the behavior which he brings to marriage. If his family love him and make him feel like a big boy capable of doing great things and being a fine acceptable person, he will be able to make a more successful adjustment in his marriage. If, on the other hand, in his early experiences he is made to feel that he is dirty, bad, inferior, he may carry these feelings of unworthiness right into marriage and beyond, unless he is helped along the way to a more adequate acceptance of himself.

Masculinity-Femininity Learnings. You were born male or female, but you learn to be masculine or feminine.[10] The first are biological inheritances; the second are ways of behaving as a member of a sex group. The masculine or feminine habits are learned first in childhood and become more and more complicated as the child grows into adulthood and gets ready to be married.

People used to say that children imitate adults. Now it seems that something stronger than imitation is at work impelling them so wholeheartedly to take over the behavior of others. As an individual finds people who embody the characteristics that he is seeking for himself, he tends to become deeply attached to them and tries out their ways of behavior. This process of identification starts very early in childhood. As the little boy admires the superior strength and power of his father,

---

[10] See Amram Scheinfeld, *Women and Men* (New York: Harcourt, Brace, 1944), and Margaret Mead, *Male and Female* (New York: Morrow, 1949).

he identifies himself with him and acts out his own interpretation of the grown-up man. He throws out his chest and struts like his daddy. He wears his father's hat and rubbers. He sits in daddy's chair with daddy's pipe in his mouth. He opens the door for his mother as he sees his father do, kisses her good-by, plays the man of the house as he senses the part to be, and acts out through the years the patterns of masculinity he sees his father following.

Similarly, little girls trot around after their mothers, wanting to wipe dishes when mother does, helping to sweep and dust, talking over the telephone in the same tone of voice, and often telling the same little stories that they hear mother telling. A little girl goes through the many motions of being a mother as she disciplines her dolls, dresses up, goes calling, and puts on tea parties. She takes over many of her mother's attitudes toward the man of the house and often openly welcomes her mother's absence so that she can set the table and take care of father. All this time she is building the basic attitudes of her role as a woman which she is to bring to marriage.

In childhood we begin to practice being the kinds of men and women we are to become, and at the same time begin to formulate our ideas and feelings about what we can expect of others. A girl who is fond of her strong, protective daddy develops a faith in men parallel to the fear of men which is learned by the girl whose father is harsh. The boy whose mother is kind, encouraging, and loving is a great deal more likely to appreciate women than is the man who fears them because his masculinity was undermined by a mother too ready to punish him. We learn out of our experience with these first adults both what seems to be expected of us as members of our sex and what we feel we can expect of people in general.

People do what is expected of them, if they can. The lad who is told that little boys don't cry when they are hurt, that boys must fight for their rights, who sees his father confirming these lessons in his actions, is learning what it means to be a man. If his father is a ne'er-do-well and if his mother and other influential persons try to teach him to be different by scolding him for being "just like your father," he faces the difficult task of choosing which type of man he is going to be — the type he has been identifying himself with, his real father, or the type he is being urged to become, the opposite of his father.

Our conception of the ideal woman is changing so rapidly girls can't be blamed for being confused. The girl who sees her mother getting what she wants by crying for it, and being comforted in her tears, learns that it is all right for a girl to cry; indeed, that it is the way to get along as a woman. Then as she grows older and begins to admire other women who get their satisfactions through rugged determination or more straight-forward approaches, she perceives other ways of playing the feminine role. Her choice of the kind of woman she is to become depends first of all on the type of person she is, where her deepest satisfactions lie, and how she is rewarded and punished as she tries first one and then another pattern. Many girls find it impossible to select from the contradictory alternatives a feminine role with which they can be happy. Happy is the girl who knows the kind of woman she wants to be before marriage, because it is in marriage that femininity receives its greatest test.

Our Human Needs

Certain universal hungers run through the course of human living. So powerful and so insistent are these that they cannot be denied without distorting or impoverishing the personality. These needs have been widely discussed and frequently catalogued. Whatever they are called or however they are listed, they remain the great universal needs that are sought by human beings everywhere.

Our physical needs announce themselves so specifically and unmistakably that they are widely recognized. The need for food is recognized immediately by feelings of hunger. Need for water manifests itself promptly in thirst. Organic demands for rest, exercise, elimination, relief from pain and tension, tolerable temperature, and oxygen vary in the intensity and specificity of their manifestations, yet are quite generally understood. Our attitude toward these physical needs is one of general acceptance. When we are hungry we eat, when tired we sleep, when thirsty we drink, all without embarrassment or defense.

Emotional requirements are neither so well recognized nor so accepted. Deprivations of emotional satisfactions may not show up immediately, and when they do they may appear in any one of many highly individual forms. Behavior directed toward satisfaction of emotional needs is often subtly indirect rather than obviously direct. It usually looks toward *persons* rather than toward *things*. Hence, it is more difficult to understand and to accept.

A hungry man eats without question. But an affection-starved fellow may aggressively demand attention, or he may hit his child who seems to be directing his wife's attention away from himself, or he may sulk or argue or slam out of the door or throw a temper tantrum; he may refuse to eat, or, rarely, he may take the more direct approach and cuddle up to be kissed. Any or all of these behavior expressions of his needs may be unrecognized or ignored by all but the highly sensitive wife. Indeed, he may be further deprived by being punished for actions not acceptable to his wife. So his hunger goes unsatisfied, and he, just as needful as before, makes his adjustment around his deprivation. Prolonged or intense neglect of emotional hungers distorts the personality. Patterns of hostility or discouragement or both develop when the person feels chronically that he must fight for what he wants in a hostile world.

Learning to recognize and meet satisfactorily the emotional needs of each other is a challenge for married couples. Although there are differences among individuals, two types of emotional needs are so universal that they are common to all of us: the need for love and the need for a sense of personal worth.

We Need Love. Love is not just an adornment of life about which we sing and toward which we turn as we begin to go dating. We need love throughout all our lives. Love is as necessary for us as are sunshine and fresh air for the tomato. With love and full acceptance we flourish, and grow strong and happy; without them we develop fears and other symptoms of ill health. As Dr. Benjamin Spock says [11] "this is not just sentimental talk. It is a fact that infants who have long been starved for company and affection . . . may wither in body and spirit. They lose all joy in doing things and seeing people. . . . Such tragedies are rare. But they prove that love is as vital as calories. . . ."

Children recognize many ways of being loved. They warm to mother's words of approval and try even harder to be worthy of her love. They watch for signs of affection on the faces of those around them and direct most of their activities toward winning and holding adult com-

[11] Benjamin Spock, M.D., Keynote Address, Midcentury White House Conference on Children and Youth, Washington, 1950.

mendations. Their need for reassurance is most evident, however, when they have done something wrong or when they are sick or hurt.

The need for love is so strong that half-way measures rarely satisfy. We often hear a mother tell her child, "Mother loves you when you are good." She little realizes when she does this that she is threatening the child with the withdrawal of her love. Vulnerable as he is, the child will hang on tenaciously or abandon his struggle for her love completely, since it is withdrawn so easily. Actually, every child needs the affection of his parents whether or not he has earned it. When he is bad or when he displeases them he needs their love more than ever. Being loved for what he *is* rather than for what he *does* makes him feel included and reassures him that he belongs no matter what.

Adolescents pass through many love-hungry days yearning for a more adult variety of love than is available. The satisfactions of earlier days are no longer so accessible. As legs grow long, the snuggling and cuddling forms of loving are no longer feasible. Adolescents dodge their mothers' caresses at the time when they want them most, and protest their sisters' kisses with a vigor which implies their need for love. Yet it will be years before they are permitted the full affectional responses of adults in marriage. Adolescence is a period of striving for affection and acceptance characterized by inconsistency and frustration. (See the discussion of adolescent-parent interaction in Chapter Fourteen.)

Adults are more fortunate in finding the means of satisfying their need for love. Within the intimacies of marriage and in the parent-child relation there is opportunity to supply the strongest wishes for intimate response. There is, however, a two-way quality to love that is essential for complete fulfillment. It isn't enough to be loved; one must feel free to love others without fear of being rebuffed. Members of the minority groups in America, Negroes, Indians, Orientals, and others, may be loved by their intimate friends but find themselves so inhibited in affectional expressions outside their own circles that they feel chronically deprived. Likewise, unattractive persons fight the haunting fear of not being fully acceptable and may suppress their friendly tendencies toward others after many uncomfortable rebuffs. Men and women fearing that their expressions of interest in the other sex may be misinterpreted as philandering suppress them so completely that their full needs for response often go unsatisfied. A few unusually emancipated persons respond so forthrightly to others that they are able to express their affection for many persons without being misunderstood or misinterpreted. Most people today are much more forthright in expressing their feelings toward each other than was true at the turn of the century. In many ways this is a good trend that should be encouraged.

These patterns of affectional response are learned throughout a person's lifetime. The general outlines are laid down in childhood when the person first begins to respond to others. If his responses are accepted and reciprocated he learns that it is safe and good to love and be loved, and as he grows older his skills in being warm and friendly increase. As he is neglected or abused or ignored or repelled, he shrinks back into himself or lashes out toward others in ways that protect his hurt ego but fail to satisfy his need. Later reassurances from friends, sweethearts, and mate can gradually rekindle his desire to respond fully and freely again, but the retraining period is often long. The emotionally starved individual is rarely a good marital risk; for even though he needs love desperately, he has been without it so long that his own defenses are apt to repudiate it. The art of loving is learned through years of practice in loving and being loved. And like the starving man who cannot assimilate a full meal at once but must be fed slowly, in small quantities, so the emotionally deprived must be patiently reconditioned to full adult love. Grandmother recognized that she shouldn't marry a man to reform his habits. Today it is known that marrying an unhappy, lonely person in the hope of making him or her happy is equally discouraging. The old patterns of adjusting are so deeply entrenched that only exceptional skill and infinite patience can bring about satisfactory reconditioning.

In summary, we see that we all need to love and to be loved. The expression of this need changes as we mature and as we learn more satisfying ways of meeting it. We may or may not express directly the desire to be loved. Our affectional hungers often go unmentioned and unsatisfied only to betray themselves in inappropriate tantrums and excessive demands on others. But the ability to love fully and genuinely is so important that those married partners who have mastered it find fundamental satisfactions in their marriage that other less skilled persons lack, regardless of how well they may be matched otherwise.

We Need a Sense of Personal Worth. A need which parallels the need for love is the desire to feel that one is worthy of respect. Other people set the standards by which self-appraisal is made, but it is pretty much up to the individual to say which of the goals shall be his to attain. Whatever the realm of achievement may be, he needs to feel that he is a growing, progressing person.

In infancy there is ample evidence of rapid growth and motor development. The first undirected leg and foot movements are preliminary to those which propel the baby across the floor in creeping movements. That first thrilling moment when, by holding onto a chair, he first stands erect and looks his world over from the vertical rather than the horizontal plane is but the threshold of the adventure of learning to walk. Motor development is remarkable — creeping, walking, jumping; riding a tricycle, a scooter, a bicycle; then the first exciting attempts at the wheel of the family car!

Building skills also bring their satisfactions. Whether the media be cookie dough or soft pine lumber, clay or engine parts, erector sets or radio equipment, the satisfaction of making something spurs us on and brings to many a keen sense of progress. While one child finds his satisfaction in using his hands and in getting around, another may find greater pleasure in precocious mental achievements. The Quiz Kids are not only unusually bright youngsters; every one of them has grown up in a home where learning has brought unusually keen satisfactions.

Evidence of the need to feel growth is seen in the popularity of such mental sparring games as quiz shows, popular versions of psychological tests, and crossword puzzles. The reason that many men keep golf scores so religiously is that the opportunity to measure their present performance with some past achievement gives them pleasure. To feel the power of growth within oneself is a magnificent sensation. To look over the past five or ten years and see how far one has come in the ability to get along with people, in the development of a satisfying hobby, in performance in one's business or profession, gives keen satisfaction that is its own reward.

The lack of this sense of personal worth is seen in the multitude of weary-eyed wanderers who, losing faith in themselves, lose faith in others and in life itself. The beaten, hangdog attitude which anticipates failure more often than not finds it. On the other hand, the man who brings to marriage the rewards of years of achievement and growth brings with him the faith that he can work out marriage adjustments as they arise, an attribute to weigh heavily in married life.

When Our Needs Aren't Met. Life rarely gives any one of us all we want or need to be completely satisfied. What we do when our needs are not met the psychologist calls *mechanisms*. These modes of adjustment are for the most part substitutive, and rest on willingness to accept something less than the real thing. There are two general types, escape and the defense mechanisms.

The *escape mechanisms* are all characterized by displacement of attention away from the unhappy situation which produced the frustration, and are most frequently carried over from childhood patterns of adjustment. The schoolboy expresses the values of escape when he chants, "He who ducks and runs away lives to duck another day." The trouble is that running away becomes a habit and takes up more time and emotional energy than the original situation warranted. There are some crises from which one should escape, but they are far fewer than our poorly trained emotions would have us believe. Standing up to life, understanding what the problem is and accepting it, develops the mental stamina which is needed in marriage. Escape mechanisms enable the individual to alleviate the pain of frustration temporarily but do nothing about meeting his long-time needs. There are many forms of escape, the most frequent of which are:

1 Daydreaming or fantasy, in which the problem is solved by forgetting it; building air castles in which there are no problems of any consequence.
2 Walking out on the problem or running away from it, refusing to talk about it, passing the buck.
3 Retiring into oneself, being with the group but not of it, developing seclusiveness, withdrawing from contacts.
4 Regressing to infantile levels, backsliding to simpler or earlier forms of behavior which brought attention and satisfaction: bed-wetting, thumb sucking, temper tantrums, refusal to eat, and so on.
5 Becoming sick, developing illnesses that come from mental more than physical causes: headaches, stomach troubles, tics, and other troubles which enable the afflicted to run away from some difficulty.

The *defense mechanisms* are modes of adjustment by which the person bolsters himself when he feels threatened or inadequate. The individual is faced with a need, but as he reaches out to satisfy it he is frustrated by an obstacle or force which proves too great for him. Instead of making a direct attack on the obstacle he allows himself to be maneuvered into taking something less than the real thing; he may pretend he didn't want the need satisfied anyway, or may even deny the existence of the need. The defense mechanisms all have one generic factor in common: they all enable the individual using them to prove to himself that there is nothing wrong with him and that the entire blame for his difficulties can be placed elsewhere. The defense mechanisms most frequently observed include:

1 Compensation, making up for a lack by overworking one's strengths, attaining satisfaction by enjoyment in a substitutive activity.
2 Rationalization, giving "good" excuses for one's behavior instead of the real ones, justifying and defending mistakes as if they were wise decisions. Rationalization is accomplished in a variety of ways:
   a. Being a Pollyanna, pretending that everything is wonderful.
   b. Taking a sour-grapes attitude, pretending you don't want to succeed.
   c. Projecting your failure on others, seeing in them the weakness you are trying to cover up in yourself.
3 Negativism, resisting domination, a common form of defending oneself.

These mechanisms, sometimes conscious, sometimes unconscious solutions to problem situations, are rarely effective, because they are modes of adjustment by subterfuge and substitution and do not really bring the craved satisfactions. Pretending that you don't like boys when you don't have a date doesn't give you a partner for the evening nor prepare you to be more winsome another time. Nor is there any gain in blaming your lack of popularity on your mother, your clothes, or your roommate. Staying in and dreaming about being a pin-up girl with men flocking around you may be one way to spend the evening, but it doesn't get you a date to the prom. Similarly, every other mechanism tends to dodge the really effective ways of reaching the goals that you are striving to attain.

Confident persons develop the conviction that problems lend themselves to solution and choose direct ways of satisfying their needs. They are able to admit to themselves that they are hungry or lonely or angry and then deal with the situation in an acceptable way. The direct approach is learned through success in past forthrightness; it not only brings release for the moment but also establishes the habit of direct satisfaction that assures good marriage adjustment.

Growing Up as a Person

How grown up are you? Are you mature enough for marriage? You may be legally of age, but how about your emotional age? You grow up in many different ways, physically, mentally, and emotionally, and the rate of growth is not uniform. Some growth is regular, predictable, and almost unalterable, whereas some is sporadic and irregular.

Chronologically, one year from today we will be exactly one year older, regardless of what happens. We may suffer a severe illness, move across the country, get married, or just stay put, but nothing will change the regularity of our chronological aging.

Physically our growth within certain broad limits is regular and predictable. Taking into consideration wide individual differences, human development experts can accurately plot the whole timetable of growth from conception through senility. Heredity gets the ball rolling, diet and other environmental circumstances keep it going. Speaking of physical growth only, no man can add a cubit to his stature by willing it.

Mentally we move forward with new experiences and then settle onto plateaus of learning which break as we move on to the next level of growth. This staircase type of development seems to be far more rapid in our infancy when we are busy mastering the fundamentals of communication, locomotion, and general exploration than it is later on. Studies indicate that even while we are at the preschool age, mental growth is affected by our feelings about ourselves and the nature of our surroundings.[12] As we find life challenging and feel that we are able to master it, we learn rapidly and maintain a sustained pattern of mental growth. When we feel stumped or frustrated we may quit trying and stagnate at a level below our true capacity. The indications are that native intelligence is greatly influenced by position in society, by assured opportunities, by where we live and how we interpret life's opportunities. Thus the lower class lad with a high native IQ may not achieve the intellectual growth of an upper middle class fellow with very average native ability, because of the limitations in the values, expectations, and opportunities under which he operates.

Emotionally our growth is highly individual. No other area of growth is more irregular and unpredictable. Some adults are more in-

[12] George Stoddard, *The Meaning of Intelligence* (New York: Macmillan, 1943), pp. 343, 347–392.

fantile emotionally than children whole generations younger. Some emotional responses may develop far ahead of others because habits of responding to situations grow out of experience. Where there are opportunities for learning how to handle a specific situation in competent fashion, the person builds satisfactory emotional habits with regard to it. Because emotional development comes through contacts with others, it can be traced through the stages of social growth that follow.

Stages in Social Growth. As infants we were limited to the hazy world of feelings and sensations. We hadn't been anywhere yet. Our eyes focused poorly. We didn't understand what we heard. All was strange and new and unknown. Our own bodies occupied us entirely at first. We felt hungry and cold and uneasy and lashed out with kicks and screams, our whole squirming body expressing our uneasiness. We expressed our pleasure over food and warmth and a sense of well-being by cooing, gurgling, and kicking out with lusty enthusiasm.

1 *Receiving.* All this time we were entirely on the receiving end of things. We swallowed the milk that was put into our mouths. We slept and wakened and thrashed about without direction or purpose. When we became hungry we were quite intolerant, entirely unaware of the circumstances that made for delays in our feeding. Those first responses to life were explosive. By uncontrolled outcries we demanded our own satisfactions without regard for others. Many of us could point out situations in adult life which evoke the self-centered "gimme" attitude of the infant.

2 *Manipulation.* We were not many weeks old before we learned that there was a relationship between what we did and the satisfactions we enjoyed. We learned that our cries brought mother to comfort us. We discovered that our coos brought father in to play with us. By trial and error we found out what it took to get others to yield to our demands. A little later we developed elaborate systems of teasing, bribing, and coaxing as means of getting people to do what we wanted them to do. One baby learned to depend upon her dimples and sweet ways, while another, feeling less sure that her world was a friendly one, lashed out in temper tantrums when things didn't go her way. The child is supported in any of his manipulations if it is apparent that satisfactions are regularly forthcoming.

Too often adults try to get more of what they want by getting around friends and influencing people. This childish mode of emotional and social adjustment is everywhere apparent both in public and private life, and is evident in the many efforts husbands and wives make to manipulate and control their partners. Fortunately, many children outgrow these attempts to manage others, and before they reach school age are already practicing more grown-up forms of adaptation.

3 *Compromise.* When we were old enough to get hold of toys that belonged to others we trod on their rights, and trouble was brewing. The baby tricks that brought the family to our cradle lost their potency in the rough and tumble of more grown-up family interplay. Mother showed her disapproval of continual wet panties, so we tried to win her smile and avoid her scowl by keeping dry. We sensed the size and strength of our all-powerful parents and tried to win their favor by the kind of behavior they asked of us. Our brothers and sisters had to be won over by some recognition of their rights. If we wanted to play with Jimmy's fire engine, he must be convinced of the desirability of playing with our Kiddie Kar. This familiar "you do this for me and I'll do that for you" type of compromise is more mature than simple manipulation, since it recognizes the values and interests of the other. It is widespread in adult society and runs through much of marital adaptation. Yet it leaves much to be desired in comparison with more cooperative patterns of interaction such as sharing and creative cooperation.

4 *Sharing.* When Jimmy with his fire engine and Johnny with his Kiddie Kar join forces and wheel noisily down the walk in a two-man parade, they are already feeling something that is more fun than merely taking turns and exchanging their equipment. They are beginning to find the satisfactions of sharing which will be rediscovered in games, sports, and other activities that revolve around common values. Playing farmer in the dell and drop the handkerchief may not sound like fun to an adult, but such games were once exciting entrees into sharing with others, a variety of social enjoyment that is not found in solitary activities.

Sharing as a method of social adjustment starts in the family circle and continues on into adulthood. As we learn to note and respect the needs of others and to pool our resources with theirs in the pursuit of mutually satisfying values, we are beginning to enjoy the full richness of interrelationships that may be achieved by emotionally mature adults.

5 *Creative Cooperation.* Beyond the satisfactions of personal sharing lie the rewards of joining forces with others for the pursuit of interests that are bigger than any one of the cooperating partners. The couple that has found the joy of working together in community affairs taps deep wells of satisfaction that quench the thirst of loneliness. The family that lives for something beyond its own immediate wants and throws its resources into creative social projects not only gets more out of life as it goes along, but also helps each of its members attain the kind of maturity that assures them of successful human interrelationships.

Phil and Mary were such a couple. When they finished medical college they married and moved to a Southern mountain community, where they set up a much-needed hospital and clinic service. They worked shoulder to shoulder through the years. As their children came, they too became part of the project. Personal and family disputes were ironed out relatively easily, because there were always more serious things to be done together. One by one the children grew up and went on to college, into marriage, and on into their own vocations. Scattered around the world, they still keep in touch with each other and with the home folks. Phil and Mary had built their marriage on the basis of interest in and devotion to a common purpose. Their children grew up prepared in turn to establish sound marriages, and they found, in the example of their parents, that success in marriage comes from throwing themselves wholeheartedly into meaningful programs outside themselves. Seven new families now carry on the tradition of creative cooperation of losing themselves in something bigger than themselves.

Self-centered people often expect marriage to be a case of "they lived happily ever after." They frequently demand personal satisfactions to the exclusion of the larger needs of the marriage and of themselves. They are often too infantile to lose themselves in values larger than those of the immediate present. Professor Terman [18] in a study of the most frequently mentioned grievances of husbands and wives found most of them to be of the infantile order of social-emotional responses: "selfish and inconsiderate," "complains too much," "not affectionate,"

[13] Lewis M. Terman and associates, *Psychological Factors in Marital Happiness* (New York: McGraw-Hill, 1938), p. 105.

"insincere," "criticizes me," "argumentative," and so on. We conclude from the foregoing that socialization needs to be carried to the level of sharing and creative cooperation to produce personalities that will be best equipped for marriage. Marriage is not child's play but requires the values, habits, and attitudes of adults, and its satisfactions are for those who are emotionally ready to enjoy them.

Fulfillment of Needs through Changing Appetites. Maturity doesn't mean that we are all set. As long as we live we continue to grow. As we develop, our adjustments to others change, as we have just seen. We tend to give more of ourselves and to demand less of others. Yet throughout the whole life span we have needs that other people satisfy.

All living things have to get substances and energies necessary for growth from their surroundings. A tomato plant must have the proper soil and sun and moisture in order to grow at its best. A puppy must be given plenty of chance to suck and to chew, and must be kept warm and allowed to sleep and play, if it is to develop into a healthy, comfortable animal. Children as well as older people have needs that must be satisfied if they are to be healthy, strong, and happy. Many of these needs continue for a lifetime and are common to all people everywhere. Other needs are modified as the person grows older. Food, for instance, is a necessity for everyone, but the form in which it is needed changes with the years. The baby needs carefully prepared milk products that would scarcely satisfy a hungry man who craves a steak. The infant is satisfied with its feeding without table adornments, such as flowers, silver service, candlelight, or linens. The adult builds around his elemental needs for food the need for certain embellishments which tend to become part of the basic requirement. He wants not only the steak, but all the fixings.

The table that follows indicates the way our personality needs change as we develop through childhood and into adulthood. Following the need for intervals of solitude as infants, we develop needs for companionship. To our two or three companions of preschool days we add many more as we get into school; then as adolescents we mingle freely among a great many friends. Similarly our activity needs change from those of the rudimentary interaction of the nonsocialized child to those of the team play and sharing of grown-up activities. Our love needs grow from love of mother to deepening friendships of adolescence by

way of the affection within the family and the group loyalties characteristic of the school years. Our needs for attention change, too, from the
more or less constant care required in infancy. By adolescence we are
ready for the more grown-up forms of attention, such as encouragement,
and reassurance that we can carry on with a minimum of supervision.
The schematic outline of changing needs shown in the accompanying
chart is not to be interpreted rigidly but should be understood as de-
scriptive merely of the stages we attain as personality develops. Likewise, the process of developing from receiving through to cooperating
with others is one that is not determined by age alone. Adults still resort to exchange. We all like to lie back and passively receive at times.

HOW NEEDS CHANGE WITH GROWTH

Infant	Preschool Child	School Child	Adolescent	Adult
		SIGNIFICANT PEOPLE		
Family, espe-cially mother	Two or three playmates and family	Many compan-ions and family	Friends of own age group	Wide variety
		TYPES OF CONTACT		
Solitude and one or two at time	Parallel play	Group games, active play	Boy-girl activities	Many forms
		REQUIREMENTS FROM OTHERS		
Nurturing care (Dependence)	Supervision	Guidance	Encourage-ment in inde-pendence	Affirmation through inter-dependence
		RESPONSE		
Receiving	Exchanging	Sharing	Accommodat-ing	Cooperating

Marriage: The Union of Two Unique Personalities

Preparation for your marriage started before you were born. The planning and the anticipating of your parents had a part in setting the stage
for the kind of personality you have since developed.

As soon as you were born you began to learn about life and about
yourself. You learned that you were important and that people cared
about you by the fondling and attention you received. Your efforts to
grow and do things and become somebody were recognized and encour-

aged. Your mistakes were usually corrected with respect for your need of self-esteem. Your love for mother and father was returned in full measure, and the early jealousies of brothers and sisters gradually diminished. Your talents and abilities were duly pointed out, and your efforts to make something of them were praised. You learned that life was rewarding, and you developed faith in yourself and in your ability to meet it without escape or defense. That aspect of you will approach marriage with courage and eagerness.

There is, however, another part of you as a personality which is not so pleasant. Not all of your life has been equally satisfying and rewarding. You have met defeats and disappointments that have left you feeling small, insignificant, and unworthy. Eating problems in childhood may have left you convinced that you have a weak stomach. Training episodes early in your toddler days have left residues of inadequacy, rebellion, and dirtiness. You received some punishments in your youth which you didn't deserve. A baldheaded neighbor teased you about your hair until you developed a phobia about bald heads and a permanent aversion for those tresses of yours. Your mother was sometimes tired and cross and failed to notice all your hard-earned triumphs. Your father never seemed satisfied with what you did. Your sister was smarter than you and lots quicker, and you never did catch up. You nearly drowned one summer at the lake, and you prickle with fear to this day when you get near water. And so it goes. Some of these situations you recognize and understand and have already learned to take without sidetracking. Others have left their scars without any helpful indication to you of their origin, and they account in part for quirks in your personality that will make married living interesting but difficult.

Marriage is a union of two unique personalities, each with a background and a history. Your marriage partner comes with a peculiarly personal set of patterns and habits for meeting life situations that he has learned in his parental family and elsewhere. He is courteous and pulls out your chair at the table for you, because his mother made so much of such gentlemanly manners when he was younger. But he honks the horn of the car in front of the house like a drugstore cowboy, the pattern he picked up from the fellows at the fraternity house whom he idealized as a frosh. He is a whiz in chemistry; his father and he tinkered with chemistry sets in his basement from the time he was nine. But he's like a big bull in the kitchen, because little boys didn't have any business there when he was most teachable. Add all this together and put in all the other highly individualized responses to people and problems, and do you have your Bill? No, not quite.

Each of you is greater than the sum of all your habits and responses. Each of you operates around a core of feelings and beliefs about yourself. Each of you has a highly individualized personality all your own. Each of you has had a unique childhood and has been influenced in a special way by all the people who have mattered to you since then.

What do you bring to marriage? You bring to marriage all that you have ever been. You bring to marriage your needs and hopes and goals. You come prepared to mean a great deal to your chosen one. Success in your marriage relationship is dependent on bringing to the union the habit of happiness and the capacity to love and to be loved. These are attributes of an emotionally mature personality — the best possible dowry you can bring to marriage.

CHECK YOURSELF   Mrs. B. wants a new fur coat badly. She might use any of several methods to get it from her husband, depending on her stage in the socialization process. Write in for each of the methods listed the levels of socialization represented. Is it *receiving, manipulation, compromise, sharing,* or *creative cooperation?*

_____ 1 John dear, you said you wished I would fix your favorite desserts oftener. Well, I want a new fur coat so badly I'll make them every night for two months if you'll get me one.

_____ 2 We both need new coats this winter, dear. Since our budget is a little tight right now, what do you say if I earn enough extra money to get us each one?

_____ 3 I just had to have a new fur coat right away, so I bought one on your account this afternoon.

_____ 4 If we budget carefully we could have our new baby this year. We both want one much more than I want that new fur coat we were looking at last week.

_____ 5 Other husbands are proud of the way their wives look. Have you seen that beautiful mink coat Mrs. Jones is wearing? Her husband gave that to her just last week. Of course I know that you don't make as much as Harry Jones, but my tastes are so simple. Just a sheared beaver would satisfy little me.

★ KEY   4 Creative cooperation   5 Manipulation
1 Compromise   2 Sharing   3 Receiving

Readings

DUVALL, EVELYN MILLIS, *Family Living* (New York: Macmillan, 1961). Read especially the first four chapters: "What Makes You — You," "Your Development as a Teen-Ager," "How Mature Are You?" "What It Takes to Grow On," in Unit I, given entirely to exploring the personality factors in your growth as a person.

ENGLISH, O. SPURGEON, and CONSTANCE J. FOSTER, *Your Behavior Problems* (Science Research Associates, Inc., 259 East Erie Street, Chicago 11, Illinois, 1952). A wise and understanding psychiatrist helps you understand why you do what you do and how you can work through the problems you are having with yourself.

MENNINGER, WILLIAM C., *Understanding Yourself* (Science Research Associates, Inc., 259 East Erie Street, Chicago 11, Illinois, 1948). The famous Dr. Menninger discusses how you are made psychologically, how your personality has taken shape, and the mechanisms by which all of us operate when we are in tough spots.

MOORE, BERNICE MILBURN, and DOROTHY M. LEAHY, *You and Your Family* (Boston: D. C. Heath and Company, 1953). Chapters 4–8 discuss "Why We Behave as We Do," "Human Beings Learn to Be Human," "Growth Has Its Problems," "Emotions and Everyday Living," and "Emotional Climate and Emotional Habits."

NATIONAL FORUM FOUNDATION STAFF, *Discovering Myself* (Chicago: National Forum Foundation, 1955). Chapters 4–13 talk over such matters as facing disappointment, meeting difficulties, taking success, accepting criticism, being self-conscious, and handling fears and moods.

SMART, MOLLIE STEVENS and RUSSELL COOK, *Living in Families* (Boston: Houghton Mifflin Company, 1958). Husband and wife experts devote several chapters in Unit Two to helping you understand your own development as a person. Read especially Chapters 6, 7, and 8 on "Mental and Emotional Development," "Your Personality Development," and "The Development of a Way of Life."

WARNER, W. LLOYD and MILDRED HALL, *What You Should Know about Social Class* (Chicago: Social Science Research Associates, Inc., 1953). A noted social research worker and his wife tell you how to determine your social class, how your social status affects your life and what you can do about it.

CHAPTER TWO

"How can it be love at first sight?"

ARE YOU IN LOVE?

How do you know it's love?

Can you tell whether it will last?

What about love at first sight?

What are the principles of attraction?

What is the difference between love and infatuation?

$\mathcal{E}$VERYONE HAS IDEAS AND NOTIONS ABOUT LOVE. NOT ALL OF these opinions jibe, however, with what authorities have found about love feelings; so let's pull out what you think you know and see how right you are. Check each of the following statements which you believe to be true. Then compare your replies with those of the authors. If you agree with most of them, you will enjoy the contents of this chapter. If you don't agree with what the investigators believe to be true, read on and see what it is that they are driving at.

? ? ? ? ? ? ? ?   HOW DO YOU KNOW IT'S LOVE   ? ? ? ? ? ? ? ?

_____ 1 When love hits you, you know it.

_____ 2 It is possible to sometimes dislike a person whom you love at other times.

_____ 3 Puppy love is not a real love feeling.

_____ 4 When you are really in love, you just aren't interested in anyone else.

_____ 5 When you fall head over heels in love, it's sure to be the real thing.

_____ 6 There is only one kind of love feeling.

_____ 7 It is quite normal for a person to love several different people at once.

_____ 8 You never love two people in quite the same way.

_____ 9 Love that grows slowly over a long time is not as satisfying as the sudden thunder-and-lightning variety.

_____ 10 Love doesn't make sense. It just *is*.

_____ 11 Once two people find that they love each other, that settles it; they should marry as soon as possible, no matter what.

_____ 12 Love without marriage is a serious tragedy and will probably ruin one's life.

_____ 13 Loving someone besides the one to whom you are married need not wreck your marriage.

_____ 14 Before the average person becomes an adult, he will have loved many people.

_____ 15 Love isn't anything you can study or know anything about; it's too emotional.

Here are the facts:

1 (*Incorrect.*)   Love feelings are of many kinds and only rarely are of the sudden, sure nature indicated in the statement.

2 (*Correct.*)   Not only is it possible, but it is also extremely likely that people who are loved will be disliked in some situations.   Human nature has too many facets to be expected to show only the best one at all times. Disliking loved ones in some situations is a common experience.

3 (*Incorrect.*)   Although puppy love may not be a mature type of love, it nevertheless is a love feeling.   The only trouble with puppy love feelings is that, taken too seriously, they may lead to a dog's life.

4 (*Wrong.*)   Being in love tends to make other persons and things more rather than less lovable.   The truly loving person loves and is interested in most of the people he or she knows well.   If love cut off all other interests, wouldn't it tend to become monotonous?   We'll never know, because love doesn't operate that way.   We have heard, "All the world loves a lover."   The converse is also true, "Lovers love all the world."

5 (*Wrong.*)   Undergoing such tremendous emotional excitement as is referred to in the popular concept of "falling head over heels in love" is not the best indication that the feeling is true and lasting love.   Later in this chapter we will discuss some more reliable love yardsticks.   Will you wait until then for more on this?

6 (*No.*)   Of course not.   There are many, many kinds of love feelings: tenderness, passion, mother love, ecstasy, peaceful security, etc., to name just a few of the contrasting kinds of love feelings.

7 (*Correct.*)   It is normal to love several people at once.   In fact, it is one of the ways that normality is gauged.   Mate love tends to be sexually exclusive, but love in its broader sense is richly inclusive.   Love begets love and normally fosters love feelings.

8 (*Correct.*)   Just as no two persons are identical, so no two combinations of persons can be the same.   The love feelings we have for dear old

friends may be quite different from those we have in an exhilaratingly new relationship. Love for grandpa's sweetness is quite different from the vigorous mate love we feel for a marriage partner, and so on and on through the multitude of combinations possible in a lifetime of warm relationships with hundreds of people.

9 (*Wrong.*) *Satisfying* is the catch. Truly satisfying love relationships are far more apt to be of the long-term, growing variety than of the whoop-whoop-hurrah kind, which frequently dies out like fireworks after a very pretty show.

10 (*Incorrect.*) Generally love makes sense. It is governed by the same natural laws that determine all life. A love has a history that is socially determined and that modifies and directs its present and its future. The person in love may not know why he fell for this particular girl, any more than he may be aware of why he likes certain foods, or what happens to them after he has eaten them, or why they make him strong or sick or fat. But to the scientist, most of these processes are becoming increasingly understandable. So, to some extent, is this mysterious thing called love. Science, which began with a study of the stars in the skies, now is making headway in understanding the stars in lovers' eyes. Investigations tend to show that the laws of attraction are reasonable, reliable, and capable of being understood.

11 (*Incorrect.*) The popular belief in this fallacy is one of the big reasons for so much unhappiness and discord in marriage. There are so many kinds of love feelings that a person who takes this position seriously finds himself in emotional hot water most of the time. Chasing down every tempting trail after a new marriage partner is an exhausting experience.

12 (*Nonsense.*) Can you see why from the answer to the previous question? And isn't it slightly dreary to think that all of life outside of marriage must be completely devoid of warmth?

13 (*Correct.*) We've really been answering this all along, haven't we? Marriages are not so often wrecked by love as by the lack of it!

14 (*Surely.*) We all begin to love before we are out of our cradles; our own toes and fingers, our mothers, our dads, our sisters and brothers, the boy next door, the kindergarten teacher, the scout master, the new girl in second grade, Uncle Louis-who-always-brings-candy, the cub scout troop (all nineteen of them), the girl in the pink sweater, the boy who walked us home from the party — all these and many more have come in for a share of our loving. Indeed, by the time most of us are adults, we are old hands at the game of love!

15 (*No!*) If it were true, why bother with a study like this? Many successful investigations have been carried out and a great deal of information has been made available already. And that's what the rest of this chapter is going to deal with. Besides, who said that emotions cannot be understood? The way we feel about things makes some sense when we know something of the principles of human behavior in the same way that the workings of electricity become predictable to the engineer who knows what to expect. So let's see what we know about love. . . .

What Is Love?

Love is not easy to define. It is a word that covers many feelings. We may feel good, or we may feel very blue, all because we are in love. We may be tenderly protective or lustily aggressive; we may work furiously or daydream for weeks; we may worship devotedly or exploit hungrily; we may give or we may take — all in the name of love!

Love may look like its opposite, hate, when its face is distorted with vanity, possessiveness, or jealousy. One big difference between love and hatred is that love is an irradiation. It flows outward from the loving person in a warm current of feeling toward others generally. Hate, on the other hand, tends to focus on the hated one with heavy concentration. There are no more perfect loves than there are perfect persons. But, as Sidney Harris [1] says, it is the direction and not the degree that is most important. Love turned outward can always grow. Turned inward or concentrated too intensely on one object, love cannot survive its own stagnation. It seems to be this growth factor in love that assures its permanence. As Magoun so ably defines love:

Love is the passionate and abiding desire on the part of two or more people to produce together conditions under which each can be and spontaneously express his real self; *to produce together an intellectual soil and an emotional climate in which each can flourish,* far superior to what either could achieve alone." [2] (Italics ours)

Love then is fulfillment through healthy growth with and for another. It is self-realization in an atmosphere conducive to human growth. It is an emotional response to others who meet our basic personality needs. [3] Two people in love so mutually meet each other's needs that they both thrive in their "togetherness" more fully than could either alone. In this sense love grows as the personality develops, and is capable of ever-changing, ever-deepening, ever-widening involvement.

Self-Love and Outgoing Love. The Greeks had two words for love — *eros* and *agape. Eros* tends to center in sexual love. It is that love for another that comes spontaneously and longs to be reciprocated. [4] It is

[1] Sidney Harris, "Strictly Personal," *Chicago Daily News* (February 2, 1952), p. 10.
[2] F. Alexander Magoun, *Love and Marriage* (New York: Harper, 1956), p. 7.
[3] Robert Winch, *The Modern Family* (New York: Holt, 1952), Chap. 15.
[4] Esther Adams, "Eros and Agape," *Marriage Guidance* (August, 1950), pp. 6–7.

possessive and demanding. We have called it the "orange squeezer" type of love that is implied when one says "I love oranges," in which the emphasis is on one's own appetite and not concerned with the fate of the orange! Erotic love wants something in return and if frustrated may turn to hate. This is the "hell has no fury like a woman scorned" [5] brand of love . . . primarily self-love.

Agape, in contrast, cannot be frustrated because it is not demanding. It is outgoing, overflowing joy in fellowship. Its pleasure is in being and in giving. It releases the freedom of cooperation that people find in thinking, yearning, developing, and achieving together. This is the kind of love that inspires the full giving of oneself freely to causes and purposes beyond oneself. It is close to the truth that Jesus described when he said, "He who loses his life shall find it." (Matthew 10:39)

There are satisfactions of personal needs in every marriage, often rich and intense. But if there is nothing more to it than satisfying selfish needs, the marriage will not and cannot endure; for as soon as someone else appears who seems able to give more satisfaction, the partner is tossed out like last week's newspaper. Love that lasts involves a real and genuine concern for others as persons, for their values as they feel them, for their development and growth. As time goes by, those we love become increasingly dear to us. We watch their progress with joy. We are saddened by their sufferings and disappointed with them in their mistakes. Because we love them, we are able to lose some of our petty selfishness in thoughts and actions directed beyond ourselves. This outgoing type of love has capacities for infinite variety and for satisfying deep hungers within us. This is the love that builds a strong, enduring marriage.

Principles of Attraction. Very few of us know just why we like the people to whom we are attracted; our likes and dislikes are not rational or planned. The people we like are not always the folk that the social scientist would recommend for us as companions, either for a lifetime or for a few months. Yet these little-understood forces of personal attraction wield a mighty weight in the process of falling in love and getting married, and often overshadow more rational and sensible considerations in the choice of a wife or husband.

[5] "Heaven has no rage like love to hatred turned,
   Nor hell a fury like a woman scorned."
         Congreve — *The Mourning Bride*, Act III, Scene 8.

Some of the unconscious tendencies that determine our preferences for people are these:

1 We tend to like the people and the things that remind us of pleasant and comfortable experiences in our past, many of which go way back into our early childhood and are forgotten except for the powerful, unconscious role they continue to play in our choices. "I loved him the minute I set eyes upon him."

2 We tend to be repulsed by the people and the things that are associated with uncomfortable and unpleasant experiences in our past. The original painful experience may be no longer remembered, but its influence continues to deflect us from anything and anybody that resembles some aspect of that unhappy situation. "Don't ask me why, I just don't like her."

3 We tend to be attracted to those people who reassure us, do not make us feel less worthy or less able or attractive than we like to think we are. "She's just too smart to suit me," or "I can't stand him, he's always so *superior*," and "She makes me feel as though I am somebody."

4 We tend to seek the people who are considered attractive by those around us and to leave the unsought alone. "I want the kind of girl the other fellows will whistle at."

5 We tend to like those who satisfy some particularly hungry spot in our make-up. The boy who has not had as much mother love as he wanted may be strongly attracted to a mother type of girl. "I don't know why I love her. She just gives me all I need."

6 We tend both to reproduce and to repudiate the relationships in which we grew up. A boy may be attracted to anyone who reminds him of his mother and who can reproduce the feeling of the old parent-child relationships. A girl may be unable to tolerate anyone who even remotely reminds her of her father, a repudiation of the former parent-child relationships. "I want a girl just like the girl who married dear old dad," or "I can't stand her. Who does she think she is, my mother?"

The Course of Love. The girls that Ellis studied [6] reported that they first fell in love with or became infatuated with a man or boy when they were near twelve years of age. They also indicated that between the ages of twelve and eighteen they had been in love with or infatuated with more than six different men or boys. Although further research is needed in this area, general observation corroborates this finding that young people do tend to experience specific love feelings early and to be attracted

[6] Albert Ellis, "Questionnaire Versus Interview Methods in the Study of Human Love Relationships. II, Uncategorized Responses," *American Sociological Review* (February, 1948), XIII, No. 1, pp. 62–64.

to a variety of love objects of the other sex throughout the entire second decade of life.[7]

Two other investigators have shown graphically that college students are able to plot the course of their love affairs between four levels of involvement: love, attraction, indifference, dislike. The most frequently reported curve was regular, beginning with indifference, moving slowly or precipitately upward through attraction to love and then (a) dropping again to indifference (indicating that the affair had terminated), or (b) remaining at a high level of love in ongoing affairs. About one-fifth of the students both male and female reported irregular courses of love, while a somewhat smaller group showed the course of love as they had known it to be vacillating or "cyclical" (see typical graphs and percentages reporting each below).

There is nothing absolute about the data below. They are merely indications of the variable nature of love emotions among young people.

PROFILES OF LOVE EXPERIENCE *

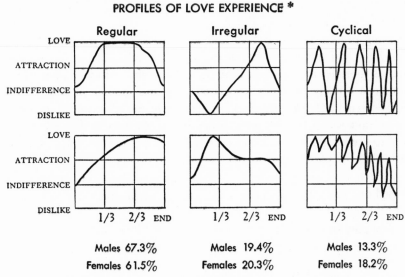

Regular	Irregular	Cyclical
Males 67.3%	Males 19.4%	Males 13.3%
Females 61.5%	Females 20.3%	Females 18.2%

* Clifford Kirkpatrick and Theodore Caplow, "Emotional Trends in the Courtship Experience of College Students as Expressed by Graphs with Some Observations on Methodological Implications," *American Sociological Review* (October, 1945), X, No. 5, pp. 619–626.

[7] Evelyn Millis Duvall, *Facts of Life and Love for Teen-Agers* (New York: Association Press, 1956). Based on thousands of questions asked by teen-age young people of both sexes.

Such findings reaffirm the importance of two other questions now to be discussed: 1. how does the capacity to love develop? and 2. how can you tell that you are in love?

Learning to Love

Love does not come as a sudden answer to life's basic needs. We develop the capacity to love gradually through years of interaction with other people. We learn to love just as we learn to eat and to walk and to read. The native tendencies and potentialities are there from the beginning. Given favorable opportunities, these capacities develop and flower; and as in all learning, first experiences set the stage for later responses. Therefore, to trace the development of the ability to love and to be loved, we must go back to the early days of infancy.

Developing the Capacity to Love. In his mother's arms the baby receives his first lessons in learning to love. As she holds him close in nursing, he feels the comfort of her supporting arms, the warmth of her body, the gratification of the satisfying milk, and the pleasure of the sucking process itself. Before long his eyes focus on her face, he sees her smile and soon manages one of his own in return. He coos back to her as she talks and sings to him. The glow of comfort he feels in her presence quickly becomes associated with the mother herself, as the baby learns that these highly pleasurable experiences arrive wrapped in the sound and the smell and the feel and the sight of his mother. Associated with all his fundamental satisfactions, this first mother-love establishes the pattern for further responses to others.

From the extremely dependent love of the infant for the mother, based on the infant's complete dependence on her for the gratification of his needs, the child develops self-dependence in many areas of his life, diffuses his "needs-meeting" among many individuals outside the family, and eventually does not need to have all his needs met through one all-consuming love. By means of trial-and-error he discovers persons whose needs to gratify others complement his needs to be gratified. His parents become alternates in his love life, and companionship love of an interdependence-of-peers sort is experienced with one or more age mates.[8]

[8] Robert F. Winch, *The Modern Family* (New York: Holt, 1952), especially pp. 396–400.

If the child is frustrated in this first important relationship, he may come to feel that he is living in a hostile world in which he must fight for what he needs; or if the outlook is too discouraging, he may lapse into the listless lethargy described so vividly by Ribble.[9] If he is neglected, handled harshly, or fed too little, the unfortunate child develops irritability instead of the glow of the happy child. He feels frustration in continued hunger, and he misses the cuddling support and warmth of the mother. He whimpers his discontent, lashes about in his discomfort, cries out in distress, and if no relief is forthcoming he may lapse into troubled, discouraged apathy.

The neglected child has been deprived of the first opportunities of feeling and responding warmly to another. He starts life, therefore, either like a bully with a chip on his shoulder or like a puppy with his tail between his legs. Years later as an adult he may attempt to compensate for his childhood deprivations by excesses and undue personal demands upon others. His early protests may continue into marriage in the form of unpredictable, little-understood aggressions toward his wife and children.

Diffusion of Love to Others. Mother may be the first love, but she is not the last! Father often enters into the affectional set-up very early. As he helps bathe and dress the child, as he comes in for a frolic before bedtime, as he tucks the infant under the covers, he too becomes an object of the child's love. Soon his voice and his step are awaited with eagerness, and his presence brings peculiarly satisfying meanings to the child. The child now responds to both father and mother with love.

The baby learns still another type of love response from children. Their play with the child is less tender; their laughter is a bit more spontaneous, their voices louder and their touch a little rougher. With them the baby learns a new type of love, hearty and carefree. The familiar roughhouse of the typical household finds the baby the gleeful center. Now he's beginning to feel one of the gang. It took mother to nurse him through early infancy. It took father to teach him that men are good and very much a part of his life. Brothers and sisters round off his early emotional education by helping him feel that he belongs, that he is one of them — a part of the family.

[9] Margaret A. Ribble, *The Rights of Infants* (New York: Columbia University Press, 1943). See also our earlier discussion of the basic love needs of children, pp. 13–15, 23–24.

Early in the child's life come other adults to strengthen and to modify the feelings built up toward parents. Relatives, neighbors, and
teachers become substitute parents as the youngster tries out his parent-
learned responses on them. These adults play important roles in the
lives of children, giving them the comforting security so needed by
youngsters growing away from early parent-child relationships. Baruch
gives a particularly clear illustration from a nursery school in the following episode:

. . . a two year old is having trouble making his adjustment in the new situation. He has been raised by his grandmother, and now his grandmother
has gone to work. He sulks at the teachers and shrugs away. But, after a
while, he navigates into the kitchen, settles himself there on a chair, and
does not wish to budge. The head-teacher, observing, suddenly realizes, "It's
the cook." As she said later, "The rest of the staff was so much younger
than the only mother he had ever known. But not the cook. She's an
elderly, comfortable, grandmotherly soul. So, we suggested that she take
over and that she give him some loving between paring carrots and potatoes.
He spent two days sitting in the kitchen, dragging the toys in under her feet,
until he got the feeling of anchorage and belongingness, and could wander
further apace." [10]

Most of us remember the warm friendly adults who made us feel
important back in those days when we went exploring for new relationships. Unfortunately, not all adults were equally friendly, and some of
us also remember the shame and ignominy of early experiences with sar-
castic, blaming persons, some of whom were teachers who shamed and
ridiculed us and rebuffed our struggling efforts to please. All too few
educators realize the importance of selecting leaders and teachers who
can take the place of parents in the molding and directing of love responses of growing children. Teachers especially should be persons who
are themselves emotionally mature enough to guide the affectional as
well as the intellectual development of their charges. The typical experience of the youngster falling in love with his scout leader or teacher
should be a happy one, guided and understood by the adults involved.
It is a further step in the direction of the mature, heterosexual love
which unites people in marriage.

Some young people become fearful of social intercourse and avoid
the very gatherings that they most crave. Others mask their insecurity

[10] Dorothy W. Baruch, "Are Teaching Techniques Meant for Children?" *Journal of Consulting Psychology*, Vol. 8, No. 2 (March–April, 1944), p. 111.

by a pretense at sophistication and play the bravado role of a "wolf." They may go in heavily for petting rather than explore the fuller personal meanings of boy-girl relationships. The trauma and the disappointment of many of these blind-alley experiences affect the ability to love and seem to be related to later marital unhappiness.

Teen-age young people who have had a hearty experience in loving and being loved in a happy family circle make these adjustments relatively successfully. There are two reasons for their success: 1. they have parents who are adequate examples of people in love, and 2. they have had years of practice in learning to respond with affection and consideration to loved ones.

Learning to Express Affection Takes Practice. Families differ widely in the ways in which their members express affection for one another. In some homes loving words and gestures are rare; in others, the children grow up from babyhood surrounded by warm assurances of love. Some married couples hide their love for each other behind a wall of reserve, while others continue to show their affection by all the small meaningful signals that develop through years of close association. Children growing up in a home where father kisses mother good-by in the morning and returns affectionately to her side in the evening learn that "papa loves mama." Children who have been taught how to express their feelings for others as they grow up, reach marriage with the fundamental skills required for living intimately with another person. On the other hand, the youngster who has never known the meaning of demonstrated love is apt to be clumsy in his efforts to express his feelings.

Elsie was such a person. Her mother died when she was very young, and she was raised by her father and his unmarried sister. Her father so mourned for his young wife that he dared not express the feeling that he had for the little girl who so closely resembled her. The maiden aunt was also bottled up, with no outlets save mournful love ballads. For years the little girl didn't know the meaning of being kissed or fondled. As she grew up and realized that other people were more overt in expressing their affection, she was shocked and vowed that no man would ever fuss around her. In the course of time Elsie found herself involved in a friendship with a fine young man whom she respected highly. They became engaged without having had closer contact than an occasional handclasp. Two weeks before their marriage they still

♡♡♡♡♡♡♡♡♡♡♡♡♡♡♡♡♡♡♡♡♡♡♡♡♡♡♡♡♡♡♡♡

DIFFERENCES BETWEEN LOVE AND INFATUATION

Love

1 Tends to occur first in late teens and in the twenties [1]

2 Attachment simultaneously to two or more tends not to be frequent [1]

3 Most cases last over a long period of time [1]

4 More slowly develops again after a love affair has ended [1]

5 Often used to refer to present affair [1]

6 Object of affection is more likely a suitable person [2]

7 Parents tend to approve [2]

8 Broadly involves entire personality [2]

9 Brings new energy and ambition, and more interest in life [3]

10 Associated with feelings of self-confidence, trust, and security [3]

11 Accompanied by kindlier feelings toward other people generally [3]

12 Joy in many common interests and an ongoing sense of being alive when together precludes boredom [4]

13 Relationship changes and grows with ongoing association, developing interests, and deepening feelings [4]

14 Accompanied by willingness to face reality and to tackle problems realistically [5]

---

[1] Albert Ellis, "A Study of Human Love Relationships," *Journal Genetic Psychology* (1949), No. 75, pp. 61–71.

[2] Paul Popenoe, "Infatuation and Its Treatment," *Family Life* (March, 1949), IX, No. 3, pp. 1–2.

[3] Albert Ellis, "A Study of the Love Emotions of American College Girls," *International Journal of Sexology* (August, 1949), pp. 1–6.

♡♡♡♡♡♡♡♡♡♡♡♡♡♡♡♡♡♡♡♡♡♡♡♡♡♡♡♡♡♡♡♡♡♡♡

AS REVEALED IN REPRESENTATIVE RESEARCH STUDIES

Infatuation

1 Tends to be more frequent among young adolescents and children under teen age [1]

2 Simultaneous attachments to two or more tends to be frequent [1]

3 Tends to last but a short time (only a few weeks in most cases) [1]

4 More quickly reoccurs soon after a given involvement has ended [1]

5 Is often the term applied to past attachments [1]

6 Tends to focus more frequently on unsuitable person [2]

7 Parents more often disapprove [2]

8 Narrowly focused on a few traits; mostly physical thrill [2]

9 Less frequently accompanied by ambition and wide interests [3]

10 Feelings of guilt, insecurity, and frustration are frequent [4]

11 Tends to be self-centered and restricted [4]

12 Boredom is frequent when there is no sexual excitement or social amusement [4]

13 Little change in the relationship with the passing of time [4]

14 Problems and barriers are often disregarded; idealization may have little regard for reality [5]

---

[4] Joe McCarthy, "How Do You Know You're in Love?" *McCall's Magazine,* Reprint, pp. 26–27, 88–90.

[5] Stephen Laycock, Director of Mental Hygiene, Canada (informal communication).

had not kissed each other. In panic the girl, now a young woman of nearly twenty-five, came to a marital guidance center for help. She shivered as she told of her fears in anticipating her marriage, of her desire to be kissed and loved by this man who meant so much to her. Yet she felt impelled to fight off his advances, felt herself freeze whenever he came near. The counselor recommended postponing the marriage until the couple could build up a more satisfactory mode of expressing their affection. After several months, the counselor with step-by-step guidance was able to open up the affectional outlets that would prepare them for the married happiness they both wanted. Elsie and her husband, even so, will probably never be as free in expressing their love for each other as couples whose childhood experiences in loving were adequate. Learning to express affection takes practice.

How Can You Know?

Love is a highly variable sentiment. It may be superficial and trivial or it may be splendid and deep. Love may be a transient appeal that disappears after a few heavy dates, and again it may foster a relationship which will become stronger with the years. It would be folly to decide whether or not to marry by the quality of the love sentiment at a given moment. In some instances the very intensity of the feeling may be a danger signal. How can you know that it's the type of love on which happy marriages are based? One of the first steps is to distinguish between love and infatuation. (See table on pages 40–41.)

Seven Ways to Tell If Your Love Will Last. There is no magic daisy petal test by which you can measure the extent or the depth or the permanence of your love feelings. Yet, if you are going to try to base your marriage upon your love for each other, you must have some criteria by which to judge whether yours is the kind of love that may be expected to last in marriage. Here are some ways to help you tell.

LASTING LOVE . . .

has *many facets:*
tender, passionate, comradely, protecting, highly specific in its focus, widely general in its diffusion.

is *outgoing:*
radiating out in its values, concerns, and interests to others' happiness and well-being.

is *motivating:*
releases energy for work, is creative, brings an eagerness to grow, to improve, to work for worthy purposes and ideals.

is *sharing:*
what one has and what one is strive to be shared; thoughts, feelings, attitudes, ambitions, hopes, interests, all are sharable.

is a *we-feeling:*
thinking and planning are in terms of "we"; what *we* want, how *we* feel, what *we* will do, rather than "I" centeredness.

is *realistic:*
faults, weaknesses, and problems are faced together as part of reality; willingness to work on building the relationship.

changes and grows with time:
time is the surest test — if the relationship has grown through many emotional climates, further association, developing interests, and deepening feelings, the chances are that it will continue to grow as long as the persons do.

By gaining insight into ourselves and into the nature of our past and present involvements, we may learn in some measure how to appraise the depth and the strength of a particular relationship. If we can love another deeply enough to subordinate ourselves to the relationship and lose ourselves in values common to both of us, we have love enough to marry on.

Readings

BURGESS, ERNEST W., PAUL WALLIN, and GLADYS DENNY SHULTZ, *Courtship, Engagement and Marriage* (Philadelphia: J. B. Lippincott Company, 1954). The famous research team discuss their findings about why John loves Mary, the real reasons why people fall in love, how love develops, whether love is blind, and why lovers quarrel, in their Part Two, Chapters 2–6.

DUVALL, EVELYN MILLIS, *Facts of Life and Love for Teen-Agers* (New York: Association Press, 1956 revision). Part Three, "Loving and Being Loved," considers the many questions young people have about expressing love feelings, telling real love from infatuation, what to do about crushes on unlikely persons, and how to get over an unpromising love affair.

ECKERT, RALPH G., *So You Think It's Love!* (Public Affairs Pamphlets, 22 East 38th Street, New York City 16, 1950). A sympathetic expert in the subject talks over the questions of falling in love, love at first sight, and finding the right person, in a way that young people find helpful.

LeMASTERS, E. E., *Modern Courtship and Marriage* (New York: The Macmillan Company, 1957). A trained observer calls your attention to our folklore about love and marriage in America and does a great deal to help you to see the difference between facts and fallacies. See especially his Chapters 3 and 4.

LEVY, JOHN and RUTH MUNROE, *The Happy Family* (New York: Alfred A. Knopf, 1938). A very wise book that has become a modern classic. You will find Chapter One especially pertinent to the material in this chapter.

MAGOUN, F. ALEXANDER, *Love and Marriage* (New York: Harper and Brothers, 1956 revision). The mature student will find Chapter 1, "The Nature of Love," especially rewarding.

CHAPTER THREE

"Well . . . Can't you say something!"

DATING

What makes a person popular?

How about petting as a pastime?

Why are some folks so slow starting to date?

What is there to do on a date besides the same old stuff?

What can you do about the fast ones?

*W*HEN YOU MARRY, YOU MARRY SOMEONE YOU ALREADY KNOW. The strange prince who dashes up and carries the blushing damsel away on his white horse is no more in evidence today than is his prancing charger. Couples find each other in contemporary society through a variety of associations that precede courtship and marriage. These paired contacts between the sexes go by the name of dating.

What Is a Date?

Young people themselves usually think of a date as a mutually agreed upon association of a boy and a girl, or a man and a woman, for a particular occasion or activity. Dating today differs from courtship, as it used to be defined, in that young people now can date each other without either of them or their parents assuming that because they date they are seriously interested in each other. They may be. But just the fact of their dating each other does not commit them in the future.

As such, dating is a phenomenon of the twentieth century. Before then it was usual for the boy to request permission of the girl's parents to "court" her before any paired association took place. Courtship implied in the eyes of the couple, the parents, and the community a responsibility for the future that the greater freedom of current dating does not.

Dating is defined differently by some observers than by others. Willard Waller observing college young people, after World War I in the East, took a pessimistic view of dating as largely exploitative and competitive. Margaret Mead and Geoffrey Gorer have since echoed these reflections. Students of the family such as Burgess and Locke, on the other hand, have seen dating as preliminary to courtship and as having functions preparatory to courtship and marriage. A third concept of dating formulated by persons working closely with large numbers of high school and college students is that dating is a value in itself both in personality development and in education for future stages of involvement and commitment. These three concepts of dating are outlined below.

HOW DATING IS DEFINED [1]

Dating as a dalliance: a time-filler [2]	Prestige in rating Status in peer group Excitement in pretended involvement Pursuit of a thrill Exploitative Capacity to love impaired Many are hurt Poor education for marriage
Dating as preliminary to courtship [3]	Opportunity for association with other sex Variety of social experience Range of social contacts Selection of compatible pairs Opportunities for choice of potential mate

[1] See Samuel Harman Lowrie, "Dating Theories and Student Responses," *American Sociological Review* (June, 1951), Vol. 16, No. 3, pp. 334–340.

[2] See especially, Willard Waller, "The Rating and Dating Complex," *American Sociological Review* (October, 1937), No. 2, pp. 727–734; *The Family, a Dynamic Interpretation* (New York: Cordon, 1938), pp. 222–235; and Margaret Mead, *Male and Female* (New York: Morrow, 1949), pp. 281–295; also, Geoffrey Gorer, *The American People* (New York: Norton, 1948), pp. 106–132.

[3] Ernest W. Burgess and Harvey Locke, *The Family* (New York: American Book, 1960), pp. 331–333.

<table>
<tr><td>Dating as a social
value in itself [4]</td><td>Enriched personality development
Broad experience
Wide acquaintance
Skills in mixing socially
Poise and self-confidence
Rational selection of friends among other sex
Prestige among associates
Satisfaction of social goals</td></tr>
</table>

Some Do Not Date

Those who take the "dating is dalliance" point of view might consider the young person who does not date as fortunate. He is not wasting his time in a time-filler that leads to nothing but pain. Apparently young people themselves do not consider the lack of dates as an advantage. Indeed one of the most frequent problems that both boys and girls raise is that of not having enough contact with the other sex through dating. The Purdue University Opinion Panel for Young People, in a systematic country-wide analysis of representative young people, reports that although some senior high school students are dating regularly, some 42 per cent of the boys, and 24 per cent of the girls in the 10th, 11th, and 12th grades seldom or never have a date.[5]

SOME YOUNG PEOPLE REPORT THEY DO NOT DATE

	BOYS	GIRLS
Never or seldom have a date	42%	24%
Frequent dates with different persons	29	27
Frequent dates with one person	8	14
Going steady with one person	16	28
Engaged	1	3
Married	2	1

[4] Lowrie, op. cit., p. 337; also Evelyn Millis Duvall and Reuben Hill, *When You Marry* (Boston: D. C. Heath and Company, 1945), Chap. 3; and Evelyn Millis Duvall, *Facts of Life and Love for Teen-Agers* (New York: Association Press, 1956), Chaps. 5, 6.

[5] P. C. Baker, H. T. Christensen, R. W. Heath, and H. H. Remmers, "Male-Female Roles as Seen by Youth," The Purdue Opinion Panel, Division of Educational Reference, Purdue University, Lafayette, Indiana, Report of Poll No. 43, Vol. 15, No. 1, February 1956, pages 2a–4a.

"I don't think boys are half as girl-crazy as people say they are."

Reproduced by permission of Martha Blanchard
from THE SATURDAY EVENING POST, October 6, 1951

The problem is greater for younger than for older youth. But there is evidence that a considerable number of out-of-school young people and college students still are not dating. More than a third of the university students in one study [6] reported inadequate opportunities for meeting members of the other sex. Attempts to analyze why some young people do not get dates uncovers a number of traits and characteristics that seem to be handicaps. Physically unattractive, geographically isolated, academically insulated, emotionally immature, and psychologi-

[6] Clifford Kirkpatrick and Theodore Caplow, "Courtship in a Group of Minnesota Students," *American Journal of Sociology* (September, 1945), LI, No. 2, p. 117.

cally unstable young people of both sexes seem to have more difficulty securing the favorable attention of the other sex than do the attractive, accessible, mature, and socially skilled young people.

Preferences in Dates. A nation-wide sample of thousands of high school students paralleling previous studies of college youth reports that there is general agreement among young people as to who is preferred as a dating partner. The seven characteristics rated highest are in the table below, in order of rank.[7]

THE PREFERRED DATE . . .

is physically and mentally fit
is dependable, can be trusted
takes pride in personal appearance and manners
is clean in speech and action
has pleasant disposition and a sense of humor
is considerate of me and others
acts own age, is not childish

Both sexes have certain patterns of conduct objectionable to the other sex. In general, boys are criticized for being less inhibited and more careless, thoughtless, disrespectful, sex-driven, and loud than their partners in dating. Girls are characterized as being less natural, more touchy, money-minded, unresponsive, childish, and flighty than the boys they date.[8]

At What Age Does Dating Begin?

Many factors seem to operate to determine the age at which dating begins.

What Your Folks Expect of You. Dating practices vary widely from family to family. There are still some fathers and mothers who so protect their girls that any man walking their daughter home is subjected to a full inquiry of his intentions. A considerable number of fathers forbid their daughters dating privileges. Other parents expect young

---

[7] Harold Christensen, "Dating Behavior as Evaluated by High School Students," *American Journal of Sociology* (May, 1952), LVII, No. 6, p. 580.
[8] Christensen, *op. cit.*, pp. 581–582.

people to "couple off" very early, with no questions asked or eyebrows raised. In fact, many parents encourage both their sons and daughters in their first dating.

ATTITUDES OF PARENTS TOWARD FIRST DATING [9]

Attitude of Parents as Reported by Students	Father toward		Mother toward	
	Son	Daughter	Son	Daughter
Prohibited or disapproved	8.5%	18.0%	7.3%	9.5%
Indifferent	70.7	62.3	57.6	39.6
Encouraged	20.8	19.7	35.1	50.9

Where You Come in the Family. Studies of the age at which young people begin to have dates indicate that their position in the family is a very important factor. Only children and oldest children are usually a little slower in getting started than are the younger members of the family. The oldest boy or girl has to break the ice among the younger set in the neighborhood. In addition, he must get the parents accustomed to the idea that going out is all right. This is especially difficult when customs are changing from one generation to the next as they are today. Parents who lived in the times when no nice girl was out after dark with a man the family didn't know well, take some plain and fancy reconditioning to be brought up to date. The older children in the family perform a real service to their younger brothers and sisters in winning the parents over to the idea of modern dating. The younger fry then come along and take advantage of all the spade work which has been done. The result is that they begin dating earlier and know more about it than their older brothers and sisters.

It is not uncommon for younger brothers and sisters to get some practice on the friends of those just ahead of them in the family. Kid brother may be a pest when he hangs around the sofa when the boy friends come calling, but he is also getting some very good tips on what to do in such a situation and how a girl whom he knows as well as he does that sister of his acts when she is on a date. Little sisters haven't quite the reputation of little brothers for having to be bought off by visiting suitors, but they usually stick around long enough to get in a few licks of practice on their sister's boy friends, and thus smooth over

[9] Adapted from Clifford Kirkpatrick and Theodore Caplow, "Courtship in a Group of Minnesota Students," *American Journal of Sociology* (September, 1945), LI, No. 2, p. 115.

some of their own rough edges before they try out their techniques on a boy who really matters. Going along for the ride with the set just a notch older is of great help in improving these skills and in getting in on the social activities about town. "Has she got a sister?" is a boost that gives many a kid sister a start.

How Friendly You Are. Friendly people make friends. In no area is this more true than in dating. The person who has learned to enjoy being with people, to be sensitive to what they do and do not like, and who has developed the skills of being attractive to others is off to a head start when it comes to getting along with the other sex. These skills are specifically learned. The little wolf child whom you have read about wouldn't have the slightest idea of what to do on a coke date . . . she couldn't even sit up to the table! Shy Sam who got his feelings hurt in second grade and hasn't talked to a girl since may be in an awkward spot when it comes to facing the terrors of a high school dance. Smooth Sue who has gone around with many friends of assorted sizes and sexes from the time she first held Jimmie's hand in nursery school has probably learned what it takes to be friendly and comfortable with all kinds of boys. In this sense, being a person of experience is quite acceptable.

Learning to be friendly is every bit as complex an attainment as learning to swim or to ride a bicycle, and maybe a little more so. You can't learn to swim without getting some water up your nose and being sure that your next breath may be your last! If you can take these first uncomfortable moments, you are soon paddling around, wondering what the early fuss was all about and feeling sure you could do a swan dive if you practiced. It is practice that makes for the poise and skills that are so universally envied in dating too.

What You Consider a Date. It would be hard for some young adults to remember when they had their first real date. Young people of both sexes mingle so freely in some of our communities that they have literally been doing things together since before they could toddle. It is becoming more and more common for grade school boys to take girls in their classrooms to a Saturday afternoon movie, or a children's symphony, or the zoo, in a pattern of behavior that has many of the aspects which in older circles is known as dating. In some neighborhoods, however, a girl is not allowed to go anywhere with a boy until she is sixteen or older, and then under supervision, and the event is regarded by the family and friends as quite an occasion. So the age at which you begin to date, as such, depends on whether you define a date as something special, over and beyond the child's play of early friendship, or whether you are willing to call any sortie of a couple a date, no matter what the maturity of the participants may be.

When You Become Mature. Recent studies of the rate and pace at which children become adults show that there is a great difference in the speed with which individuals do grow up. Generally speaking, most girls mature a little earlier than boys do, causing some tension between the sexes, especially at the awkward age along about junior high school time. Not only are the girls physically more mature than the boys of their own age, but they are ready for grown-up activities before the boys are. We know definitely that these grown-up interests, such as getting special pleasure out of being with those of the other sex, taking an interest in one's personal appearance, enjoying love stories and romantic movies, etc., follow the physical maturing of the boy or girl. The girl who is beginning to look like a woman wants to act like one. The boy who is as tall as his dad will very soon be seeking the more grown-up roles he has seen his dad and other men play. This sequence of development of the person is more important by far than his or her chronological age. In careful work at the University of California, it has been shown that as much as five years' difference may be found in the age at which boys begin to develop. Some youngsters of ten are already in the puberal cycle (period of change from childhood to adulthood, physically speaking), while others of nearly fourteen haven't yet started.[10] And the age at which boys complete their physical growth is not the same for all boys. Some are through the growth period before they are fifteen, while others may be out of high school before they achieve maturity. These individual differences are important to recognize, so that we won't expect all seventeen-year-old boys to be alike in their readiness for dating, for dancing, or any other adult activity. Girls show much the same personal variation in their development, and by the seventh or the eighth grade we find two thirds of the girls on their way to becoming young ladies — one of the reasons why they vote for long dresses and a graduation dance. Two thirds of the boys in their classes, how-

[10] Lois Hayden Meek and associates, *The Personal-Social Development of Boys and Girls with Implications for Secondary Education* (New York: Progressive Education Association, 1940), p. 34.

ever, haven't yet started on the cycle of growth that is to carry them into manhood.

This general tendency for girls to grow up before the boys of their own age leads to another interesting occurrence — girls usually date boys a little older than themselves. Boys, conversely, prefer girls younger than themselves as friends and dates. This tendency carries right through the dating, mating, engagement, and marriage periods and is

STAGES IN DATING DEVELOPMENT

Hit-and-Miss Childhood Groups

Determined largely by family, neighborhood, and community opportunities, the geographical "range" to roam provided, and the amount of supervision.

Cliques

Cliquelike groups formed by both boys and girls for which they feel deep loyalty but which change in nature and membership very readily.

Fleeting Affinities

The coke date, the "being walked home from school" involvements characteristic of the junior high school and high school age, types of temporary try-outs with each other across the sex line on a couple basis, called "playing the field" by some.

Going Together

A recognizable couple formation in which a boy and girl show preference for each other over a period of time, perhaps for just a few weeks, the "Jane is going with Jim" stage.

Mixed Couple Formations

Constellations of several previously identifiable couples who start going round together in groups of several couples, attending basketball games together, coming to the proms together, visiting one another's homes as a group — the "sets" we see in every community.

Going Steady

Couples who find their own status as a couple taking precedence over other alignments.

Choosing "The One"

Selection of a permanent partner with the "understanding" that engagement and marriage will develop naturally.

known as the "age gradient." Unfortunately, few of our schools and communities have made adequate provision for this mingling of the sexes of different age groups, making dating more difficult than it is where young people of different ages have ready access to each other in everyday work and play situations.

When a person starts to date is not nearly as important as how he begins. The factors determining the onset of his dating practice operate in many ways to influence the progress of dating for him. But more important by far is his willingness and ability to learn the rules and skills by which success is attained, because no one is born popular. Social success is a learned art, and learning is hard and long for most of us. In the last analysis, then, the ability to understand and accept the whole dating scheme is more important than the age of starting.

Although the forms and patterns of dating vary widely in different sections of the country, there is a general pattern of development that is interesting. It appears in tabular form in the table on page 55.

How Many Kinds of Dates Are There?

We not only go through a process of several stages in our dating experiences, but we have many kinds of dating relationships within any one period. These experiences are distinguished by the meanings and feelings they arouse, as we shall see in the following analysis:

Old-shoe familiarity is characteristic of dates with old pals and friends who are enjoyed as comrades, with very little of the excitement of novelty or the thrill of "being in love." She is just "good old Lillian" to him and is taken for granted in much the same way he takes his sister or his maiden aunt.

Glamor dates are made of different stuff. They are something of an achievement. Being seen with a "glamor girl" is a feather in his cap. Similarly, a girl is envied as having made a "catch" if she is seen with someone who rates high among her friends.

Blind dates and **pick-ups** are more scary, in a sense. There's the feeling of being on your guard at the same time that you probe around to see how far you can go. There's the disadvantage of being afraid to be stuck with a dud, but the advantage of being able to try out your skills on someone who doesn't have to remind you of possible failures later. They are good experiences but risky on the whole, both in feeling tones and in results.

Difficulties arise when romantic ideas press you to look for the "one and only" behind every blind date, with the consequence of disillusionment and disappointment, and inability to enjoy the real situation for what it is worth.

Growing friendships deepen and widen their bases through the opportunities of dating. The couple get to know each other, and discover new aspects of their own changing relationship that give the date more meaning and charge it with an increasing depth and variety of feeling. This kind of date usually leads to something, though not always the altar. It may be just the basis for a lifelong friendship.

Where to Go and What to Do on a Date

Keeping dates from becoming monotonous is one of the difficulties of modern dating. "Where can we go?" "What can we do?" "What can you do?" "What can you do that's fun at home?" are pressingly urgent questions for many young people. Few of our cities and towns have provided the kinds of facilities most young folk enjoy. All too often there is nothing but the movies, the pool halls and taverns, and the dance halls open for the casual dater. In some communities Teen Canteens, Community Centers, Teen Towns, etc., have sprung up as hangouts and recreation centers for the young people of the town. There with a juke box, soft drinks, ping-pong tables, and a kitchenette, young people of dating age dance, drink cokes, pop corn, and swap lines, and develop the skills that are necessary to get along with each other. But for the town without such a community hangout, what is there for young people to do when they get together?

For the outdoor girl and boy there are many possibilities: skating, hiking, the walkie-talkie date, cycling, swimming, gardening, hunting for nature specimens of all kinds, picnics, to say nothing of all the outdoor games and sports from croquet and tennis to golf and horseback riding. Making equipment for a favorite sport is great fun. The couple that spent all one summer building a little rowboat got a thrill that will make boating forever afterwards exciting. Setting up an archery set in the back yard may be as interesting as using it afterwards. There are innumerable pursuits which the creative-minded couple can explore together.

Stay-at-home dates can be made interesting by the couple who can think of home as encompassing more territory than just the davenport.

Scrapbook of Army-Navy Humor

"Since you're new at this, Anderson, maybe you'd better
just tag along and watch."

The kitchen has real possibilities for group or couple dating. Making up a batch of spaghetti, trying out a recipe for Hungarian goulash, or beating up an old-fashioned coffee cake have been known to keep dating young people interested for several hours at a time. There is nothing dull in the clowning around and deciding what to make, or the who-will-do-what that precedes the actual culinary endeavor itself. Refreshments are no problem when friends make their own. Even the cleaning up is fun with big Arthur behind the best chintz apron, and everybody behind plans for next time. It's no wonder that some groups of young people have worked their way through the United Nations Cookbook in a series of kitchen dates around the calendar.

Attics yield materials for parades in costume and impromptu plays and skits. The dining room table is just the spot for a series of group table games where several couples can participate at once. Games suggested by such agencies as the National Recreation Association and the publishers of *Handy* are especially good.

Living rooms adapt themselves well to a variety of dates. Piano games, singing old favorites and new hot numbers, amateur orchestras, parlor games of the more grown-up varieties such as Elsa Maxwell so ingeniously devises and which are described from time to time in popular magazines, reading aloud, and a galaxy of other activities around common projects can be fascinating. One couple entertained friends by providing a large cotton square which they were all to decorate with gaudy block printing made from cut potato halves (each person making his own design) dipped in a fabric paint. It took all evening, but was it fun! And you should see the table cloth that resulted. . . .

Radio to the imaginative couple will suggest not just listening, nor even dancing to its rhythms, but also working out slogans and sending in questions to stump the experts. A dozen other ventures into creative twosomeness can be interesting and rewarding, even if the sponsor doesn't come across with a check by return mail. A person armed with such ideas will be welcomed into almost any home. He will find that dating this way can be great fun, and that he doesn't have to be the center of attention to have a good time.

Where to go and what to do depends not only on the wealth of local resources but even more on the ability of those who date to make use of what they have. Going to the museum doesn't have to be stuffy. Going to a concert isn't necessarily prosaic. What takes any activity out of the area of the humdrum is to give it focus. "You must see *this*," "Don't miss *that*," are quite different in interest appeal from the lackadaisical, unfocused suggestion, "Do you want to go downtown?" or "Would you like to make something?" This pepping up of the dating activities comes with experience and learning as does everything else. Take your time. Plan your campaign. And have fun!

What about Petting?

Do you have to pet to be popular? No question is more universally asked by young people who want to rate and to date and yet are interested in a variety of dating activities beyond the sheer sex-exploration level. To answer the question wisely, a categorical "Yes" or "No" is not adequate. Rather, let us look for answers to certain subquestions, an understanding of which will give direction to the final personal choice.

Why Do Young People Pet? Young people discussing this problem give the following reasons for premarital petting:

It seems to be expected of you.
The rest of the crowd are all doing it.
You need some assurance that you are desirable.

Where else can you get a little loving? Most young folk are too old to be fondled by their parents any more, and too young to enjoy the caresses of marriage.

It's exciting.

Sure it's sex, but what's wrong with that?

It's something to do . . . most dates are a bore without it.

How else can you know you are compatible?

What's Wrong with Petting? There seems to be some agreement among both young people and understanding adults that too frequent and too promiscuous petting has hazards that most folk like to avoid. Briefly listed, these difficulties are:

Petting often rules out other activities.

It tends to overemphasize the physical aspects of the relationship.

It may limit the choice of companionship.

It may give rise to feelings of shame and guilt (our own early training and the standards of the communities in which we live see to this).

It rouses sex feelings and then leaves them unsatisfied.

It leads too often into premarital sex intercourse with the threats of unwanted pregnancy and feelings of regret.

It makes good marriage adjustment difficult, especially when the petting has been too promiscuous and too deeply established as a pattern of behavior.

Although there are very real dangers of going too far in the petting game before marriage, few people are so constituted that they can refrain from expressing affection when they feel it. Between people who love each other deeply and who are sharing rich and meaningful experiences, some physical expression of the love each feels for the other is desirable. When these expressions of affection become sex-tinged they need not terrify the intelligent couple, but should merely serve to indicate the potency of the force which attracts them to each other.

Occasionally a young person may be so strictly brought up that he develops feelings of disgust and comes to avoid all physical contact with others. Elsie (p. 39) was such a person. She came within weeks of marriage without ever having been kissed by either her lover or any other man. Consequently, she was in panic over the prospect of the impending intimacies of marriage. The counselor she consulted had to recommend a postponement of the marriage until the couple had paved the way more adequately for the marriage that was to come. Such a case is unusual, but aspects of it are sufficiently common, especially among exceedingly nice girls, to make one aware of the dangers of too much prudery as well as of an excess of license in the sex field.

Do You Have to Pet to Be Popular? No, you do not! Popularity that rests on a reputation for petting is not as satisfying as popularity which comes from the attraction of a pleasing personality. Popularity is a nebulous concept involving all the complexities of what makes a person attractive to others: appearance, abilities, responses, attitudes, charm, and specific skills. In dating success all of these play a part, but large numbers of young people from all sorts of settings agree that the element of friendliness is of primary importance. The person who has developed the habit of being friendly, who is genuinely interested in people and eager to know them better, who sees girls as interesting personalities to explore and understand as whole personalities, who likes boys for what they are, who has had many pleasant experiences with a wide variety of people in the past so that he meets new ones with eagerness and anticipation rather than with fear and hostility, who feels that people like him and that they will like him better when they know him better — this is the type of person, old or young, boy or girl, who will enjoy popularity. This kind of person makes people feel comfortable when he is around; he doesn't threaten or antagonize; he enjoys people and they enjoy him, and he will always be a welcome companion. His friendliness is all he needs to get through to other people.

A person with skills also has alternatives to petting. The girl who can do things goes places. If she can swim and dance and play a decent game of tennis and bridge, or can sing or play an instrument and carry on a live conversation, she is invited out more often, goes to more places, meets more people. Such skills are developed by the processes of learning and are worth the effort for the person who would be a popular, successful dater.

When They Are Either Too Slow or Too Fast

What do to with the "dumb bunny" who answers in monosyllables and leaves the whole burden of the date on you is a puzzler. One constructive possibility is to take the situation as a challenge and see what your social skills and insights can do to help the other person have a good time. Loosening up a shy, reserved girl to the place where her eyes are shining and she's having a good time with you brings rewards that even the Smooth Suzy can't guarantee. Girls as USO hostesses and YWCA volunteers have done an excellent job of making lonesome, reserved, and uncomfortable boys feel at home.

Dealing with the fast ones is quite another thing.[11] Wolves don't always go in packs or pick on the Three Little Pigs. There are she-wolves who are dynamite and Lone Wolves of both sexes who can cause plenty of trouble when allowed to roam too fast or too far. Everyone can develop protective devices and methods of rechanneling the on-slaughts of such exploitive folk. The dangers are not great for the young person who has had some previous understanding of the existence of such exploitation across the sex line, and who has been able to arrive at a decision as to the values worth holding. The greatest danger in dealing with a fast worker is that young people aren't sure themselves just how far they are willing to go. A song of a generation ago phrased it clearly if not too prettily when it moaned, "Her lips tell me 'No, No,' but there's 'Yes, Yes' in her eyes." This inner indecision is what causes the trouble; a preconceived set of values will carry one over many emer-gencies. The temptations of the moment are effectively met only when they are not desirable in terms of what they will cost. Today this holds for both sexes. There was a time, not too long ago, when it was the girl who was expected to uphold the standards for both of them. Now, when many girls are so open and active in their dating relationships, boys too have to learn the skills of holding to the line in the face of vigorous campaigns.

Boys are often baffled by the lack of understanding shown by girls. As they put it, "Why do really nice girls lead you on so far and then aren't willing to do anything about it?" Woman's sexual response is so general and diffused that frequently she does not even know that she is being aroused, and even more frequently is quite unaware that her be-havior is arousing the boy beyond the boundaries which she herself would wish to maintain. It therefore falls to the boy, who is more quickly and recognizably awakened, to share the responsibility for con-trol. Needless to say, there are elements of mutuality here that the cou-ple who care for the long-time relationship will perfect with practice.

[11] See especially, Evelyn Millis Duvall, *Facts of Life and Love for Teen-Agers* (New York: Association Press, 1956), Chaps. 7, 12, 13.

Going Steady

Couples go steady for a number of reasons. In many sets, it's the only way to get around. You must have a steady in order to rate invitations to the activities of the young crowd. Then there is a certain "social security" in knowing that you can count on someone when things come along for which you need a partner. Many girls find that going steady insures them getting to the season's games and dances with far more reliability than comes with "playing the field." A sense of personal security in having someone to belong to means a great deal to some people. Others find that getting and holding a steady is a way of showing himself and others that he can do it: it tends to be a symbol of achievement. Going steady is a good way to get to know each other. Moods and manners change as contacts multiply. Each member of the couple can see how the personality of the other reacts to the ups and downs of daily living far better when going steady than in more fleeting contacts. The reason for going steady most frequently assumed is that the couple love each other and would rather go together than with any other possibility. But behind the story of many steadies lies an element of accident that the couple itself often senses clearly. Ray took Betty to a couple of movies and then to the school prom. By that time friends of both had them paired off in their thinking. Sally gave a party and expected Ray to bring Betty. Soon the habit of going together was so well fixed and expected that they were going steady without the benefit of any particular choice or decision in the matter. All too often the members of such accidental relationships go all the way to the threshold of marriage with a minimum of interests in common. Going steady becomes a habit which is difficult to break.

CHECK YOURSELF   In the discussion immediately above on "Going Steady," underline as many phrases as seem to describe why people go steady. How many do you have? (There are 8 in all; see KEY for listing.)

★ KEY   Answers in order of their appearance in the text.

7 The couple love each other   8 Element of accident
4 Personal security   5 Symbol of achievement   6 To get to know each other
1 The only way to get around   2 To rate invitations   3 Social security

---

While there are valid and quite reasonable advantages in going steady, there are also factors worth looking into which indicate that it may be unwise to go steady too soon.

First, starting to go steady too soon lessens opportunities for exploring the field. After all, we spend much of our lifetime going steady with our one and only. The chance for knowing enough members of the other sex well enough to make a real choice of a life partner comes during the dating period. Shortening the period of exploring possibilities by settling prematurely on any one person may create a feeling of having missed something important.

Second, confining our entire interests to a single person during the time of social and emotional maturation limits the scope of our responses and self-understanding. We all respond differently to different people. By interacting with a wide variety of people, especially of the other sex, we discover facets of our own personality that otherwise might lie dormant only to be awakened after marriage, in some cases with distressing confusion. Specifically, a fellow should have had the emotional experience of being with a girl who made him feel tenderly protective, with another who gave him a pleasurable feeling of being mothered, with another whose hand he could clasp with a feeling of hearty comradeship, with another whose feminine appeal sent his blood to his face and his heart to his throat, with another who made him as comfortable and easy as a sister, and perhaps with still another who brought forth a pleasant combination of all these feelings in a satisfying mixture.

Third, one of the most uncomfortable problems to be worked out by steadies who start too soon and go on too long is that which arises when one takes the other seriously while the other is tired of the relationship. Breaking off may prove to be so difficult that the couple will remain together only because of the dread one has of hurting the other.

How to Break Off with a Steady

Our romantic compulsion to hold together has shut off frank discussion of how a relationship that is unpromising may be broken comfortably and with a minimum of pain. There are three practices in general use today: 1. The *love-'em-and-leave-'em* variety is characteristic of one method which is quick, easy, and effective. A relationship which was there yesterday just isn't today, because one of the couple just doesn't respond any more. He doesn't call her or drop around. She isn't in when he calls, if she is the one who is through. The difficulties of this method are that, although it is effective, hurts are inflicted both to the feelings of the one who has been so summarily jilted and to the conscience of the one who did the running away. 2. *Agonizing discussions* about how washed up we are; "if only you would do so-and-so we could go on still"; tormenting memories about how happy we once were; the break drags on uncomfortably, with hopes rising and falling sometimes for months. Grandpa had a point when he mused, "If you have to cut off the puppy's tail do it in one blow." Yet a certain amount of preparation and some explanation are usually helpful. 3. The *easing-off* type of break includes some understanding on the part of both members of the couple of what is happening, and an acceptance of the situation before the bond is completely severed. Some day people will be much wiser about these things. In the meantime we all can be more aware of both the need to sever certain relationships and the necessity of building the skills that will be most kind and effective.

Dating as Preparation for Marriage

Dating has a value as preparation for courtship, engagement, and marriage in addition to its value as recreation and play. The patterns and habits that are built up during the dating days are to some extent those which carry over into the courtship and engagement. A man bosses his wife very much as he did his fiancée in dating days, that is, if she acceded to that arrangement. Dating should be educational, but it may turn out to be miseducation.

Who makes the decisions on a date? Is it the boy who always decides where they will go, what they will do, how much they will eat? Or is it the girl who holds this balance of power in her skillful little fist? Can a date be democratic, each one contributing to and receiving from the relationship those things which he can and should? Does joint planning of activities spoil the fun? Can surprises be mutual? Does taking turns in running things help any in dating? Or does one person need to show who is boss and play that role down to the bitter end? These are basic problems too involved to be solved here, except to point out that role-taking begins in the dating period and sets the stage for later marriage and home management.

Money matters especially are often a problem. Why is it that boys always expect to pay a girl's way when they go out together? Even though a girl may be earning as much as or perhaps even more than the boy, why does he feel that he should "take" her? To realize how entrenched this custom is, just listen sometime to a group of young people discuss the pros and cons of sharing expenses on a date. The consensus almost always is that it just won't work . . . "the girl will feel funny," "the boy's ego can't take it," "the girl can make it up some other way," are the typical comments. Girls have been so conscious of having to wait until boys ask them for a date for which they will foot the bills, that recently girls have developed considerable skill in perfecting devices for asking men to functions where the girls carry the financial and social burden. Girls band together and put on a party to which they invite their own partners or a "bunch of boys," who are given all the courtesies of guests with none of the usual financial burdens assumed by men in mixed company. Inviting the boys out to the house for an evening, to come to supper, to share theater tickets that grandma just happened to have, to use "a pass to the ballgame dad gave me" are typical of the kinds of ruses now in common usage. The problem doesn't end there. It will pop up again early in marriage and become one of the areas for adjustment in establishing the new home. The whole problem of working wives is often not so much a matter of the wife's being out of the home for part of the day as it is a question of whose money it is that she earns. Do her earnings go into the family budget as do her husband's, or are they to be labeled as hers alone?

We conclude that dating in America is not a thing apart from the rest of life. It grows out of childhood friendships, out of customs, and merges into the involvements of courtship and engagement in a process which we will describe in later chapters.

Dating May Be Preparation but It Is Also Fun

The account of dating which you have just read emphasizes the values which come with learning the skills of boy and girl relations. You aren't born popular; you have to learn how to do the friendly things which will endear you to people. The speed with which you grow in competence depends on the encouragement given by your family, your eagerness to learn, and your rate of emotional maturation.

Just as there are all kinds of people, so there are many kinds of dates — informal old-friend dates, blind dates, formal dates, and so on. Each takes imagination and ingenuity to carry off right; each is a challenge to the growing person. Those who have read this chapter will see how many things there are to do on a date besides the same old stuff.

Dating has been explained as education in the discovery of emotions and their control. Sexual urges, unruly tempers, and needs for affection come to the fore out of the new experiences of dating relations. Participants come to find that gestures of affection enrich their relations if tied in with the discovery of common interests and goals. Out of dating, then, should come not only the ability to love and be loved, but also the alternatives to petting.

Finally, dating proves to have value in training young people in the art of democratic give and take. Girls are allowed more initiative in dating than they were in old-fashioned courting days and often stage events in which they assume the costs of the party. This equalitarian relationship carries over into later courtship, engagement, and marriage relations and makes for a more democratic marriage and family life.

Readings

BLOOD, ROBERT O., *Anticipating Your Marriage* (Glencoe, Illinois: The Free Press, 1955). Chapter 1 takes up the motives for, and the functions of, dating — random and steady dating, "dates for the dateless," and how dating foreshadows marriage. Although this is a college text, the mature high school student will get a great deal of value from it.

BURGESS, ERNEST W., PAUL WALLIN and GLADYS DENNY SHULTZ, *Courtship, Engagement and Marriage* (Philadelphia: J. B. Lippincott Company, 1954). Part One: "Dating in the Modern Age," reviews relevant findings that have to do with dating from an extensive study of one thousand couples through their courtship and into their marriage. Recommended for the interested mature student.

DUVALL, EVELYN MILLIS, *The Art of Dating* (New York: Association Press, 1958). This book is written for young people, around thousands of their questions about dating. Each topic is dealt with frankly, using what research evidence there is and the attitudes of young people to the situations where youth surveys make them available.

FORCE, ELIZABETH S., *Your Family Today and Tomorrow* (New York: Harcourt, Brace and Company, 1955). Mrs. Force, experienced teacher of high school marriage and family courses, writes to and for youth. See especially her "The Dating Ladder" on page 108 in Chapter 7.

KIRKENDALL, LESTER A., and RUTH FARNHAM OSBORNE, *Dating Days* (Science Research Associates, 259 East Erie Street, Chicago 11, Illinois, 1949).

This excellent pamphlet contains check tests on which you can rate yourself on how you measure up as a good date, and where you stand in your present relationship.

LANDIS, JUDSON and MARY, *Personal Adjustment, Marriage and Family Living* (New York: Prentice-Hall, 1955 revision). See especially how the Landises treat the questions of uncertainties during dating, and standards of behavior in dating, in their Chapters 5 and 6.

LANDIS, PAUL H., *Your Marriage and Family Living* (New York: McGraw-Hill Book Company, 1954 edition). Professor Landis devotes three chapters to dating: 4. "How the Sexes Differ," 5. "Personality Needs and Dating," and 6. "Dating for Experience."

CHAPTER FOUR

In Deeper than Ever

BECOMING INVOLVED

How do you get in so deep?

Are lovers' quarrels normal?

Do friends push the couple even closer together?

Should girls be given more freedom in getting their man?

What about dating bureaus?

7 HE COURTSHIP PROCESS TODAY REFLECTS THE INCREASING MUTUAL-ity of the man-woman status. At one time courtship referred to a process of persuading, or courting, during which the swain-in-love won the affections of his fair lady who was ostensibly not in love. Courtship today has been preceded by casual dating in which little or no commitment is expected, and consists less of a persuading period than a process of mutual involvement leading to a formal commitment in engagement.

Dating, courtship, and engagement are general terms used popularly to denote varying degrees of commitment in the sifting and sorting of the sexes into marrying couples. There is some appearance of orderliness in the stages from lesser to greater degrees of involvement.

Individuals may shift within these stages of involvement experiencing some of the stages and not others. Some are arrested at an intermediate stage and find it difficult to progress beyond that point. The wary bachelor and the uncoquettish spinster are examples.

Persons high on the popularity scale may keep several affairs going concurrently. Generally as the stage of involvement progresses the number of relationships maintained decreases sharply. Courtship, as we use the term in this chapter, begins with the stages of involvement in which the field has narrowed down, and one relationship has taken precedence over all others.

In the pages which follow, the social psychology of courtship involvement unfolds. Dating *activities* and *skills* constituted the focus of the last chapter. In this discussion we shift to the *relationships* and bonds of sentiment which grow up *between dating individuals*.

Several forces are at work to forge the bonds of sentiment which change the pair from a casual twosome to an engaged couple. Powerful

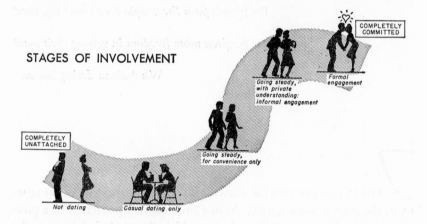

STAGES OF INVOLVEMENT

COMPLETELY COMMITTED

Formal engagement

Going steady, with private understanding: informal engagement

COMPLETELY UNATTACHED

Going steady, for convenience only

Not dating   Casual dating only

physical attractions are at work in heterosexual dating. Pride in having and holding are anticipatory of mutual ego-involvement. Finally, shared activities, whether recreation oriented or work oriented, create bonds of sentiment which are strangely strong. As these three processes support one another in the interactions of steady dating, courtship, a process of mutual involvement, ensues.

The Involvement Process [1]

The involvement process begins in dating, at which time there may be little serious intent, and ends in a climax of powerful emotional responses which are most evident in the engagement and honeymoon

[1] We present the following discussion with acknowledgments to Willard Waller, who first developed the approach we are taking in his book, revised by Reuben Hill, *The Family: A Dynamic Interpretation* (New York: Dryden Press, 1951), pp. 176–190, and urge you to regard it as typical only of the middle class courtships in America. No single courtship conforms in all details to the picture we shall present, but thousands approximate it in one or more ways.

periods. Human beings act upon one another emotionally when they are thrown into intimate relations. As emotions build up in one they are communicated contagiously to the other. Unless there is opportunity for release, the climax which is attained may reach great proportions. Here is the way it looks in the anger response: A mother may start the morning gay and relaxed, with a song on her lips, and may hardly notice the noise and bickering of the children. All too typically, frustrations pile up as the day gets under way. She finds the toaster doesn't work, the coffee cream is sour, her husband gets up late, is touchy and critical, and dashes off without kissing her good-by. The hot water faucet was left on all night and so there isn't any hot water for her dishes. She bears all this with patience and forbearance, but at 9:30, a half hour late already, the cleaning woman calls to say she's sorry but she guesses she won't be able to come today because Mrs. B. needs her to clean up after a party. The mother's forbearance cracks wide open, and a disproportionately heated anger response is unleashed. The cleaning woman doesn't understand it and is hurt. "She was such a nice lady all the other days, I wonder what's eating her?"

Courtship is a summatory process which builds up in much the same fashion, with many little experiences, some pleasant and some irritating, each affecting the other, and leaving the parties more involved than before. Each person becomes increasingly committed in his own eyes and in the eyes of the other. Once reaching a certain level of intensity, the process gets a movement of its own. It creates its own demands and needs, and each member finds himself more and more in need of the other to satisfy the new appetites which have been developed. The process tends to be irreversible after a certain momentum is reached, and the couple find they can't stop with being just good friends.[2] Some insightful couples have described the experience as not unlike an emotional build-up which occurs in a religious revival. The religious feelings mount as persons interact emotionally. The emotions of the more excitable in the congregation build up the slower, and, eventually, all experience conversion and the calm which comes with being sure they are right.

What are the specific components of the involvement process in this movement from casual dating to the emotional climax of engagement? When the brake is taken off a car on a hill, the car may start slowly

2 *Ibid.*, p. 181.

enough at first, but there are the possibilities of excitement even at the beginning. The components of the courtship process are present in the dating period, but are kept in leash by powerful inhibitions until the man, at least, is economically and psychologically ready to take the consequences of emotional involvement.

Coquetry. The involvement process begins with coquetry, behavior which invites to amorous adventure. It is seen in the toning up of the organism which occurs when boy and girl meet. The smile of the boy when he sees a pretty girl is automatic, and he takes her in with a glance which leaves nothing out. Her blush is evidence that she knows he sees her, and her own coquetry is expressed in her sparkling eyes and flashing smile. Both sense the coltish impulse to kick about with their feet, which they suppress in favor of tossing the head, laughing, and giggling.

Coquetry is found in all cultures and has been described beautifully in the literature of many peoples. Its tricks are legion. Small hints of interest are given, and hints of erotic possibilities with alternate advance and recession; great interest is followed by mock modesty, by teasing. Teasing is one of the main techniques of coquetry by which tension is stimulated in the other person to a higher level; the impulse is to chase and be chased, but never quite to catch or be caught.

The Line. In America a familiar accompaniment and expression of coquetry is "the line." The line is an exaggeration of our feelings, as if the feelings we exhibit in coquetry were not enough. It is used by both sexes and is called variously "handing her a line," or "laying it on"; among the Irish it is called "blarney." When you first meet a girl you profess to be greatly impressed by her charms, and you hand her a line. You don't expect to be taken too seriously or you will take flight. But you want to be taken somewhat seriously, and so does she. Neither knows how much is line and how much is sincerity.

The line was especially well developed by the lovemaking knights of Arthur's mythical court. Much of our line is outright copying of these lovers of old, and it is best done in parts of the South where, relatively speaking, women still occupy a somewhat exalted position. The typical gallant young Southerner at the slightest provocation can string a line of sugared words and compliments which will delight any female listener.

The line covers up real emotional involvements by exaggeration. Under the soft words may be conflict, because each has the uneasy feeling that he is being tricked. Each avoids being caught by the loaded words of the other — each wishes, however, to dominate the fantasy of the other and to set him to dreaming.

Each tends to become involved in his own line, which he comes to believe in part, but each worries because the other doesn't reveal the extent to which he is sincere. A sense of insecurity arises from not knowing just where they stand, and the lovers quarrel.

Lovers' Quarrels. The line finally becomes so burdensome that it has to be broken through, and the crisis comes in a good quarrel followed by crying and releasing of tension. Each reveals in the process how much he truly cares for the other, and the pair come to take themselves more seriously. The quarrel tends to redefine the situation upward. Quarrels of alienation, in contrast, leave the relationship weaker than it was. The typical lovers' quarrel builds up to a new level of commitment. The pair make up with a glorious sense of satisfaction and are more involved than before.

Common Interests. Quarrels leave the pair still using the line, but with more security and with a tenderness developing that wasn't there before. Each is surer of the other and both reach out to claim things which tie them together. Common interests further love involvements by giving the pair a common universe of discourse. The lovers can exclude the rest of the world, and they feel a sense of superiority as they talk on and on about things they understand better than anyone else in the world.

Increasing Intimacy. Coquetry enhanced by the mutual interchange of lines and the build-up of common interests brings the pair increasingly together. The line alone encourages physical intimacy, and love gestures confirm the sincerity of the verbal "I love you." The other person becomes a bona fide love object to be reckoned with — not just another date, but a person with feelings. Feelings of tenderness develop, and the lover finds himself more sincere than before, and impressed with his moral obligation to the other who believes in him so implicitly.

Idealization. Another component of love involvement, which owes some of its development to the line, is idealization. In the line all the desirable characteristics of the other are stressed to the exclusion of the annoying or disturbing characteristics, and it is not uncommon for young people to become so enamored of the love object that they come to believe their own line. The lover forgets his sweetheart's crooked teeth, her so-so complexion, and her stringy hair, and remembers only her lovely eyes and regal carriage. The greatest compliment a lover can be paid is to be told, "You're different." Waller tells the story of a young man who was very conscious of a wart on his chin and went to the expense of an operation to remove it. After it had healed, he presented himself to his fiancée. "Notice anything different about my face?" The moment was embarrassing; she had never noticed the wart in the first place.

Idealization results in each replacing the other with an imaginary person to whom he reacts. Separation for brief periods tends to accentuate this process. Absence makes the heart grow fonder, because the real person's presence gives way to the imaginary one. Each feels troubled that his own weaknesses are not seen, but doesn't try too hard to expose them. Unfortunately for later adjustments, the greater the idealization, the greater is the disillusionment which must follow in the marriage period. But couples should remember it was their imagination which cheated them, not marriage!

Couple Unity. In the midst of this process couple unity develops. Favored by the development of common interests which act to exclude the public and to give the pair a feeling of superiority, the couple reach out and seize upon evidences that they were meant for each other. One couple in the course of their daily walk simultaneously focused their attention upon a certain mountain peak glittering in the sun and called it "their mountain." They took every opportunity thereafter to admire this symbol of their unity. Years later they returned to the exact spot to get another view of the mountain which had come to mean so much to them during their courtship period.

Early in the development of unity, rings or other articles will be exchanged to crystallize and render tangible that elusive "we feeling" which they sense but can't describe. As each leaves the other, he carries away a reminder of their growing unity. It is as if the exchanged articles could somehow summon the presence of the loved one, and the separation is thereby made more bearable. As the couple see more and more of each other, they may express a growing sense of unity by wearing similar clothing to inform others that they belong together.

Another development in this process is the growth of a special lan-

guage between the two, which they alone can understand. They develop their own idioms, pet names, and inflections which tend to alienate any third person and make him realize that two is company but
three is a crowd. Left more and more together, the pair build up a
shorthand language of symbols which obviates the necessity of complet-
ing sentences. Conversation is speeded up tremendously. Their language may look and sound to the outsider like a combination of nudges,
knowing winks, and half-finished sentences, with poorly repressed mirth
at things the outsider doesn't think funny at all. The jokes are hardest
of all for the intruder to understand. They can be fully appreciated
and understood only by the couple themselves. The jokes grow funnier
the more frequently they are repeated, because they develop unseen
nuances and are attached to other associations of a pleasant nature in
the relationship. In summary, the process of developing pair unity is
one of building a separate history and culture which the pair alone can
understand. The relationship is stabilized in direct proportion to its
success in throwing the pair on its own resources and in excluding,
thereby, rivals and other members of the public.

Friends Encourage a Public Announcement. All of these activities of
the couple have not escaped the eyes of friends, who play a very important role in furthering love involvements. Whenever a young man and
young woman appear together, even in the casual dating stage, they risk
being identified as a likely marriage pair by well-wishers. Friendly gossip — "We hear that Bob and Mary are getting serious" — gets back to
the ears of the participants. Gossip columns of community and campus
newspapers are widely read and further the public's identification of the
pair. There is something about being identified by the public which
changes the relationship. The sense of moral obligation on the part of
the man, particularly, is a function partly of what the public thinks of
his affair. Yesterday he might have been asked by a relative of the girl
what his intentions were; today his conscience asks him the same question and is quite as effective in furthering his feeling of obligation to
clarify things. The talk of people acts as further pressure to drop the
exaggerations of the line and become more sincere in the relationship.
"People are saying we are going steady but you haven't said a word
about it. Margaret even asked me if we were engaged. The nerve. . . ."
They quarrel, and in making up, many of the problems concerning their

status which have given them the jitters are cleared up. The discussion and redefinition of the situation enables them to explain satisfactorily to themselves and to the public where they stand.

The public plays its part in clarifying the situation by treating the two as a unit, arranging for them to be together, inviting them to social affairs together. When a friend meets one member of the couple, he asks about the other member and expresses inferentially the hope that all is well between them. The pair come to feel that the public approves of the match and expects something to come of it. This sanctioning in itself has a pushing effect and changes the nature of the relationship subtly but effectively. Much of the exciting novelty of the relation is lost, but in its place comes a sense of responsibility and stability. If the pair are emotionally built up to a certain point, all it may take is a suggestion from a friend that they act as if they were engaged to crystallize the situation. It seems only natural and right to make a public announcement of their involvement, and a formal engagement takes place.

Variations from the Typical. As we have already warned, no single courtship will necessarily embody all of the components described, and many individual courtships will vary greatly from the pattern just pre sented. Young people who have come through courses in marriage and the family rarely take the line as seriously as described here, with the result that they build up fewer illusions about each other and indulge in relatively little idealization. Indeed, the courtship remains much more on the companionship level, and the emotions tend to be enjoyed on the spot rather than built up toward an explosive release at the honeymoon stage. These couples carry over into marriage fewer illusions about one another but nevertheless develop considerable fondness for each other as persons. They rarely build up ideas of the other as the incarnation of perfection so characteristic of those who have gone in for extreme idealization.

The courtship pattern followed by young people in isolated rural areas may also vary greatly from that of the middle class urban couple described in the foregoing pages. Rural courtships may conform more closely to those of the last generation and move more naturally and easily from keeping company to serious courtship to engagement and marriage. Each step in the process is well marked. Moreover, the couple have probably known one another for so long that there is little possibility of extreme idealization. The line is not likely to take such exaggerated form and would not be taken seriously if it did.

A third variation is seen in the courtships of war and postwar couples who have telescoped the dating and courtship and engagement periods in favor of immediate marriage.

These three variations from the patterns regarded as typical of the courtship process remind us of the range which exists in America. A more detailed consideration of the changes in courtship patterns which have occurred in the last three generations may give us the perspective we need to understand courtship today.

Changes in Courtship Patterns

The finding of a mate, and the details of arranging the betrothal, was until frontier days the prerogative of parents, and still is in many countries. Freedom of choice in this country dates from the days when all the eligible men and all the eligible women were known by the entire community. Young ladies knew from childhood the men who might come "a-courtin'." Rarely would a stranger be permitted to compete for the hand of a local belle. Freedom of choice was limited to the local eligibles and was therefore safe enough.

In the more settled towns of the Atlantic seaboard the problem was handled with prosaic formality. A formal introduction was followed by careful supervision of the relationship. A good girl refused to talk to any man who had not been first vouched for by a friend, and even then she consulted her parents for their approval. This system operated to limit the contacts of genteel young ladies to a relatively select group of eligible young men and discouraged social relations between ineligible women and men of good birth. Girls in those days had fewer opportunities to circulate, but the conditions under which they met men were conducive to the type of prolonged acquaintance necessary to judge men as potential marriage partners.

Today, there is less likelihood of marrying one's first love, and somewhat greater opportunity for exploring the field to find what one's preferences are.[3] Under the contemporary system, if there are years of

. [3] A study which reveals clearly differences in courtship patterns in three generations is Marvin H. Koller's "Some Changes in Courtship Behavior in Three Generations of Ohio Women," *American Sociological Review*, Vol. 16, No. 3 (June, 1951),

professional training ahead, it is possible through dating to maintain contact with the opposite sex until marriage proves feasible.

A number of trends in courtship customs can be established from the contrasts between the beginning and the middle of the 20th century:

TEN RECENT TRENDS IN COURTSHIP CUSTOMS

1 Dating and courtship begin at earlier age
2 More frequent contact between the sexes
3 Dating and courtship last until later at night
4 More privacy for dating and courting pairs
5 Less supervision and chaperonage
6 More general acceptance of "going steady"
7 Wider range of patterns of intimacy and sex play
8 Many more discussable topics during dating and courtship
9 Higher readiness for education and guidance in courtship
10 Courtship culminates earlier in engagement and marriage

Difficulties in the Courtship System

Our somewhat unique pattern of freedom of choice has survived as an integral part of the courtship system today, but the community and neighborhood controls which helped it work in the colonial days have largely disappeared, particularly in cities. Blind dates are followed more often than not by regular dates without the slightest reference to the possibilities of parental approval or disapproval.

Another way of looking at courtship is as a device to sort out the compatible from the incompatible pairs of young people and provide the steps for leading the former to marriage and the latter back into circulation. If we had a courtship system which meshed well with the other parts of our changing culture, we should have fewer unhappy marriages and obviously many fewer divorces. The divorce rate is closely tied up with the number of poorly mated pairs who become engaged despite a minimum of common interests, and whose experiences in the engagement period are too superficial to reveal incompatibility. What

pp. 366–370. Koller studied 111 grandmothers averaging 78 years of age, 118 mothers averaging 48 years, and 140 married daughters averaging 23 years of age. The daughters reported over four times as many dates per week as their grandmothers. They circulated more widely and considered more men seriously as spouses before settling on the man they finally married. The earlier generations averaged longer engagements (11 months, 9 months, and 6 months respectively), but covered less territory in their premarital discussions and agreements.

has happened to our mate-finding machinery to break it down so completely?

Freedom of Choice Breaks Down. The courtship system of free choice has broken down as America has become urbanized. The conditions which produced the system of free choice have disappeared, and it is incumbent upon social engineers to devise new machinery or streamline the old. Sufficient research has been made regarding the situation to show the directions social planning for courtship should take. One authority lists four general needs: 1. the need for more initiative in courtship by girls; 2. the need for removing restraints upon the employment of women, such as the ban on married teachers, so that they would not be limited in their selection to men who could immediately provide full maintenance; 3. the need to increase opportunities for circulation of young people among several groups for a more varied experience and deeper companionship before a selection is made; and 4. the need for premarital counseling services to enable individuals to utilize the resources at their disposal.[4]

In frontier days men greatly outnumbered women, and the passive role of women did not seriously handicap them in obtaining desirable husbands. Today the sex ratio is reversed in many areas, and nowhere are there very many men to spare. To meet this changed situation, the initiative in courtship should be taken more equally by both sexes. We grant the right of a woman to equal education and to equal freedom of choice of vocation and profession; at least the trend is in that direction. It is inconsistent, then, to continue the traditional courtship practice just because it is traditional. The newer findings of mental hygiene specialists indicate that the passive method by which women must lie in wait makes for greater frustration and more neurotic adjustments than the active program of pursuit permitted, as yet, for men only.

Today we recognize that a person of either sex must become marriageable if he or she hopes to find a satisfactory mate, appeal, attract, and win a spouse by getting into the ongoing courtship competition as an eligible young man or woman. Becoming marriageable involves developing personal qualities that are pleasing, and acquiring the social skills that make for competence in relationships with the other sex.

---

[4] See Joseph K. Folsom's discussion of the limitations of our present courtship system, and his suggestions for improving it, in his book, *The Family and Democratic Society* (New York: Wiley, 1943), pp. 531–543.

Recommended Improvements

The proposal to increase greatly the opportunities for circulation of young people among several groups for a more varied experience and deeper companionship before making their selection strikes at the heart of the courtship problem. Gone are the limitations of the past, the barriers of formal introductions and parentally controlled courtships, but the facilities for bringing young people together in an atmosphere that is conducive to courtship have been slow to make their appearance. The need is particularly great in the larger cities where contacts between people are usually transitory and superficial. Letters such as the following are not uncommon in the collection of requests received by social agencies:

. . . I'm definitely disgusted with myself for not being able to go out and find romance as others do — but frankly, it's reached the point where I'm actually becoming morbid over my social deficiency — the more I try to fight it, the further back I seem to go. I don't know of anyone that can actually be of any constructive help, my friends are as much in the dark as I am when it comes to getting a girl friend. . . . When quitting time comes at the office, I hate to leave because it only means a lonely and empty evening. . . . Psychiatrists have told me, get married, it will give you a new set of social values. . . . Really that was just rubbing it in, because secretly that is what I've always wanted more than anything in life. . . . What I want isn't unreasonable — it's the very essence of society — it's no more than millions of couples since time immemorial have accepted as a matter of fact. . . . Chicago ought to have one of these [introduction services] for fellows like me.

There is a holdover of the romantic notion that the first meeting of two lovers must seem accidental and that their love must be confirmed by the evidence of fate having brought them together. There remains, therefore, a certain amount of resistance to the devices invented by more ingenious young people to widen their horizons, such as dating bureaus, dating exchanges, introduction services, and acquaintance bureaus. Dating bureaus on college campuses have sometimes failed because they attract mainly those most in need of an introduction service. Once students identify the bureaus as containing mainly the names of the socially inept, the project falls through, even though many may have been helped. Introduction services in large communities have usually fared better. Young men and women coming into the big city often need help in establishing themselves in congenial social groups. Churches and social agencies make a contribution as well as commercial introduction services. Established primarily to widen the circle of acquaintances rather than to arrange marriages, these services have succeeded where more formal arrangements have failed. The director of one such service described his clientele as composed of normal young people of fairly high education who, though able to find some companionship, were eager to be more selective in regard to tastes and interests. The conclusions and recommendations contained in his report are distinctly quotable:

. . . they were an exceptionally fine type of young people, and their high average education, as well as conversations I had with them, indicate they approached the idea with a minimum of emotional resistance against the "stigma" of a dating bureau (which, after all, it was) and especially against a plan using a methodical, scientific approach to something which is not, under present social customs, ordinarily susceptible to anything but the usual haphazard, accidental, inspirational, romantic approach. In other words, these young people were better qualified than the average to perceive the breakdown of the older system and the necessity of something new and better.

As a result of the experience obtained from the experiment . . . I have come to the conclusion that the difficulties might be overcome fairly well. The *method*, consisting of tests, rating, references, and matching according to principles developed in recent researches (referring here to such tests as the Moss-Hunt-Omwake Social Intelligence Test, the Pressey Senior Classification test, and Bernreuter Personality Inventory furnished by the Psychological Corporation and to the researches of Dr. Kelley) is, I believe, fundamentally sound. If we are going to accept people as they are, and try to find the best combinations under those circumstances without trying to change people themselves, something of this very nature must eventually be adopted. . . .

The *procedure*, however, should be thoroughly revamped, in the light of current social customs. It appears to me that the principal emotional resistances are as follows: 1. the fear (often based on past experience) of getting "stuck" when on a "blind date," 2. the dislike of anything that approaches romance and luck from a "cold-and-calculating" angle, based (*a*) on the scientific methods employed and (*b*) on the fact that it was necessary to make a charge for the service, which was self-supporting.

Therefore, any new plan, if it is to succeed in numbers reached, must operate on a non-profit, unintentional basis. It occurs to me that this would be done best by adopting the program in some already existing organization which is of such a nature that the interviews and tests can be given ostensibly for some regular purpose of the organization.[5]

The advantage of this social invention, which is no more incredible than the first television, is that it may be adapted with success by church groups, youth agencies, and counseling services as part of their youth service programs. These agencies are rapidly building up staffs of workers competent to carry out the procedure of a "friend-finding" bureau (interviewing, personality inventories, card indexing, and so on). The resistances to the procedure can be circumvented at first by the suggestions made above. The results should be a greatly improved courtship and mate-finding system for America.

Ideally, young people should have abundant opportunity to meet members of the opposite sex with a variety of interests and tastes and from a variety of economic and social backgrounds. They should, however, become sufficiently well acquainted with perhaps a dozen persons to determine whether there is a basis for marriage. Here, indeed, is another area in which social invention is needed: many more boys are met than formerly, but girls know few of them on a basis adequate for judging their availability as husbands.

Dating and courtship may be the period of shuffling and pairing the players into what appear to be compatible twosomes, but the engagement period is the first official test of the pairing. When courtship is successful in bringing together congenial young people the engagement is likely to be less stormy. In any event, the engagement occupies the bottleneck position through which most marriages-to-be pass, and one of its assignments is to discourage mismatings. Our attention shifts at this point, then, to the engagement.

Readings

BOWMAN, HENRY A., *Marriage for Moderns* (New York: McGraw-Hill Book Company, 1960 edition). One of the first marriage texts to deal directly with the problems young people face as they approach marriage, this book can be heartily recommended for today's mature student.

DUVALL, SYLVANUS M., *Before You Marry* (New York: Association Press, 1959 edition). This step-by-step guide to a happy marriage is based upon the 101 questions young people most appropriately ask themselves before they marry. Chapter 2 is particularly pertinent here.

[5] Report of Joseph Clawson of New York City in Joseph K. Folsom, *The Family and Democratic Society* (New York: Wiley, 1943), pp. 542–543.

MAGOUN, F. ALEXANDER, *Love and Marriage* (New York: Harper & Brothers, 1956 edition). Chapter 7, "Courtship," deals with such topics as the search for love, outgrowing dependent love, avoiding courtship mistakes, emotional dishonesties, and how to be analytical about oneself and one's personal love relationships.

MOORE, BERNICE MILBURN, and DOROTHY M. LEAHY, *You and Your Family* (Boston, D. C. Heath and Company, 1953 edition). See particularly the discussion of the functions of courtship in Chapter 11, "The Next Step is Courtship."

WALLER, WILLARD, and REUBEN HILL, *The Family: A Dynamic Interpretation* (New York: Dryden Press, 1951). Chapter 10, "Courtship as an Interactive Process," discusses many of the topics taken up in your chapter in greater detail, and as such is well worth the time and attention of the superior student.

CHAPTER FIVE

Does Every Engaged Couple Have Doubts?

GETTING ENGAGED

Are short engagements better than long ones?

Once you are engaged, what are your obligations?

What can an engaged couple do to prepare themselves for marriage?

What sorts of engagements ought to be broken?

Should engagement mean monopoly?

$\mathcal{G}$ETTING ENGAGED, AS WELL AS THE INTERPRETATION OF ITS OB-ligations and duties, varies tremendously from couple to couple. For many it is regarded as an end in itself, like a degree or a diploma, rather than a period of preparation for greater responsibilities in marriage and family life. For many it is dominated by the thrills of novelty and new experience rather than by the solving of problems and testing of personalities.

This chapter is designed to open the eyes of couples who regard engagement simply as a hurdle before marriage. We hope to show that the betrothal has values of its own, and that time invested in a conscientious engagement returns dividends in more successful marriage later on. It is a necessary bridge between the irresponsibility of youth with its "single blessedness" and the married responsibility of adults.

The courting relationship to begin with is fairly casual, and there is little pain involved if a rupture occurs in the relation. By engagement time the couple has been caught up in a whole series of involvements through the use of the line, occasional love gestures, idealizations, and lovers' quarrels. Couple unity builds up out of common interests and the growing feeling that they are meant for each other. Friends take notice and encourage them to think of themselves as engaged. They are identified in the public's eyes henceforth as a potential married couple, and they are aware of the necessity of conforming to social expectations.

Engagement from a Man's Point of View

Engagement is commonly thought to be mainly of concern to women. According to the articulate male critic, engagement is a matter of putting up with a whim of the fiancée in order that she may have her quota of parties and showers, and that she may rate the society pages and may be duly congratulated and feted on her good fortune. She often supports him in this viewpoint by insisting that a girl gets married only once, and she has a right to all the attention and excitement she can get out of the preparations which attend the engagement period. Partly due to this attitude, many couples have married without bothering with engagement at all. Just what are the advantages of an engagement which a man should consider, for he is more frequently the offender in bypassing this period as needless ceremonial?

There are real advantages to the man of a full and complete engagement period, which hold in many instances for his fiancée as well:

1 The engagement may save a man from being dazzled by the supposed glamor of his fiancée, since it gives him opportunities to see her without make-up, over a period of time. It is the more enjoyable because it is conducted in everyday clothes instead of Sunday best.

2 The engagement may enable a man to become better acquainted with the thinking of the emancipated woman of the twentieth century. He may find that the present edition will not play the same submissive game his mother has and that she expects to be accepted as a person in her own right. If he wants a wife who will baby him as mother may have done, he may need to look elsewhere.

3 The engagement gives him an opportunity to get acquainted with his fiancée's family and to have his fiancée accepted by his family. In-laws are valuable assets, and their approval is most necessary. If they disapprove, they may act as a wedge to separate him from his wife when the first crisis develops.[1]

---

[1] Studies of marriage success list "approval of parents" as one of the important factors in marital happiness. See Ernest W. Burgess and Leonard S. Cottrell, Jr., *Predicting Success or Failure in Marriage* (New York: Prentice-Hall, 1939), pp. 168–

4 The engagement gives him time to arrange his financial affairs and to get ready for the economic burden of marriage.

5 The engagement may give him insight into the relative responsiveness of his fiancée. Even though there be a minimum of sex experimentation in the engagement, such deficiencies as frigidity, lack of capacity for demonstrating affection, and childhood fears will show up in the normal love play of the engagement.

6 The engagement gives the man a chance to see whether there is any possibility of sharing his business and professional interests with his wife-to-be. This is an important factor in the early years of marriage as both are struggling to attain a secure economic position.

7 The engagement gives the man who wants children the opportunity of noting in more detail his affianced's attitudes toward children and child rearing. (Not all women want children, you know.)

8 The engagement gives a man a chance to slip into his role of husband gradually and to learn some of the ropes while still in the engagement period. Nothing succeeds like success, and the engagement enables the novice to succeed by starting him out with premarriage problems and inducting him slowly into the complications of married life.

Woman's Point of View

The feminine reader will recognize here many values of an engagement which, when transposed, hold equally well for her. She should be aware also of the unusual opportunities the engagement offers for prolonged discussions of mutual interest. She can feel perfectly free, now that she is engaged, to express her desires and aspiration in marriage. She will want to find out the attitudes of her fiancé toward the role of the wife as homemaker or worker outside the home, his point of view on the issues of housing, extramarital friendships, handling of money, and so on. The initiative which a woman properly takes in this discussion is com-

---

170. In America we are inclined to dispose of the mother-in-law and other in-laws by a system of avoidance. Any story commiserating the victim of in-law interference is sure to get a laugh or a headline; see for example the following clipping from the *Detroit News:*

"Tom took his wife and two children out to spend a week with her parents in the country, while some repairs were being made on the house.

"At week-end the repair job wasn't finished and Tom telephoned to suggest that the missus extend her stay for a few days.

" 'I will not,' she hissed. 'You come right out and get me. I can't stand living with in-laws any longer.'

" 'What do you mean?' asked puzzled Tom. 'They're not my folks; they're yours.'

" 'Well,' said Mrs. Tom defensively, 'after you're married they're all in-laws.' "

ing to be recognized frankly. There is little today that is considered "unladylike" as a topic of discussion between two people who plan to marry each other. Since the engagement period has been characterized as the period during which the idea of marriage with this particular mate is being explored as a working hypothesis, such discussions are especially pertinent during this interval.

A third reason for the engagement is to test the sincerity of the professions of affection which occur so frequently in the courtship period. The newly engaged want to be assured that the professing of love isn't part of the line, that this is really love. The girl wants to feel the tenderness of her affianced without the threat of rivals to disturb her. The members of an engaged pair inevitably bring from courtship certain resentments, memories of injustices and painful jealousy, as a result of the insecurity of the relation in competitive courtship days. Now is the time to bring out on the table the unresolved differences and conflicts which have heretofore plagued the relationship. Each can now speak his piece with more security. There are no longer rivals who might take immediate advantage of any temporary alienation. It is no longer necessary to jockey for position. The line, which was used originally to cover up the insecurity of the participants, can now be put aside. People leave the pair alone a lot more now, so they can be quite frank about themselves. The period can be one of personality testing and can also be one of exploration and experimentation.

Finally, the young woman knows that it is no longer primarily her parents' job, but hers, to investigate the background and future prospects of the man to whom she is engaged. Presumably she has made certain investigations during the courtship period, or she would not have become engaged. Within the privacy and intimacy of the new relationship the more detailed double checks on their reactions to each other are invaluable. It is incumbent on the pair to carry on this exploration in our crazy-quilt society, because there is no guarantee that our present mate-finding machinery has brought together individuals of similar backgrounds.

What, in summary, can the engagement do for our hypothetical courtship couple that warrants any further postponement of their marriage? The engagement has possibilities as a stage for getting better acquainted without the fear of rivals' cutting in, as an off-stage setting where the line, the wisecracking, and the kidding of the courtship may be exchanged for the more honest and earnest discussion. It has possibilities as a testing ground for the congeniality of personalities, as a school for solving differences and finding areas of agreement, as a waiting period for the doubting Thomases with their misgivings, and finally as a trial period with the public watching and judging. All the processes welding a couple together in courtship continue with greater force in engagement, but they operate with less uncertainty, because there is less danger that the relationship will be disrupted. The engagement period makes possible the continuation of these processes which make for solidarity to the point where the relationship can withstand the crises and the responsibilities of marriage.

Length of Engagement

How long should the engagement be? This is a frequent question in marriage classes. As we have pointed out earlier, each engaged couple is unique in experience and background, and each interprets engagement somewhat differently. To answer the question of length of engagement would require an intimate acquaintance with the history of the individual engagement pair. Much depends, for example, on the length of acquaintance before engagement and the degree to which the couple may have undertaken the personality testing and problem solving functions in the pre-engagement period. Many students who have read books or attended classes on marriage problems discuss during courtship questions which other couples less well oriented postpone for the engagement.

In both the Burgess-Cottrell and the Terman studies of marriage success already cited there appears to be a positive relationship between length of engagement and marital happiness.[2] The longer couples were engaged, the studies showed, the more satisfactory was their later marital adjustment. Actually, these statistics may reflect more than appears on the surface. There probably was a selection of the hardier couples of superior character who could survive a long engagement. We have no adjustment scores for those couples whose engagements were broken because they attempted to prolong the engagement beyond a sensible point.

[2] See Lewis M. Terman and associates, *Psychological Factors in Marital Happiness*, p. 198; and Burgess and Cottrell, *op. cit.*, p. 167.

The highest happiness scores in the Burgess study went to those married couples who had been engaged for two years or longer before marriage. Only 11 per cent of this group showed poor marital adjustment, while of those who had been engaged less than three months 50 per cent showed poor adjustment. The mean happiness scores of Terman's couples went up steadily in relation to length of engagement, reaching a peak among those who had been engaged five years or longer. One of these authors concludes from his findings that companionship rather than romantic love forms the best sustaining force for a mutually satisfying love relation. He apparently questions the lasting quality of a relation based primarily on romantic love, suggesting that there should be an opportunity for the relationship to mature over a considerable period of time before marriage.[3]

The case for fairly long engagements need not rest on these statistical studies of marriage success alone. There are obvious values in engagements which are long enough to prepare couples for marriage. Engagements need to be long enough to act as a screening device to alienate and separate incompatible couples who would otherwise marry, only to separate more painfully after some years of marriage. The answer to the question of length of engagement is given best, not as a definite number of months or years, but in terms of the indefinite "long enough." The engagement, then, should be *long enough* to perform the many functions of testing, discussing, learning, fighting, and loving which underlie successful marriage. If the student requires a more specific figure, it is probably safe to state that the engagement should rarely be shorter than six months and rarely longer than two years, depending on the length of previous acquaintance and the extent to which the engagement functions have already been started in the courtship period.

How long an engagement is too long? Henry Bowman has established rough criteria which may be helpful:

An engagement is too long if an excessive amount of nervous tension is generated; if the couple experience a sense of frustration; if they become more than usually tired of waiting; if they grow discouraged; if they become indifferent to each other; if they begin to accept the *status quo* as a substitute for marriage and lose interest in the latter; if the engagement constitutes more than a relatively small fraction of the total period from meeting to wedding. . . . We wish to counteract the opinion so commonly expressed

[3] Burgess and Cottrell, *op. cit.*, p. 168.

among students to the effect that on the basis of a few months' courtship a couple may without risk enter upon an engagement of several years' duration.[4]

Engagements in the Face of Separation

An important variable to be considered in computing the length of the engagement period is that of distance, which all too frequently separates the engaged couple. The engagement of individuals parted for long periods of time because of war, employment, prolonged professional training, or other enforced absences is hardly to be compared with the engagement of young people actively pursuing the job of mutual exploration and problem solving day in and day out. Can the functions of engagement be satisfactorily carried on by correspondence?

In the ideal engagement, separation immediately after the announcement would hardly be contemplated. Rather, the announcement should normally be followed by a series of mutual investigations during more or less constant association. The pair needs time to win the approval of the families, relatives, and friends of both parties. This necessitates being seen in public together long enough for people to say, "I think they make a fine pair; they ought to hit it off nicely." The support of the public is not to be disregarded, even in these times, and it is hard to obtain public support of the marriage-to-be by correspondence. There are, however, several young couples who are working out their engagement duties quite conscientiously by correspondence. How are they doing it?

First, every effort is made to keep letters full of information about day-to-day experiences which tell about the changes in personality. The correspondents go in for frequent exchange of candid photographs and snapshots. These keep the couple up to date on physical appearance (new clothes, changes in weight, etc.) and give a visual picture of the places and people each is meeting. These tokens will later act as a source of common experience to tie the couple together.

Second, the couples find that some questions may be discussed more deeply and somewhat more objectively by correspondence than in face-to-face chats; for example, attitudes about children, money, religion, a wife's working, the use of leisure time, and the place of sex in marriage.

[4] Henry Bowman, *Marriage for Moderns* (New York: McGraw-Hill, 1953), p. 249.

Letters most certainly should not preclude many face-to-face talks on these subjects at some later date, but during the separation they do serve to clear up many questions.

A third device used by successful correspondents is to refer to particularly enjoyable books and newspaper and magazine articles as a means of getting the reaction of the other on questions of mutual interest. "I read an interesting article which you would enjoy. Remember your resistance to women working? Tell me what you think of it."

Finally, the correspondents should make relatively little effort to spare the other person the daily details of living. Realistic correspondence keeps the avenues of communication open frankly and honestly, and holds to a minimum the building of illusions of sweetness and light when things are actually going pretty poorly. This is an art which needs to be worked at — how to write what is happening without arousing anxiety, and yet not encourage illusory ideas by telling too little.[5]

Certain of the engagement functions will have to wait, to be worked out satisfactorily until the pair is reunited. The aspect of marriage preparations which has to do with living together in intimate association is an art and takes practice; the skills of getting along together must be learned. Engagement by correspondence prepares only for a marriage in which most contacts are by correspondence and might be good preparation for marriage with a traveling salesman. For normal, settled, married living, however, there is no substitute for daily association over a period of time to learn the art of resolving conflicts, of cooperative planning, of joint functioning, all of which are learned only by doing.

CHECK YOURSELF   Which of the following problems might lend themselves to effective discussion by correspondence?

_____   1 Problems of child spacing
_____   2 Choice of a place for the honeymoon
_____   3 The quick temper of one of the partners
_____   4 Source and stability of the man's income
_____   5 Changing of religion
_____   6 Handling a mother fixation problem

★ KEY   1, 2, 4, possibly parts of 5.

---

[5] Confession of misdeeds, of past missteps, is quite another problem and will be discussed later in the chapter.

In brief, in the face of prolonged separation many of the functions of the engagement may be satisfactorily carried on by correspondence, but a period of association should be planned for before marriage to work out the problems of intimate relationships which remain.

Should Engagement Mean "No Stepping Out"?

Many of the questions which are raised about the engagement center around what is fair and just to expect of betrothed couples separated over long periods of time. Should engagement mean monopoly? Is it fair to date men other than the affianced? What are the risks of being misunderstood and perhaps having the engagement endangered thereby?

There should be no question about the engagement's being an amorous monopoly. Otherwise the relationship is no engagement and should be dissolved. There must be a recognition of the devotion each has for the other to the exclusion of rivals. Does that preclude dating others when the couple are to be separated indefinitely? This problem is one for each couple to work out in the light of their own attitudes and needs. Some couples will find it to their advantage to continue dating while separated, regarding it as recreation and as a valuable social experience. Couples who have doubts and mixed feelings may well decide to forego the experience of dating others until their own engagement is more firmly established emotionally.

In a survey of this problem at the University of Wisconsin, 65 per cent of the 608 students studied disapproved of stepping out, and only 14 per cent approved. The balance were undecided. The Wisconsin students were reacting, however, to a situation which differs greatly from wartime absences, where engaged couples are separated for long periods of time. At Stephens College Henry Bowman reviewed the problem of dating among engaged students who attended colleges in widely separated towns. He concluded: "In general, it may be said that, unless there are weighty considerations to the contrary, such students should date, even while they are engaged." [6]

Since a large proportion of social activities everywhere are organized around couples, it is important to have a partner in order to participate. To miss all these activities is to give up valuable social experience in understanding individuals of the opposite sex. After marriage the husband

[6] Bowman, *op. cit.*, p. 253.

will not abstain from social contact, but will find himself constantly in association with persons of both sexes at parties and professional gatherings. Moreover, sooner or later he must learn to accept members of the opposite sex as persons rather than as potential marriage partners. He will want to be able to associate with them genuinely without the implication of amorous inclinations. If the engagement is sufficiently established to permit dating without fear of emotional competition, the individual couple being best equipped to judge, then dating may well be in order. Such dating, moreover, may help to relieve the strain of separation. Bowman adds, "It is also a good test of the couple's devotion, for if their love and trust cannot withstand a simple test like this, they are not ready to marry and their engagement is insubstantial." [7]

Several suggestions might well be made to make dating while engaged less hazardous and more enjoyable: 1. Dating should be for recreation or pleasure without amorous interest in the other person. 2. Dating should not be limited to one person exclusively. 3. Dating should be with the full understanding and approval of the affianced. 4. Dating should not be expected to come up to the standards of enjoyment of dating with the affianced, and unfavorable comparisons should not be made. The casual date is purely for recreation and convenience, whereas dating the affianced has the added lift of the love relationship which quite naturally increases the enjoyment.

Revealing the Past

Another question which frequently troubles young people entering upon an engagement is how much of the past should be revealed to the other. In the Wisconsin survey referred to previously more reluctance to reveal the past was found among women than among men; 29 per cent of the women disapproved and 33 per cent were undecided; 24 per cent of the men disapproved and 33 per cent were undecided. This gives some clue to the nature of the problem. Wisconsin women did not wish to reveal the past, which might reduce their chances of consummating a marriage, and many men felt the same way about themselves.

Frank discussion should be the order of the day during the engagement period; indeed, that is one of engagement's major functions. However, there is no obligation to rattle all the family skeletons in a

[7] Bowman, *op. cit.*, p. 254.

recital of past misdeeds and foolish indiscretions. These would be much better taken up with your marital counselor or minister or family physician or another trained specialist who will hear them out without becoming emotionally involved.

Whatever cards are put on the table should be laid down before the wedding. What items that might have a bearing on the couple's future should come out in the frank discussions of the engagement period? Certainly these: 1. a previous marriage and any financial obligations which that might entail; 2. hereditary or other defects which might involve reasons for not having children; 3. a history of tuberculosis, heart disease, venereal disease, mental breakdown, etc.; 4. an imprisonment record; 5. debts or similar obligations which might handicap the marriage.

How Much Intimacy during Engagement? [8]

One of the most difficult of all the questions of the engagement period is the one of the extent of physical intimacy. Some caressing and expressing of warm affection is normally desired and is definitely helpful in the processes of preparation for the intimacies of marriage. But while some lovemaking is desirable, full expression of the sex urge in premarital sex intercourse has hazards of guilt and shame which are extremely difficult for many couples to overcome. So the question inevitably comes up, "How far shall we go?" It is wise to have some kind of understanding on this matter so that each can notify the other of the proximity of the boundaries already set. Such understandings may naturally emerge out of the contacts themselves. If Jim laughingly whisks Mary off his lap with a gentle reminder that she is too much for him at the moment, Mary may understandingly accept both her attractiveness to her fiancé and his response to her. When recognized in time, such experiences need not be as frustrating and tantalizing as they are later on in the love play.

Not long ago one of the authors worked with a group of engaged couples in outlining the symptoms of "time to stop and do something else" that may be helpful to the student: 1. when either is flushed and uncomfortable; 2. when either senses an urgency to continue the petting; 3. when either finds himself or herself restless and sleepless for

[8] For other discussion of the issues of intimacy before marriage see the discussion of petting in the chapter on dating, pp. 59–62.

extended periods after being together; 4. when the love play is an unpleasant memory with aspects of shame or guilt; 5. when being with the loved one is fun only when there are physical contacts. The student will be able to add his own guideposts to these general ones in setting up his own boundaries for engagement conduct.

Emotional Involvement. The engaged couple who decide to wait for marriage before consummating their union need such practical guides to keep their lovemaking within the bounds they have set for themselves. By assuming responsibility for matching their standards with their conduct they may enjoy a sense of their strength as a couple that augurs well for their marriage. They may genuinely prefer to wait for the permanence and security that marriage provides rather than threaten their engagement with the negative feelings that premarital sex relations might bring.

Unfortunately the history of couples who establish full sex relationships outside of marriage is not always encouraging to read. Even engaged couples who have agreed on marriage plans find full sex relations bring unanticipated consequences. The pangs of conscience are something they expect and know how to handle because they expect to be married soon. They put up with these in order to experience immediate satisfactions of complete intimacy. The experimenting couple, however, expect their love to be strengthened by their increased physical intimacy. But there are many indications that their idealized images of one another may be shattered thereby, that the sense of mystery, the aura of holiness, will vanish. Interest in the other wanes at the end of the chase, and the tensions of unrequited sex lose their titillating power as they are released, and the couple realize that they have "gone the limit." These ingredients of the romantic complex are lost simultaneously with the recurrence of guilt feelings. Because they are conditioned to expect romantic love as a necessary prerequisite to marriage, its lessening is interpreted as meaning that they were really not meant for each other, that the engagement should be broken off so that they may hunt for someone else.

As we shall learn in later chapters, much the same transformation of emotional relationships takes place within marriage and partly for the same reasons. When romance wanes after marriage, however, it is not so hazardous. By then the ties have been formally sanctioned through the wedding ceremony, the couple has established a common household with its many satisfactions and interlocking functions.

If the experimenting couple is not engaged, and has no plans for marriage, the emotional involvement may be fully as complicated. Once a couple attains a state of satisfactory sexual union, either the boy or (more usually) the girl begins to wish for something more permanent. If the relationship is satisfying, one or the other tends to become involved emotionally and begins to press for marriage. The member who is postponing marriage is thereupon frightened, and a bitter quarrel may ensue. The break at that point may prove disastrous to them both. But such is the nature of the sex relationship. If it is satisfying there will inevitably result profound emotional involvements that are not counted on. There is no halfway house; it is all or nothing at all.

Sex relations can be fully satisfying, only under circumstances which make possible the full and rich development of its emotional involvements. If the physical aspects were all, those who know how to guard against physical dangers of disease and pregnancy might safely have as free a sex life as an alley cat. But they are not. Because of the emotional elements, the temporary affair is almost all risk and little promise. Sex requires for its satisfaction a complete response of the whole personality. As a general policy, this means marriage. A couple can go the limit, psychologically, only within the security of a sound and permanent marriage relationship.

Responsive Integrity

One of the aspects of freedom is the winning of unqualified acceptance of other persons. Once an individual recognizes within himself the capacity to work with others as persons rather than as potential sex objects, he frees himself for much wider and more varied relationships with members of the opposite sex. He sees the possibilities in exploring personality, in sharing points of view and collaborating in creative work, all of which possibilities are closed to the person hampered by the feeling that every friend must be fondled and caressed to be enjoyed.

The "wolf" (male or female) whose aims are sex-directed, in contact with any member of the other sex, is often not so much sex-starved as he is in need of ego-bolstering. The girl who leads a man on to prove to herself that she can, is often so insecure as a woman that she must constantly prove to herself as well as to others that she is desirable. The heart-hunter usually collects conquests because he or she needs evidence of personal power. When satisfactions outside of sex become possible, a girl does not need to measure her success by whether she got "him" to kiss her or not; the man no longer requires physical submission as proof of his acceptance.

More fortunate are those persons who are free to know and enjoy and to love a wide variety of fine people of both sexes in a variety of situations, for theirs is the love that frees them for further growth of personality. As such emotional growth takes place, mate love is enhanced rather than challenged, since the sex channeling of affection remains exclusive while the emotional responses grow richly inclusive. Such persons have what is called *responsive integrity*.

Responsive integrity is the ability to respond to another person honestly and as a whole person without having to block off or deny basic aspects of the self. If we are honest we must admit that we find all sorts of people attractive and lovable. The desire to attract and be attracted to others does not cease with marriage. Conscience tells us that we belong exclusively to one mate; so the tendency to feel guilt, shame, and a denial of our real feelings dams up the out-going responses. As long as this repression is successful we cannot allow ourselves to respond honestly to others. If, on the other hand, the emotional currents become so strong that they overflow the limits set by the conscience, they may set up a whole sequence of unacceptable behavior. Neither alternative is wholesome, since both prevent us from responding as a whole; either we must deny our feelings of affection, or we must break with our own ideals of right and wrong. Responsive integrity enters in when we accept our feelings for others, when we learn how to channel them in ways that are acceptable, and to enjoy wholesomely and freely the emotional satisfactions of our relations with others. Refusing to admit our dislike or our love for another does not lessen the potency of the feeling. Repression only masks the emotion, which somehow, someway, must burst forth eventually with accumulated force and vigor.

But responsive integrity does not mean going around with emotions unbuttoned, letting feelings spill over as they will without control. Necessarily involved is a great deal of self-imposed restraint and control to keep expressions of feelings within the bounds of the particular relationship. The gushy girl who fusses around her brother does not share as much of him as does the sister who expresses her affection in more acceptable, sisterly ways. The touchy person who flies off the handle shares fewer confidences than the poised, unshockable one with whom people feel safe. Self-control for the sake of the recognized values of the relationship allows more freedom of access to others than is granted the less disciplined, who find themselves in emotional hot water much of the time.

Take Sue and Emma, for instance. They both admire and work closely with an attractive married man in their office. Emma flashes her lashes and maneuvers for compliments and opportunities to be close to him. She goes to great lengths to let him know that he touches off her affectional responses. Yet she cannot win. If he responds to her advances, he will either be turned away from her by his own feelings of guilt, or he will take advantage of her availability without the loyalty and permanence most girls need to make sex satisfying. Or by completely succumbing to her seduction, he faces the possibility of the breaking up of his home, which would inevitably be fraught with guilt, some ostracism, and pangs of conscience. More likely he will find her advances uncomfortable and take steps to remove himself as far as possible from her silly, one-sided flirtation.

Sue, on the other hand, just as honestly admits her interest in her colleague. But she lets her affection stimulate her productivity in the job they are doing together. She throws herself wholeheartedly into doing the kind of work that he will admire and that will do credit to them both. She expresses her admiration for his achievements in this way and so spurs him on to greater creativity. Theirs can be a growing relationship with a depth and breadth of permanence, because neither threatens the other with demands that are not intrinsically a part of their own working relationship.

Responsive integrity, then, means wholehearted response to others through the avenues provided by the particular relationship. Responsive integrity is established when a person, accepting both his impulses and his conscience, exerts the self-controls that allow him freely to channel the full power of his feelings. It is one important aspect of emancipation, of freedom to grow, because it opens up to him opportunities for friendships and working relationships with men and women which might otherwise have to cease with marriage's traditional exclusiveness. Persons with responsive integrity can frankly recognize that real affection is a source of motivation in working with other people and that the enjoyment of work and play with others need not be followed by sexual contact.

When both members of the couple have developed responsive integrity in their relationship with each other as well as with other persons, they can be emotionally honest with each other. Each now knows just where he stands with the other. Both can dare to be truly sincere about the real feelings, doubts and questions he has about the engagement.

Every Engaged Couple Has Doubts

Engagement uncovers almost as many problems as it solves. Fortunate indeed is the couple that does not end the probation period with many doubts and mixed feelings. The disillusionment spoken of so frequently as occurring during the first year of marriage may come before the wedding ceremony as a result of the questions raised in the engagement period. Still, it is probably better to face these realities all along the way than to meet them unexpectedly in early marriage.

An engaged couple will do well to recognize at the outset that they will have occasional misunderstandings and that these tiffs will be accompanied by mixed feelings and inner doubts. These differences need not be a source of shock, however, if the couple expects them to occur and concentrates on developing machinery for ironing them out, instead of dwelling on the seriousness of the conflicts.

Engagement is entered into by most people in America during a transition period in life between adolescence and adulthood, when most young people face doubts and uncertainties. Those who are engaged may make the mistake of ascribing these feelings of uneasiness to the engagement and the new relationship. Realizing the fact that everyone in this stage of life faces many problems may help relieve the situation for some; part of the difficulty is just that of growing up.

One other source of doubt may be in the discrepancy between the flesh-and-blood person and the dream the affianced has built up. Uneasiness that you are not as wonderful or competent as he or she thinks you are is understandable. And, from another angle, many disturbances occur as one discovers in the engagement period the trick his imagination has played upon him. Bitter and painful quarrels may ensue which are hard to resolve.

The fact that no couple faces marriage with absolute knowledge and conviction of its ability to survive the crises ahead remains a source of

"How can we be mental companions if you're not ready
to eat when I am?"

insecurity throughout engagement; the jittery couple applying for a marriage license is an American stereotype. Anticipating difficulties built up from stories of trouble passed on from adults makes for mixed feelings about marriage itself, and the prospective bride and groom say, "We are all right now. Why can't it go on like this indefinitely?"

Elopement as an Escape. Some couples facing the usual doubts of engagement feel they may escape part of the responsibility by eloping. An elopement is just as much an impulsive escape from the realities of engagement and marriage as the hysterical breaking of an engagement on

the eve of the wedding. Although conflict with parents is frequently
the alleged cause, the desire to escape reality appears prominently. The
elopement is usually carried off in haste, is inappropriate to the situation, and bodes poorly for marital happiness. Paul Popenoe studied a
group of 738 elopements and found that they were divided among those
who eloped because of parental objection to the marriage, those who
eloped to avoid publicity, those who eloped to escape elaborate, expensive weddings, and those who eloped because of pregnancy. The marital adjustments of the eloped couples were observably poorer than those
of couples married regularly. Apparently their escape from doubts and
inner conflict was poorly conceived — they "jumped from the frying pan
into the fire."

There are objections to elopement quite apart from the escape element. The eloping couple are bypassing the testing and exploring functions of the engagement period, during which the gradual preparation
for marriage occurs. They are running out on whatever problems make
their elopement seem like a good idea. They are avoiding their social
responsibility to all members of both families. Furthermore, they are
alienating their in-laws and friends whose support they will need frequently in the days ahead.

Breaking the Engagement

There are two ways to *escape* from an engagement, one by an elopement and the other by a complete break. Both represent escapes from
inner misgivings and doubts; they differ merely in the direction of the
escape.

Yet one of the most important functions of the engagement as a social institution is to eliminate from marriage those matchings which
cannot stand the experience of intimate association. Within our culture the only trial period before marriage is engagement, which is to say
that there are many engagements contracted which should be broken
before marriage. A high rate of broken engagements is preferable to a
high rate of divorce and desertion.

The engagement should be entered into with the realization that it
might be broken. If this possibility is recognized in the beginning, the
break will be less severe for both persons. Even so, the habits of association are as difficult to cast off as any other bad habit, such as smok-

ing or drinking, but a broken engagement is less painful than a separation after years of marriage.

What are reasons for breaking an engagement? In general, any crisis which changes the basis on which the engagement was launched justifies a re-evaluation, with sufficient discussion to arrive at an agreement as to the proper course to follow. This is good procedure in any pair relationship, whether it be engaged partners, marriage partners, business partners, or research collaborators. All find it necessary to review their relationship whenever crises occur, in order to keep the partnership intact. There is strong concensus that the following reasons justify re-evaluation of the engagement, with the possible agreement to sever the relationship: 1. recognition of fundamental feelings of alienation arising as a result of the more intimate relations of engagement; not just doubts and misgivings, but strong feelings of incompatibility; 2. recognition that the engagement was made originally under pressure from relatives or circumstances, and that the main reason for refraining from breaking the engagement is the fear of publicity; 3. recognition that either member of the pair is emotionally dependent on parents and too immature to stand the rigors of marriage; 4. changes in the economic future due to serious accident or health breakdown or similar disaster affecting ability to earn a living and carry on the functions of parenthood.

These reasons for breaking the engagement will be rejected in individual cases, but they should not be rejected because of fear of publicity, fear of admitting that one has made a mistake, fear of homicide or suicide threats, fear that the break will ruin the other's future. "In the great majority of instances, suicide threats never get any further than the self-pity stage, and relatively few are ever carried out." [9] Threats of vengeance or of suicide sprees exhibit a type of immaturity that would be highly undesirable in a marriage partner and are ample reasons in themselves for breaking the engagement.

There are two reasons for allowing the girl to announce the breaking of an engagement. First, she needs to maintain face among her friends and loses status in terms of marriageability unless she is permitted to issue the announcement of the break. Second, no breach-of-promise suit can be carried out successfully against any man if the woman has announced the dissolution of the engagement. Established historically

---

[9] Bowman, *op. cit.*, p. 260.

as an indemnity for the woman whose opportunities for marriage were impaired by the broken vows, breach-of-promise suits still occur occasionally. The promise to marry is a legal contract, the breaking of which gives grounds for suit for damages; and as recently as 1929 a Michigan court awarded $450,000 in a breach-of-promise suit. One of the happy results of the improved status of women in our society is the growing feeling of disfavor toward breach-of-promise suits.

CHECK YOURSELF   Which of the following engagements should be re-evaluated with the possibility of a definite break?

_____ 1 John, engaged to Eunice, was in service and has been missing in action for almost two years.

_____ 2 Bob is Catholic, Jeanne is Protestant, and neither will change religion; they avoid the subject after three months of engagement.

_____ 3 Jim has returned from two years in the interior of Brazil, broken in health, quite possibly a permanent invalid — wishes to break his engagement of five years' standing with Eloise, since he will be unable to support her and a family in his condition.

_____ 4 Jack has broken three engagements and is on the verge of a breakup of the fourth with Georgene, of whom his doting mother disapproves.

_____ 5 A week before the marriage Susan meets quite accidentally the former wife of Frank, her fiancé, and learns details of his life he has never told her. His family assure her everything will be all right — Frank was only seventeen and infatuated — this time it will be different.

_____ 6 John swears he will commit suicide if Dorothy breaks their engagement; he waves a revolver to prove it.

★ KEY All should be re-evaluated.

Building the Engagement into a Marriage

The engaged couple expect to make a success of their marriage. All their plans are laid with that expectation in mind, and the public supports them in their resolutions. Some day there will be special orientation classes in every community in the country to which engaged couples will wend their way, to be introduced to marriage as the civilian is processed into army life and as the soldier is processed back into civilian life. Great industrial plants consider it important to give their new employees weeks of orientation into their policies and objectives, as well as into the ways of behavior in the organization, before entrusting them with free access to the plant. Marriage is worthy of even more careful attention. Some communities are now offering classes for engaged couples, and there are classes in over five hundred colleges and universities. In time young people everywhere will be able to receive such instruction. For Sally and Bill who have just announced their engagement, there are many helpful books and pamphlets available, as well as several tests and prediction scales, which are suggestive to the couple planning for a successful marriage. You, like Sally and Bill, may find many of your questions discussed further in the books that are listed at the end of each chapter.

Premarriage Counseling and the Premarital Examination. In addition to study and testing, the engaged couple preparing for marriage will find available professional premarriage counseling services. Few people attempt to build a home without consulting an architect. Even where they have their own ideas about a house, sensible people consult an architect to have them checked carefully. The same point of view is rapidly becoming current with regard to marriage, which also is given design and symmetry only after careful planning and study. Premarriage counseling is becoming increasingly the source of sound professional appraisal for the prospective bride and groom. Intelligent couples are saying, "Nothing's too good for our marriage," and the careful planning which their premarriage interviews stimulate gives them a head start on less careful students.

Premarital counseling often starts early in the courtship period and continues throughout the engagement. In addition to marriage prediction scales which test the similarity and compatibility of home and family backgrounds as well as certain social factors, the premarital guidance center will have available other personality tests which prove important in determining the emotional readiness of individuals for marriage.

Our earlier discussion of personality in marriage should have proved the necessity of understanding the nature of your own personality as well as the personality of the person you will marry. These tests in the hands of a skilled psychologist can be extremely revealing. Suppose they reveal emotional dependence and nervousness, with tendencies toward blues and depressions. The counselor may advise remedial attention just as the physician would advise a couple to postpone having a baby until a kidney infection cleared up. The couple will not want to take a chance on marrying immediately, but will recognize that the period in which these questions are best cleared up is during engagement, not after marriage.

Some counseling centers describe their premarital guidance as "premarital counseling." Actually the guidance program may take weeks and sometimes longer if problems are uncovered which deserve detailed attention. The premarital counseling is a personal course of instruction, adapted to prepare young people for marriage by giving special attention to the individual background and specific needs of the couples concerned. In general, it includes: 1. a review of the personal and family backgrounds in an effort to locate the important factors that may influence marriage and avert avoidable mismating; 2. a study of the characteristics of the person, the temperament, disposition, and other emotional inclinations and attitudes, by means of interviews and tests; 3. specific sex instruction geared to clear up misconceptions, questions, and fears; 4. instruction in the healthiest approach to marriage, its problems and responsibilities as well as its possibilities for growth and development; 5. conferences and consultations with both members of the couple, and separately at the discretion of the counselor (group conferences after classes in marriage and family courses also provide helps to the engaged couple anticipating marriage); 6. a thorough physical examination and conference by the examining physician of the center; and 7. a review of the couple's plans for how they will carry out their joint aspirations in their life together. As such, premarital counseling is one way of utilizing professional skills to objectively appraise the resources an individual couple brings to marriage.

Social and Legal Requirements for Marriage

There are certain minimum social requirements for marriage which the engaged couple will find enforced by public opinion today. Some of these are also legal requirements in many states, and include laws about age, race, mental and physical defects, previous marriages, and divorces.

In America there are fifty-one different jurisdictions with laws governing or limiting marriage, and the couple will do well to familiarize itself with the legal requirements in its state of residence. No two sets of state laws are exactly alike, although there are a few regulations that are general throughout the United States.

In most states the engaged couple would legally be denied a license if either party fell into any of the following categories: 1. already married; 2. first cousins; 3. insane or feeble-minded; 4. under age — generally under fourteen for girls, eighteen for boys; 5. having a venereal disease; 6. members of different races — white-Negro and white-Mongolian combinations prohibited regionally, determined by states.

CHECK YOURSELF Which of the following conditions would result in the couple's being denied a license in most states?

_____1 Habitual drunkenness	_____ 6 Under twelve years of age
_____2 Already married	_____ 7 Tubercular
_____3 Epilepsy	_____ 8 Prison record
_____4 Feeble-minded	_____ 9 First cousins
_____5 Pauper	____10 Venereally diseased

★ KEY 01 '6 '9 '⁴ '2

Most marriage legislation puts into written form regulations which have existed before in unwritten form as custom and public opinion. Bigamy, incest, child marriage, and miscegenation were under ban long before they became prohibited by law, and offenders were summarily dealt with for violating such social regulations by the effective controls of excommunication, ostracism, and "riding him out of town on a rail."

In addition to the legal requirements, which are for the most part stated in negative terms, we have social requirements more or less enforced which represent the desired levels at which marriage should take place.

SOCIAL REQUIREMENTS FOR MARRIAGE
Willingness and ability to carry out the matrimonial obligations of:

1 Sharing a common residence
2 Sexual access
3 Sexual fidelity
4 Conjugal kindness
5 Adult responsibility for homemaking
6 Financial support of dependents

What has been said about the engagement in this chapter which would bear repeating in quick summary?

1 The pattern in engagement is the best preview available premaritally of the marriage pattern for any given couple.

2 The optimum length of engagement is best stated as "long enough," — to perform the many functions of testing, discussing, learning, fighting, and loving which underlie successful marriage.

3 All the processes welding a couple together in courtship continue with greater force in engagement, but they operate with less uncertainty, because there is less danger that the relationship will be disrupted.

4 The engagement provides opportunity for maximum planning, learning how to make jointly choices which both parties can accept and support individually.

5 The engagement operates as a preventive of divorce since in breaking up those matchings which cannot stand the experience of intimate association, in effect it brings about a divorce before marriage itself.

Readings

BURGESS, ERNEST W., PAUL WALLIN, and GLADYS DENNY SHULTZ, *Courtship, Engagement and Marriage* (Philadelphia: J. B. Lippincott Company, 1954). Part Two: "The Engaged Couple," presents popularly the findings of an extensive study of hundreds of men and women from their engagements into their marriages. See especially the data on broken engagements in Chapters 12 and 13.

DUVALL, EVELYN MILLIS, *Family Living* (New York: Macmillan, 1961). Chapter 13, "Your Engagement Plans," discusses specifically the future plans that are laid during the engagement period, and how they are aided by premarital counseling and review.

DUVALL, SYLVANUS MILNE, *Before You Marry* (New York: Association Press, 1959). A book written entirely for engaged couples and persons at the threshold of marriage.

LANDIS, JUDSON and MARY, *Personal Adjustment, Marriage and Family Living* (New York: Prentice-Hall, 1955 edition). Chapter 12 discusses such things as readiness for and purpose of the engagement, engagement as preparation for marriage, and moral behavior during engagement.

LeMASTERS, E. E., *Modern Courtship and Marriage* (New York: Macmillan, 1957). Chapter 8 is particularly helpful in outlining what should happen during engagement to assure the happiness of the marriage, and problems that come up in the engagement.

MACE, DAVID R., *Marriage: The Art of Lasting Love* (New York: Doubleday and Company, 1952). A wise and sympathetic counselor guides Jim and Catherine through some of their engagement questions, in Chapter 2, "Are Engagements Necessary?"

SMART, RUSSELL and MOLLIE, *Living in Families* (Boston: Houghton Mifflin Company, 1958). Chapter 10, "Engagement Leads to Marriage," treats especially well what is to be learned through engagement, by both members of the couple.

CHAPTER SIX

World's Fair, 2000

WILL YOURS BE A HAPPY MARRIAGE?

What type of couple marries most happily?

Do opposites attract?

Will you be ready for marriage?

What about marrying while still in school?

Should you marry before he has finished his military service?

*A*S A YOUNG AMERICAN IN THE TWENTIETH CENTURY YOU ASSUME, of course, that you will get married and live happily ever after. You hear about unhappy marriages, separations, desertions and divorces, but those happen to "other people" and not to persons like yourself. If you feel very much in love you may assume of course that you will be eternally happy in each other's arms. As a matter of fact, the way you feel about each other at the moment has very little to do with how happy your marriage will be. Factors that show up as significantly related to happiness in marriage you should know about, as an educated person as well as a possible marriage partner.

What Type of Couple Marries Most Happily?

Until fairly recently no one knew very much about what makes for success or failure in marriage. Good marriages were "blessed," and unhappy marriages were "doomed," with few knowing anything about why some worked out well while others failed. In recent years thousands of marriages throughout the United States have been studied in an effort to discover the factors that make for happiness or unhappiness in marriage.[1]

One scholar has listed the factors discernible before marriage that are most highly associated with marital success, arranging them by order of the extent of their confirmation in several studies, as follows:

PREMARITAL FACTORS ASSOCIATED WITH HAPPINESS IN MARRIAGE

1 Happiness of parents' marriage
2 Adequate length of acquaintance, courtship and engagement
3 Adequate sex information in childhood
4 Personal happiness in childhood
5 Approval of the marriage by parents and others
6 Engagement adjustment and normal motivation toward marriage
7 Ethnic and religious similarity
8 Higher social and educational status
9 Mature and similar chronological age
10 Harmonious affection with parents during childhood [2]

Such findings as these from studies in the prediction of happiness in marriage are statistical averages derived from the study of many thousands of actual marriages. It is important to realize that for every finding reflected in this table there are numerous marriages that are happy even though they do not possess the quality listed.

To the extent that the factors in the preceding rank order can be measured before marriage, the general matrimonial risk of a person may be calculated much as life insurance companies compute the life chances of an individual applicant for insurance from actuarial tables. Just as you could prove the insurance company wrong on its prediction of your life span, by stepping in front of a fast-moving truck, or by compensating for a weakness by health-building routines, so too you can "beat the marriage prediction scales" by facing your problems squarely and determining to work through your marriage successfully.

---

[1] See especially Ernest W. Burgess and Leonard S. Cottrell, Jr., *Predicting Success or Failure in Marriage* (New York: Prentice-Hall, 1939); Lewis M. Terman and associates, *Psychological Factors in Marital Happiness* (New York: McGraw-Hill, 1938); Ernest W. Burgess and Paul Wallin, *Engagement and Marriage* (Chicago: J. B. Lippincott Company, 1953); and Harvey J. Locke, *Predicting Adjustment in Marriage: A Comparison of a Divorced and a Happily Married Group* (New York: Henry Holt & Company, 1951).
[2] Clifford Kirkpatrick, *The Family as Process and Institution* (New York: Ronald Press, 1955), p. 350.

Your chances of having your marriage happiness score come to you from an electronic computer such as that illustrated at the beginning of the chapter, are not very great. It may be the year 2000 before social science research has progressed to that degree of ability to predict a particular marriage's chances for happiness. But, even if you can't get your happiness score with any great degree of accuracy, you can look at the most important factors and see how you, and you and your partner measure up on each of them. This gives you a sense of where your strengths are, and where to find the weaknesses which may cause you trouble.

The five areas for review that occur and recur as important to marital happiness in study after study are: 1. personality and temperament, 2. cultural and family backgrounds, 3. sociability and conventionality, 4. response patterns, and 5. attitudes toward sex.

1 *Personality and Temperament.* Terman has found that marital happiness is largely determined by one's all-round happiness of temperament.[3] Happiness of temperament is not to be confused either with Pollyanna-ish or sugary attitudes or with the happy-go-lucky disposition. Non-neurotic, permissive, adaptable, cooperative individuals can live comfortably with any but the most disagreeable mate. Certain types of personalities would find almost any marriage unbearable. Marriage brings with it situations which are frustrating, perplexing, and burdensome. Personalities which thrive under stress are said to have high aptitude for marriage.

Johnson and Terman, in a study of several hundred marriages, identified personality features that distinguish the happily married, the unhappily married, and the divorced. The unhappily married woman comes off badly in comparison with the divorced and the happily married. She lacks the warm sympathy and emotional balance of the happily married woman, and the rugged individualism, ambition, and efficiency of the divorced. "She is inclined to be egocentric, irritable, and intolerant . . . She is neurotic, indecisive, and unmethodical . . ."[4]

The unhappily married man "differs from the happily married man

[3] L. M. Terman and M. Oden, *The Gifted Child Grows Up: Twenty-Five Years Followup of a Superior Group* (Palo Alto: Stanford University Press, 1947), Chapter 18.

[4] Winifred B. Johnson and Lewis H. Terman, "Personality Characteristics of Happily Married, Unhappily Married, and Divorced Persons," *Character and Personality*, Vol. 3, June, 1935, p. 297.

in being less amiable, tolerant, and sympathetic, less interested in social welfare activities, and more irritable, moody and seclusive. He differs from the typical divorced man in showing less initiative, self-confidence, and personal ambition, and in his greater tendency to conservatism." [5]

Childhood background, including the happiness of parents' marriage, the history of happiness in childhood, and the disciplinary policies of parents, all appear significant in later marital happiness. One's apprenticeship in the intimacies of family living starts in the parental home. If it has been inadequate or unhappy or distorted, the training for a happy marriage must usually be obtained elsewhere: in the homes of friends, relatives, or from counseling and formal schooling. Young people whose home experiences have been unhappy are often highly motivated to avoid similar mistakes in their own marriages, and to make great strides under proper guidance.

There is a great deal of evidence to indicate that the person who gets married and lives happily ever after is usually the person who has learned how to be happy long before he married. He had a happy childhood, and has continued to find more satisfaction than dissatisfaction with life and with himself. He has developed the habit of happiness that influences the mood of his marriage as well as of his personal way of life.

2 *Cultural and Family Backgrounds.* We tend to love, and eventually to marry, people like ourselves. It isn't an accident that doctors marry nurses and farm girls marry farmers. The more a boy and a girl have in common, the more likely they are to meet. Once they have met, the more traits they have in common, the more apt they are to marry. This tendency to marry someone who has social traits similar to one's own is called *homogamy*. Studies have shown that homogamy is overwhelmingly predominant over heterogamy (the marriage of dissimilar people). Two investigators [6] studying the social characteristics in a thousand engaged couples found that all but six of fifty characteristics showed more resemblance than dissimilarity. The factors studied included religious affiliation and behavior, family background, courtship behavior, conceptions of marriage, social participation, and family relationships. The table on page 117 provides a listing of the factors found most frequently to be more similar than dissimilar among the thousand engaged couples studied.

[5] *Ibid.*, p. 297.
[6] Ernest W. Burgess and Paul Wallin, "Homogamy in Social Characteristics," *American Journal of Sociology* (September, 1943), pp. 109–124.

FACTORS SHOWING GREATEST SIMILARITY AMONG ENGAGED COUPLES *

Courtship Characteristics	Age at beginning of courtship Number of going steady experiences Number of persons consulted about engagement
Conceptions of Marriage Held	Attitude toward married women working Attitude toward having children Number of children desired Attitude toward divorce
Family Attachments	Happiness of parents' marriage Attachment to father Attachment to siblings
Religious Behavior	Religious affiliation Church attendance Active membership
Social Habits and Participation	Drinking habits Smoking habits Leisure time preferences Extent of participation in organizations

* Drawn from research study by Burgess and Wallin, *op. cit.*, tables 1–6, pp. 113–122.

A popular novel clearly describes how parents of a couple react to differences in religion and social background. The daughter of a socially prominent family is attracted to a young lawyer of another religious faith. A scene with her father and mother ensues, in which the parents try to tell their daughter why they object to her choice:

"Why?" he repeated, looking at her. "All right, I'll tell you why. I don't want my daughter to go through life neither flesh, fowl nor good red herring, living in a kind of no man's land where half the people you know will never accept him, and half the people he knows will never accept you. I don't want a son-in-law who'll be an embarrassment to my friends, a son-in-law who can't be put up at my club and who can't go with us to places where we've gone all our lives. I don't want a son-in-law whom I'll have to apologize for and explain and have to hear insulted indirectly, unless I can remember to warn people off first."

"We want you to marry someone — someone like us. Someone who'll fit in and whom we can" — Margaret Drake caught her breath, then managed to say — "can all be proud of," and suddenly shoving back her chair, she got up and left the room.[7]

Similar reactions are found among young people themselves. There is no denying that marital choice is affected by the similarity in attitudes and backgrounds. Pair unity develops with the formation of a common language and common goals. It is the couple's excuse for excluding the rest of the world and is possible only where the members start out with many things in common.

Do Opposites Also Attract? According to current folklore, the secret of mating is to select someone who will be exotically different in make-up. Jack Sprat should marry an overweight woman so that together they can lick the platter clean; Beauty must marry the Beast; and Abie his Irish Rose. The tales go even further in that they point out that opposites have a fatal attraction for one another, that brilliant men marry the beautiful but dumb, that brunets seem drawn to blondes. To date research proves that these generalizations are fallacious. They may be based more on the visibility of the exceptions than on an accurate counting of the total marrying public. Correlations of some magnitude are found between couples as to height, age, weight, intelligence, ethnic and occupational background, and geographical area of residence. The correlations with regard to temperament are not so marked; indeed the findings are often conflicting. The tendency for a person to find a mate whose personality complements his own, whose temperament meets his own basic needs, is called the principle of complementary needs.

Cultural homogeneity of backgrounds simplifies the forging of workable family routines, facilitates the arrival at mutually acceptable solutions to problems, and increases the likelihood of quick and open communication when one's needs are not met. You will find a detailed discussion of mixed marriage in Chapter 15, to which we commend your especial attention if you are contemplating an inter-faith union.

3 *Sociability and Conventionality.* Sociability, or the tendency to join with friends of both sexes for companionship, is highly associated with marital adjustment. It is linked in our list of factors with conventionality of social behavior: attendance at church, and conservative political leanings. In America there is apparently some stability obtained from conforming to the expectations of the community, having the mar-

[7] Selection from Gwethalyn Graham Erickson Brown, *Earth and High Heaven* (Philadelphia: Lippincott, 1944).

riage ceremony performed by a minister or priest, and maintaining affiliation with a church. This is the sense in which we can safely generalize,
"Good people make good marriages."

4 *Response Patterns.* The capacity to give and receive affection, as
measured by replies to questions on demonstration of affection, is associated with success in marriage. Love based on companionship and a
community of interests and activities appeared in happy contrast with
love relationships based on romantic infatuation and highly individualized interests. Companionship based marriages were usually of longer
acquaintance before marriage. The response patterns appear to be derived partly from parental family experiences and partly from the history
of one's past pair relationships in dating, going steady, and engagements. Strong attachment to the father, some similarity between parent
of opposite sex and the affianced, and approval of the marriage by the
parents reflect the pleasurable history of parental relationships ante-
cedent to marriage. The capacity to give and receive affection probably
stems directly from this series of attachments.

There is fairly strong evidence that attachment to one's parents is
associated with good marriage adjustment. Lack of conflict with parents
is favorable to marriage success. Other expressions of emotional attachment such as equal intimacy with both parents, regarding the parent of
the other sex as attractive, and lack of attachment to one's siblings are
only slightly correlated with good marital adjustment.

Since we carry into our new relationships the memories and methods
of adjustment of our older relationships, it is not surprising that many
findings show a correlation between the way one has responded to others in intimate relationships and the way one finds or fails to find happiness in marriage. In short, if you have learned to love and be loved, to
be lovable and loving before marriage, the chances are that you will
bring this warmth of love to your marriage, and through it find happiness.

5 *Attitudes toward Sex.* Sexual adjustment in marriage depends
much more upon psychological than upon physical factors. Marriages
are therefore more likely to be satisfying in this realm where the first
sex information has been received from parents rather than acquired on
the street. Parental frankness in answering the questions of children

BACKGROUND FACTORS IN MARITAL SUCCESS

Favorable	Unfavorable	Unrelated
PERSONALITY CHARACTERISTICS		
Permissive and considerate attitudes — *both*	Lacks self-confidence — *husband*	Extraversion — intraversion
Cooperative attitudes — *both*	Combinations where man day dreams and woman does not	Friendliness or offishness
Compatibility of temperament	Combinations where man feels inferior and woman does not	
Combinations where neither is neurotic	Combinations where woman makes friends easily and man does not	
Combinations where both are intellectually superior	Prone to argue points — *wife*	
	Determination to get own way — *wife*	
	Unhappy temperament, pessimistic — *both*	
	Variability in moods — *both*	
	Feelings easily hurt — *both*	
	Self-sufficiency in facing troubles alone — *both*	
CULTURAL AND FAMILY BACKGROUNDS		
Similarity of cultural backgrounds	Dissimilarity in cultural and family backgrounds	Number of siblings
Similar educational achievements	Wife's cultural background higher than husband's	Birth order in family
Father of high occupational level — *both*	Residence in the city during childhood	Differences in educational achievements of parents
Firm but not harsh home training — *both*		Modernist or fundamentalist religious beliefs
Happiness of parents' marriage — *both* (Not true for Negro couples)		Economic circumstances at marriage
Happiness of childhood — *both*		
Conservative home backgrounds		

Frequency of attendance at church and Sunday school (Not true for Swedish couples)
Number of friends — *both sexes*
Residence in single-family dwellings
Socially conservative

Unconventionality with respect to religion, sexual ethics, drinking
Religiously inactive

Number of persons with whom one has "kept company"

RESPONSE PATTERNS

Love based on companionship
Length of acquaintance before marriage
Similarity between parent of opposite sex and affianced — *both*
Strong attachment to father — *both*
Self and mate enjoy engaging in many activities together

Romantic infatuation as basis of love
Disapproval of marriage by parents — *especially husband*
Conflict with father — *both*

Amount of "petting" before marriage
Fear of pregnancy

SEX FACTORS

Sex information received from parents first — *both*
Frank and encouraging attitudes of parents toward child's curiosity about sex — *important for husband*
Similarity in sex desires
Orgasm capacity in wife
Amount of pleasure wife experienced at first intercourse — *wife*

Premarital intercourse by either or both (low but negative relationship to subsequent marital adjustment except in case of Negro and Swedish couples)
Prudishness and excessive modesty — *wife*
Fear of sex — *wife*
Husband-wife differences in strength of sex drive

Sex techniques used
Frequency and duration of intercourse
Degree of pain experienced by wife at first intercourse
Methods of contraception used

about sex and in giving them adequate information tends to develop healthy attitudes toward the sexual experiences in marriage. These in turn are undoubtedly related to achieving similarity of sex desires, developing orgasm capacity in the wife, and other tasks of sex adjustment in marriage.

The double chart on the preceding pages gives in outline form the chief background factors associated with happiness in marriage. Remember as you review them that these are research findings, and therefore not decisive in any one instance in any actual case.

Will You Be Ready for Marriage?

Marriage is not child's play. You have to be grown up enough to assume the responsibilities and to enjoy the privileges of marriage. You should be mature enough to have outgrown your childhood dependencies and to be ready to stand on your own feet, make your own decisions and live your own life before you can join forces with another human being in marriage.

Census figures show without question that the teen years are the riskiest of all ages for marriage. Those who marry when they are between fifteen and nineteen years of age have three and one-half times the rate of divorce and separation as the marriages of persons between twenty-five and twenty-nine years old.[8]

A number of studies of marital success agree that very youthful marriages have more than their fair share of instability. Good marital adjustment is positively associated with the husband being at least in his mid-twenties according to a full half dozen research studies. Good marital adjustment begins with wives at earlier ages in all studies, with nineteen to twenty-one being the minimum ages for good adjustment.

The number of birthdays you have had is not as reliable as a measure of your readiness for marriage as is your maturity as a person. A particularly thoughtful listing of evidences of maturity is provided by Henry Bowman in his discussion of age at marriage, adapted into table form on the opposite page.

[8] For a summary of what research has found about early marriage, see Lee G. Burchinal, "Young Marriages — What We Know about Them," Chapter 4 in Evelyn M. Duvall and Sylvanus M. Duvall, eds., Sex Ways — In Fact and Faith (New York: Association Press, 1961), pp. 69–83.

A MATURE PERSON *

1 profits by his own experiences and the experiences of others
2 has some knowledge of social life, how it is organized, what the requirements are for living in a society
3 has a reasonable respect for authority and tradition
4 lives in a world of reality
5 faces an unalterable situation with poise and minimum of conflict
6 uses the present rather than the past as a point of departure
7 accepts his chronological age for what it is
8 is independent of his parents in his ability to make decisions
9 does not easily take offense at slights
10 accepts the responsibility for his own acts
11 controls his behavior, acknowledging possible undesirable appetites in self but controls them
12 operates on the basis of principles rather than pleasure or pain
13 has an attitude toward sex, love, and marriage compatible with adulthood

* Modified and adapted from Henry Bowman, *Marriage for Moderns* 4th Edition (New York: McGraw-Hill, 1960), pp. 92–115.

This list places heavy emphasis on "self-mastery and self-integration," which adolescents often lack and which college students still find troublesome. The process of achieving mastery over one's urges continues into chronological adulthood. This means that many young people marry while still unfinished in this respect — marriage becomes for them a "finishing school." From Bowman's table you can identify at least five expressions of self-mastery and integration:

Self-accepting: accepting one's body, one's sex, name, color

Self-directing: establishing one's own goals, making one's own decisions

Self-understanding: knowing self, who am I, who would I be good for, why do I do as I do, what are my limitations

Self-confidence: feeling adequate to handle life situations, jobs, school, and marriage

Self-control: able to manage one's tensions, to postpone satisfaction, to sustain pain and disappointment

Self-integration in this multiple sense is the product of a process of growth and development which begins in infancy and continues through the progressive differentiation of personality into childhood, adolescence, and adulthood. It begins with the first *recognition of self* as different from *things not self*, an achievement of high order. It continues with the discovery of areas of life over which he, the child, has power and autonomy and areas where he is dependent upon others. His first power assertions are seen as he takes control of his own physiology in refusing to defecate, to eat, and/or to sleep, differentiating between the things *I do* for myself and things that must be done for me.

Recognition and acceptance of sex differences occurs early in the building of one's sense of identity; I am a girl like mother, not a boy like father; or I am a boy like father, not a girl like mother. Now the self has grown from an undifferentiated something into a gender of a recognized form. To get approval, the child discovers he/she must act right — that there are different ways for boys and girls to act; and *self-control* tied to one's gender becomes valued. Boys further differentiate themselves from girls in the activities they engage in, placing heavy emphasis on physical prowess, skills in *doing things*, playing with *things*, toys, trains, trucks, or playing at occupations like soldiers, cowboys, all clearly masculine in orientation. Girls elaborate by contrast the nurturing roles, playing with dolls more than they do with things, imitating the mother-child relation, and less frequently they undertake occupational games such as playing school or nurse. This may account in part for the fact that college men tend to judge their marriageability by their economic and occupational competence (Am I competent to earn an adequate living?), whereas girls gauge their readiness for marriage more by their ability to make a man happy and to facilitate the interpersonal relationships socially and within the family.

For both sexes there comes with maturity a sense of self that makes it possible to associate intimately with others without being personally threatened. As you find satisfying answers to your own deepest questions — "Who am I?" What is life, and where do I fit in?" "What kind of person am I and what can I do?" — you gain a sense of your own identity as a person. This inner assurance of selfhood is necessary, says Erikson, before young people can cope with the problems of intimacy.[9] As you achieve your own identity by going beyond the simple self-placement you learned as a child — to accept your name, your ancestry, your gender, your body, your status among others — and come to feel secure deep down within yourself about who you are and what you

[9] Erik H. Erikson, *Childhood and Society* (New York: Norton, 1950), pp. 227–231.

can do, you become ready to merge with another intimately. In Erikson's words,

"When once you know who you are, you are not afraid to fuse with others and become fully intimate, that is in sexuality and in love. . . . Otherwise early marriages are often used by the partners to fight for their identity. Many young marriages break up over this point." [10]

Self-development sufficient for marriage, then, involves that level of maturity that has enough ego strength so that you do not have to fight for your selfhood in constant intimate relationships with your mate. Your ego is strong enough to stand alone without defenses to safeguard it and without constant reinforcements to prop it up. You know who you are securely enough so you can gracefully encourage your partner to reveal himself. You are free to enjoy each other for your differences as well as your likes, because each of you is first of all a socialized human being and accepted as such, each by the other. Self-development continues throughout the marriage, stimulated by creative interaction, in seeking to solve the problems of marriage and parenthood.

Education and Marital Success. Of even more relevance to readiness for marriage than age is education, insofar as it reflects adequacy of preparation for marriage and parenthood. The question of when to marry may be put in terms of readiness to leave school for marriage and homemaking, or for marriage and gainful employment. Census figures for white couples in the United States as a whole demonstrate that divorce and separation are twice as great for young people who fail to finish high school as for college graduates.[11] Marriage adjustment is noticeably better among couples with education beyond high school according to a number of studies.

High School Marriages. To hear some people talk you would think that getting married while still in high school is becoming *the* thing to do. Actually only a relatively small percentage of young people marry during their high school years. In studies of thousands of high school students in California and Nebraska, the proportion of girls marrying

[10] Erik H. Erikson, in *Healthy Personality Development in Children* (New York: The Josiah Macy Foundation, 1952), p. 93.
[11] Paul C. Glick, *American Families* (New York: Wiley, 1957), p. 154.

grade by grade was not substantial until the senior year, as you see in the table below. Many fewer boys, about one-tenth the figure for girls, marry while in high school. The majority of girls who marry while in high school marry out-of-school young men. Only seven per cent of the California girls married boys in the same school.

A COMPARISON OF PROPORTION OF HIGH SCHOOL GIRLS MARRIED
IN CALIFORNIA AND NEBRASKA

GRADES IN 1954–1955	NEBRASKA STUDY * PER CENT MARRIED	CALIFORNIA STUDY † PER CENT MARRIED
10th Grade	3.1%	2.4%
11th Grade	7.2	4.0
12th Grade	14.9	5.7
Number of Students Studied	3,456	108,198

* Kenneth L. Cannon, "Report of Study of High School Girls Who Marry under 19 Years of Age," mimeographed report, University of Nebraska, Lincoln, Nebraska.
† Judson T. Landis and Kenneth C. Kidd, "Attitudes and Policies Concerning Marriages among High School Students," *Marriage and Family Living*, Vol. 18, May 1956, pp. 129–136.

The advice given by these married high school students to others who might consider such a step was interesting. Three-fourths advised graduating first or arranging to finish high school after marriage. They saw a high school education as insurance for getting a job now or in the future, and as of help in raising a family. Girls who married while still in school have given other young people some quotable advice:

"I would tell them to wait until they have graduated because even if they think they are ready for marriage, I don't think they are."

"Both graduation and marriage are important in your life and I would want to be sure of doing both jobs as well as possible; therefore, I think they can be done best separately."

"Wait and go with more than one fellow, because I went with only this one. Make sure you are good and ready."

"Do not go steady with one certain fellow until the last of your senior year."

"Make sure you want to spend the rest of your life with this person."

"Don't ever let anyone talk you out of graduating from high school. Even if you don't graduate with high honors and maybe you'll never need a job outside of being a housewife but you'll always be proud of yourself for graduating, you'll never regret it." [12]

High school marriages are handicapped in special ways by the circumstances under which they are undertaken. Cutting short one's formal education, freezing one's economic potentials, and shortening the period of preparation for marriage and parenthood are obvious consequences of such young marriages. If high school marriages are going to increase in number, there should be attention given to education for marriage and parenthood in the early years of high school to assure its availability before marriage occurs. Certainly anyone contemplating a high school marriage will do well to take whatever marriage and family courses are offered and to read what materials are available before it is too late.

Marrying While in College. It is much more likely that individuals will reach the conclusion that they are ready to marry during the college years than while still in high school. Emotional and intellectual maturity are presumably further advanced. The maturing experiences of holding full-time summer jobs and part-time positions while in school, as well as opportunities to fill adult positions in church and community organizations, are much greater during the college years. Dr. Robert O. Blood suggests that young people need to do a certain amount of dating, getting the full sense of being "free and single" before settling down. For them the years of high school and college give a sufficient amount of independence so that by graduation time getting married looks pretty good. He writes, "The feeling that marriage is an attractive proposition does not develop out of thin air but follows when people have drunk deeply of the 'heady wine' of freedom, have found it good, but are ready now for something more nourishing." [13]

For many people this readiness to settle down comes during the college years despite lack of money, parental disapproval, and student sta-

[12] These quotes have been drawn from two reports, Cannon, *ibid.*, and Joel Moss and Ruby Gingles, "A Progress Report of a Longitudinal Study of Early Marriages in Nebraska." Paper presented at Midwest Sociological Society meetings, Minneapolis, April 1958.

[13] Robert O. Blood, Jr., *Anticipating Your Marriage* (Glencoe, Illinois: The Free Press, 1955), p. 157.

tus. The attitude toward college marriages has changed markedly since World War II. The G.I. college marriage provided a model for the non-G.I. student to follow, and today from ten to twenty per cent of college students across the country are married. Students in professional schools of medicine, law, and in graduate schools are even more marriage-prone, and few colleges can now avoid the pressure to provide apartments for married students on a par with the dormitory accommodations they provide for single students.

Married college students suffer more financial pressure than single students, since it costs more to live and there is the ever-possible baby. They have more time pressures because they usually must combine work and study, and experience a drastically different social life than available for unmarried students. Marriage requires shifting from the on-campus activities of single students to the more informal and intimate activities of friends and neighbors in the dwelling units. The married student is perhaps more aware than the person who waits until after college to marry, of the advantages of "single blessedness" which he has given up, while the majority of his classmates are participating fully in these collegiate privileges.

From the studies of college marriages it is apparent that they are no longer considered precarious, but that they are qualitatively different in form must be recognized. To marry in college successfully requires high adaptability and an acceptance of a drastically cut level of living compared with single student life. Couples economize in order to marry, and scrimp even more severely when children arrive. They must be willing to accept graciously occasional help from parents and to sharply curtail their social life. Even more important, they must be willing to pitch in together to get their work done and to make their marriage a successful companionship.

Marrying While He Is in Service. In recent years the timing of when to marry has been aggravated by the imperatives of military service for young men of marriage age. It would be generally conceded that the wise couple postpone their marriage until schooling and military service have been completed and a position with a future has been secured. But not everyone wants to do the prudent thing when a decision like marriage is to be made. What are the alternatives facing couples with military service ahead for them?

A number of alternatives face today's couple. Shall they marry at once or postpone marriage until the intensive early part of the military service is past? If they marry immediately, shall she follow him so that she may have as much time as possible with him or shall she stay at home and work things out separately during his stint? Or, would it be better to dissolve the engagement entirely and return them both to circulation, with the understanding that they will keep in touch during his service and renew their engagement when and if they are both free to marry and live together in marriage?

Many fear that the separation imposed by military service might break up their relationship if they do not marry. The vision of the availability of other attractive persons is worrisome. Some marry to assuage their doubts about the staying power of the relationship. The girl doesn't entirely trust her man, nor does she trust herself. The young man has similar doubts. In wartime such marriages have been called *war marriages*, because they are characterized by haste, impulsiveness, and a sense of urgency. It is quite true that had these couples waited, their relationship might not have survived the separation. Each would have become lonely and started dating others, and possibly would have eventually drifted into other involvements.

Other couples marry during military service because their relationship has matured to the point where marriage is surely indicated. They have completed their schooling and have been engaged long enough to prove the quality of the relationship and can face marriage in military service as a special challenge. They do not welcome the separations which military service requires, but they don't fear them, because they have ways of keeping the relationship actively growing while separated. Having been acquainted over a long period of time and having explored one another's lives through an adequate engagement, they have a host of things they can write to each other about during their separation.

One could argue against marriage until one's obligations to the military have been fulfilled, unless the call to service comes at the climax of an adequate courtship and engagement which would have eventuated in marriage, call or no call. Timing of the marriage decision at best should not be a function of the urgency of war, the possibility of separation, or the advantages of a secure officer's pay, but should weigh more heavily on the readiness of the two persons as individuals to assume the responsibilities of marriage.

Happy Marriages Don't Just Happen

You have to be good marriage material to be happy in marriage. You have a far greater chance of finding happiness in marriage if you have learned the habit of happiness long before you get married. This is probably why those who come from happy families, with pleasant relationships with members of their families are known to make a go of marriage more predictably than those whose history has not been so favorable. If you have developed the capacity to give and receive affection freely, and to respond intimately to another person, your chances are enhanced by that much for finding love in your marriage. Good marriages are made by people who have their roots deep in spiritual values beyond the moment, and whose lives are devoted to interests outside their own immediate satisfactions. If you are conventional in your beliefs and practices, both belong to and are active in your church, the studies show you have a better than average chance of being happily married.

The evidence is overwhelming that you will find it easier to marry someone who comes from the same general background as you yourself. Mixed marriages can work, but they almost always require more maturity and working out than marriages of persons whose religious affiliations, social status, and cultural backgrounds are similar. When opposites in background and attitude attract each other, it is apparently only temporary, because most of them don't marry each other. Exceptions may be found in the area of personality needs, where opposites with complementary need patterns may possibly mate with mutual fulfillment.

You have to work at the job of being married. Whatever your background, your marriage is yours to build sturdy, strong, and satisfying. Your determination to succeed, to overcome handicaps and to put your assets to work for you can make the difference between happiness and unhappiness in your marriage. Just as you have to work at any other job you undertake if you are to find satisfaction in it, so too you must accept the challenge of marriage if you are to find fulfillment within it.

Readings

BURGESS, ERNEST W., PAUL WALLIN and GLADYS DENNY SHULTZ, *Courtship, Engagement and Marriage* (Philadelphia: J. B. Lippincott Company,

1954). Part 3, "What Makes a Marriage Succeed," reports basic findings of an extensive study of the question in easily read Chapters 1–17.

DUVALL, EVELYN MILLIS, *Family Living* (New York: Macmillan, 1961). Read especially Chapter 11, "Will You Make a Success of Marriage?" and Chapter 12, "When Are You Ready for Marriage?" interpreting for the senior high school student what science says about happiness in marriage.

KIRKENDALL, LESTER A., *Too Young to Marry?* (New York: Public Affairs Pamphlets, 1956). Professor Kirkendall talks over the pros and cons of early marriage, and the problems the very young couple face as they approach marriage, in one of the best brief statements on the subject to date.

LOCKE, HARVEY J., *Predicting Adjustment in Marriage* (New York: Henry Holt and Company, 1951). A brilliant research reporting on a comparison of a divorced and a happily married group to find out what factors make for happiness in marriage. Read especially Chapters 9, 10 and 11 for the kinds of persons who marry most happily.

SMART, RUSSELL and MOLLIE, *Living in Families* (Boston: Houghton Mifflin Company, 1958). Chapter 11, "What Makes a Successful Marriage," helpfully considers such areas as fitting two lives together, emotional maturity as essential, and the place of sharing in the marriage.

WALLER, WILLARD, and REUBEN HILL, *The Family: A Dynamic Interpretation* (New York: Dryden, 1951). See Chapter 17, "Marital Success," for descriptions and a critique of marital success studies and a review of adjustment throughout the marriage. This treatment is especially rewarding for the able student.

CHAPTER SEVEN

"Please, Miss Larve, just say 'I do.' "

WEDDING PLANS

How formal does a wedding have to be to be right?

How do you decide whom to invite to your wedding?

What do you do first in getting ready for a wedding?

Who pays for what?

Just how flexible can you be and still have a nice wedding?

$\mathcal{U}$NLESS YOU WANT TO BE MARRIED IN THE CITY HALL, OR BY A Justice of the Peace with all the haste and impersonality involved in such a marriage, you will need to make some wedding plans. Most girls look forward to some kind of wedding. However, many girls and most men do not want a very large formal type of wedding. You do not need to elope to avoid such a wedding. There are simple, inexpensive weddings that are satisfying at the moment and that will bring warm memories long afterwards. But of whatever type, a wedding has to be planned to be effective.

When you marry, you may not have much choice about the kind of wedding yours will be. In some circles, the bride's mother takes over almost completely and manages everything from the first invitation to the last detail with only occasional reference to the preferences of bride and groom. Your wedding may have to conform to the expectations of your father's friends and associates or be according to rigidly prescribed forms. Or, you may find yourself being married in the chapel of a military post, either with strict formality and full military honors, or in the stark simplicity of a ceremony arranged at a moment's notice.

Setting the Wedding Date

The date of your wedding may have to be set at the time of a military leave or a long-awaited vacation from work. Then all your plans and arrangements are made around those dates as soon as they are fairly definite. If there is some flexibility, the bride usually sets the date that will come at a time when she is not menstruating, and allows time to get her clothes ready, and wedding arrangements completed. She talks over possible dates with her fiancé and together they choose a wedding time that will be most convenient to them both.

As soon as the couple has selected a tentative date for their wedding, it is wise for them to clear it with both immediate families, to rule out the possibility of a conflicting date of importance, and to reserve the date definitely in family plans. This is not too early to contact the church, chapel, or club to make sure that it may be reserved for the hour of the wedding, unless of course this is to be a home wedding. Which brings us to the question, what kind of wedding is it to be?

Types of Weddings

The type of wedding you have depends upon many factors: 1. your own hopes and dreams through the years; 2. the amount of money you want to spend; 3. the families you both come from, their wishes and interests and social standing; 4. your location with particular reference to the kinds of places suitable for a wedding; 5. the number of friends and relatives you want to invite; and 6. the amount of time you have to plan ahead for the wedding.

Weddings range all the way from simple informal affairs to large formal pageants. You may choose the type of wedding that best fits your situation from any of the following general patterns with whatever modifications make the occasion most meaningful to you.

1 *Small home wedding* with only members of the immediate families present, and whatever decorations, music, and refreshments seem suitable. Such a wedding is the least expensive in time and money, and can follow the individual wishes of the couple more freely than other types.

2 *Informal chapel wedding* to which only immediate relatives and close friends are invited, with the couple receiving their guests in the foyer

following the ceremony. Although there may be no reception as such, the immediate wedding party may go somewhere for a wedding breakfast afterwards if they wish. This type of wedding can be easily arranged, kept as simple as the couple desires, is inexpensive, and can be quite lovely. One modification of this is for the wedding to take place following a regular service in the bride's church, to which the guests come as soon as the previous service is over. This is convenient for organist, minister, and many guests. The altar is already decorated, and extra arrangements are kept to a minimum.

3 *Small wedding in church, home, or club* to which members of the two families and friends are invited, followed by a reception, that may include a longer guest list, if desired. The reception may take place in the church parlors, in the home, the club, or in some other suitable place nearby. The longer guest list may be for the ceremony itself with only a few chosen friends and family members invited to the reception that follows in another place. When the reception is held at the place of the ceremony, all those attending the ceremony are invited to the reception as well.

4 *The home, garden, or club wedding and reception* for everyone in the same location. In this type of wedding there is a flow from the ceremony to the receiving line to the refreshment tables with all guests participating. This may be an elaborate affair of *The Father of the Bride* variety, or it may be a simple ceremony under the trees in the yard or at an altar improvised inside. A sit-down wedding breakfast, a buffet supper, or simple refreshments of the stand-up sort, around whatever menu is appropriate, is chosen depending upon the number of guests, the accommodations, personnel to serve, and of course the budget.

5 *Formal, or semiformal church wedding,* followed by a small home or club reception to which only a few friends and the two families are asked. Here the pomp and splendor are in the ceremony, with the secondary interest in the reception. This can be as elaborate or as simple as the bride and her family may desire. The formal ceremony itself demands both time and money to be in accordance with traditional form. A wedding consultant to advise on the costuming of the wedding party, decorations, wedding processional, the recessional, and all such details, can be a great help in the formal wedding, which to be proper must conform to convention.

6 *Large, formal church, cathedral, or synagogue wedding,* followed by home, hotel, or country club reception to which all wedding guests are invited. Here, money is no object, and the bills may total many thousands of dollars. This may represent not only the family's investment in the couple, but as is often the case, is one way of attaining or maintaining social position and/or cementing business interests. Such a wedding lies outside the scope of this writing. Professional wedding services are in the business of arranging large formal weddings down to the last detail, under contract for a suitable fee.

Whom to Invite and How

It is usual for the family of the bride to invite the guests to the wedding. As soon as the decision has been made as to the type of wedding it will be, the bride and her family, in consultation with the groom and his parents, make out the list of persons to be invited. If the wedding is to be a small home affair, with only members of the immediate families present, the matter is a simple one except in problems of close relatives by blood or marriage who have been cut off from the family by distance, divorce, or estrangement. It is wise to invite all such family members as is at all possible. To exclude them from such an important occasion is often to widen the breach and to make for feelings of guilt and uneasiness among those present. Whether or not they are included, the decision should be the joint responsibility of all the family members planning the wedding.

Members of the immediate family and close friends may be invited to the small home, or informal chapel wedding, personally by the bride or her mother, by word of mouth, telephone, telegraph, or informal note, whichever is most convenient. In this case, announcements of the wedding are sent to all other relatives and friends as soon as the ceremony has been performed.

Guests to formal or semi-formal weddings are always invited by engraved wedding invitations according to prescribed forms available at the engravers. These are mailed from three to four weeks in advance of the ceremony. The order should be placed with the engraver about six weeks before the mailing date. Outside envelopes in the quantity decided upon may be secured from the engraver at the time the order is placed, so that addressing may be done in pen and ink at home while the engraving is being completed. If the list is very long, it is well to alphabetize it and check for duplicates and omissions before addressing the envelopes.

The engraved invitation may be used also in informal weddings to which a considerable number of guests are being invited. If engraving is too costly an item in the wedding budget, there is a form of raised printing that is frequently used instead of engraving that is much less expensive. The same general forms, dates for mailing and other customs are followed.

On the outside envelopes go the full names and addresses of the guests. Both husband and wife are invited as a Mr. and Mrs. unit, except in a case like the following. When the entire office force goes as a group to a wedding of one of its members at or close to office hours, it is not expected that the husbands and wives of members of the office staff will be invited.

If there is some question about the correct address of the guest, the return address of the sender may be included on the outside envelope; otherwise it is not necessary.

Names of members of the family not specifically indicated on the outside envelope may be written on the inside envelope of the wedding invitation, so that it may be clear just who it is that is being invited. In the case of a couple with two children, for instance, the names of each one of the four would be listed one under the other on the inside envelope. It is not necessary to invite the children to the wedding, but if one is invited, the other(s) should be included except for some important reason. Names of other relatives (brothers, sisters, mothers, etc.) living in the same residence may similarly be included in the listing of names on the inside envelope, or, somewhat more properly, they may receive separate invitations. It is usual for family members at different addresses and for members of an engaged couple to receive separate invitations.

Unless you put R.S.V.P. on the invitations to your wedding and reception, your guests are under no obligation to reply. So, if you need to know the number of guests to be expected, be sure to indicate on the invitation that a reply is expected, including the address to which the reply is to be sent, if there is apt to be some question about it. Replies to formal invitations are usually written in the third person and mailed first class. Informal invitations may be acknowledged by a simple note, or verbally by telephone, or by person to person.

If you have a considerable number of acceptances and regrets to keep track of, you will need some kind of system that will give you an accurate count. One bride-to-be simply set two boxes, one marked "YES" and the other "NO," on a convenient table. As replies came in the mail, or were given members of her family, they were dropped into the "YES" box if they were acceptances, and the "NO" box if regrets. Her tallies of each gave her a basis for an estimate for the caterer, and a final figure of total response. *Tip*: Always plan for a few extras; you never can tell!

Announcements

Engraved (or raised printing for economy's sake) announcements of the marriage are sent to all relatives and friends who did not receive an invitation to the wedding. Announcements follow a slightly different form than invitations, examples of which are available to serve as models at any stationer's or engraver's office. Lists of persons to receive announcements are collected from both bride and groom and their families, compiled and checked for duplicates as is done for invitations. Envelopes are personally addressed in pen and ink at home while awaiting delivery of the announcements and the inside envelopes. These may be prepared ahead. But, they are not mailed until after the ceremony, usually by some member of the bride's family. An "at home" card giving the address of the newly married couple and the date by which they will be settled may be enclosed with the announcement, or included in it, for the convenience of those who may wish to call, or send wedding gifts to the couple.

As with the invitations, the bride's parents' names are the first named on the announcement. In cases of death or divorce, the remaining parent's name alone is correct. When the bride is a mature woman long out of her parental home, she may announce her own marriage quite properly according to forms already developed and available as models.

If, for some reason, the formal announcement is not desired, either the bride or some senior member of her family may write to relatives and friends not present at her marriage, telling them about it, and thus announcing it informally. Likewise, the groom or one of his parents writes members of his family and friends about the wedding as soon as convenient.

Wedding Gifts

As soon as invitations are out, wedding gifts begin to arrive. Each one should be personally acknowledged by the bride just as soon as possible. With all the other things she has to do as the wedding date approaches, some sort of system will help. It is wise to plan ahead on where gifts will be kept and how they will be displayed. As each gift arrives, it is labeled with a number corresponding to that which the bride writes for it in her gift record along the following headings:

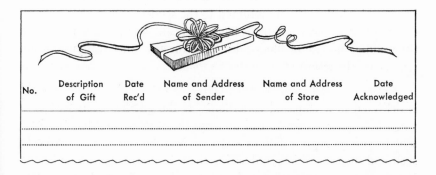

No.	Description of Gift	Date Rec'd	Name and Address of Sender	Name and Address of Store	Date Acknowledged

Such gift records appear in the back of wedding books given brides by some stores, or she may make her own in any way that seems most convenient for her to keep her gift record straight.

When a gift arrives, the bride may wait until her fiancé drops by before opening it, if they enjoy opening gifts together. Or, she may open it and enter it into her record at once, carefully preserving the card, and perhaps the packing slip from the store from which it was sent. (WARNING! Many gifts are multiple, so wrappings should be searched carefully before they are discarded.) If she keeps close by the spot where she unwraps her gifts such items as pen, note paper, stamps, and her address book, she will find that it does not take too long to immediately acknowledge each gift as it arrives. It is gracious of her to specifically mention the gift and express her warm appreciation for it and tell how she plans to use and enjoy it.

Returning Wedding Gifts. It sometimes happens that a couple will have no use for a gift that has been sent them. One couple received seventeen sugars and creamers, only a few of which could be expected to be used. In such a case, and in all other cases where the gift does not fit into the plans of the couple, it may be returned to the store from which it was sent and exchanged for something more suitable. It is therefore wise for the bride to save the packing slips and the inner box in which the gift comes, for use in case it is to be exchanged. In a situation like this, the bride may acknowledge the gift as usual, being careful not to say anything to offend or hurt the sender at the same time that she avoids telling a falsehood. She can always express her gratitude for being remembered without mention of the possible inappropriateness of a gift.

In the event that the engagement is broken, after wedding gifts have been received, the gifts are returned to the senders with a little note indicating that the wedding plans have been cancelled. Postponement of the wedding in case of illness, death, or for any other reason does not necessitate the return of the gifts.

Broken or Undelivered Wedding Gifts. What should you do if a gift is delivered in a damaged condition? If the gift has been sent by a store, it is quite proper to call or write the store saying that the item sent to you on such a date as a gift by Mrs. So-and-So has arrived in such and such condition, and asking them to pick it up and replace it. If the package was wrapped and sent from home, it is best to say nothing about its condition when acknowledging the gift. If the giver asks you specifically about the gift, of course you will have to tell her.

The undelivered gift is another cause for frequent embarrassment. Aunt Mary told Jane that she was sending her an electric toaster for a wedding gift. The wedding is long since over, and still no toaster, nor further word from Aunt Mary. Jane needs a toaster, but hesitates to buy one when Aunt Mary still might send it as she volunteered. What should Jane do? One real possibility is that Aunt Mary ordered the toaster to be sent as a gift, and the store failed to fill the order. Jane might operate on this assumption and, writing a pleasant note to Aunt Mary, mention her anticipation of receiving the toaster that Aunt Mary said she was sending. If Aunt Mary wonders why no acknowledgment of her gift has come, she can either have the store check its records, or she may tactfully ask Jane if the item has been delivered. Such a fol-

low-up on either the giver's or the receiver's part is a kindness when
carefully managed.

Suggestions for Wedding Gift Selections. Many stores offer prospective brides a service, in which the bride goes over the stock and selects
those things that she would like to have. The store then lists these, including her choice of silver pattern, household china and glassware,
color schemes, etc., so that those who wish to send some suitable gift
may choose from the list of possibilities registered with the store. This
assures the sender of giving something that will be appropriate, and the
bride and groom of receiving things that they want and can use.

Friends and family members often ask either the bride or her mother
what would be acceptable as a wedding gift. It is quite all right to reply
specifically if it is done in such a way that the sender is given some
latitude for the cost of the item. For instance, if the giver indicates
that she would like to send silver, the name of the pattern selected may
be given her so that she may add a piece or as many pieces as fit her
budget. Or, a list of several items of varying costs may be suggested.
In answer to the direct question about the acceptability of some specific
item: "Would you like an electric iron?" the reply may be frank appreciation or rejection of the suggestion; e.g., "Oh, we'd love one, thank
you," or "Thank you, it's a grand idea, but Ted's mother has already
sent us one."

In answer to the question, "Is money an acceptable wedding gift?"
Emily Post says "No," listing as her reason the fact that the money is
spent and the couple has nothing definite to remember the sender by.
However, many couples who marry today find money a highly acceptable gift in many instances. Some couples are not able to establish a
household of their own for some time. For them the problem of stor-
ing wedding gifts may be a difficult one. Other couples go to housekeeping in limited quarters where there will be no place to put many of
the things that they get for their wedding. Most young couples start
out with limited finances that must be stretched as far as dollars can
go and, knowing just what they need and what they can do without
for a while, can possibly more wisely spend the gift allotment than
could all but their closest associates.

One possible compromise between Emily Post and modern expedi-
ency is the giving of a United States Government Bond, which may be
turned in for cash at once if needed, or "salted away" as a gift of se-

curity from the sender until it matures, or until it can be used to purchase some much needed item for the new household.

Clothes for the Wedding

Your wedding clothes and those of your guests will be in keeping with the type of wedding yours is to be. Procedure for the formal wedding rigidly prescribes the clothing worn by bride, groom, and all members of the wedding party. More simple weddings allow considerable latitude within certain general conventions. Wedding clothes do not need to be expensive to be appropriate and effective. They may be as elaborate as the bride and her family may choose.

What the Bride Wears. The bride chooses her wedding outfit as the keynote theme of her wedding. If the wedding is formal, her dress will be in traditional white or near-white in some suitable fabric, with a train from three to seven yards in length over which falls the wedding veil from the bridal headpiece of fabric, flowers, or jewels in keeping with the period and style of the gown. Depending upon its elaborateness the formal wedding gown may cost anywhere from several hundred to several thousands of dollars. To be right, it must be carefully fitted.

Any bride-for-the-first-time may wear a traditional white wedding gown no matter what the type of her wedding. For the informal wedding, the bride's outfit may be a simple floor length model and either no train or one of a yard or so in length, with a veil that is finger tip length caught in a simple fabric headpiece, or a garland of flowers. She may wear the wedding dress that she has inherited from her mother or grandmother, carefully fitted to her figure. She may buy her gown and veil, or have it made for her, or as some gifted girls do, she may make it herself. The cost may be as low as a few dollars and her time; or it may mount up depending upon the quality of the material, the professional fitting needed, and "the name" of the designer.

The bride may choose to wear a ballet length gown in white or pastel color. Or she may wear a street length gown in some soft becoming color and fabric. Or, she may select a well-cut suit and blouse with which she would wear hat and gloves. Shoes and other accessories are chosen in keeping with the rest of her outfit.

Outfits for the Bride's Attendants. There are just two rules for what bridesmaids should wear: 1. bridesmaids' costumes are in the same pe-

riod as the bride's, and fit into the wedding theme that she has set.
2. bridesmaids' costumes are alike, except possibly in color. Fabric,
styling, and accessories harmonize with the costumes worn by the bride
and her attendant.

The matron of honor, or the maid of honor (if unmarried) is the
personal attendant of the bride and chooses her costume to complement
that of the bride. She may or may not wear a hat or headpiece depending upon the nature of the costume. When gloves are worn they are
long with a short-sleeved dress or short with a long-sleeved dress. Her
flowers may be in any harmonious color and style. Her outfit is usually
slightly different from that of the bridesmaids' but harmonizes in color
and styling.

The flower girl, usually a child of the family or close friends, wears
a dress like that of the bridesmaids or one that is of the same general
type, with suitable accessories.

The Groom and His Attendants Dress Alike. Whatever the type of
wedding, the men of the party dress alike. At the formal evening wedding, the groom, his best man, and the ushers all wear full dress suits:
"White tie and tails." For the formal daytime wedding, cutaway coats
and dark gray striped trousers, gray tie and gloves are prescribed. A
simple wedding calls for dark blue suits, white shirts, plain ties, and no
gloves for the men of the wedding party. In summertime, informal
white jackets and dark blue trousers are sometimes worn at informal
weddings.

Only the men's boutonnières are different. The groom's lapel blos-
som is usually white, while those of the groom's attendants may be in
color. The groom's boutonnière may be somewhat more elaborate
than the best man's and the ushers'; some little distinction marks the
groom as "the man of the day" apart from his attendants.

In some circles suits of the same material for bride and groom have
been popular. The color usually is some shade of blue, although there
is no reason why some other color becoming to both could not be
chosen. Black is rarely worn at weddings because of its association with
mourning. Brown and gray suits for men are not usual at weddings, but
there is no absolute rule that forbids them. In general, although there
are conventions about what is proper to wear, the choice is up to the
bride and groom whose wedding it is!

Calendar

OF THINGS TO DO

The Wedding Planned Well in Advance

THREE TO FOUR MONTHS BEFORE THE WEDDING

• Set the wedding date (in consultation with members of both families in so far as is possible).

• Consider possible types of weddings suitable to your situation and choose the kind of wedding you both and your families can agree would be best.

• Select the place for the wedding and reserve it for your date.

• Consult your minister, priest, or rabbi about your marriage and wedding plans.

• Make arrangements for the reception, reserving the date, determining in general the kind of food, who will prepare and serve it, and the number of guests in round numbers.

• Choose your wedding attendants and invite them, specifying the definite date and the type of wedding.

• Select the color scheme and general motif of the entire wedding, keeping in mind the season of the year, the type of wedding chosen, the budget, and your own preferences.

• Plan bride's wedding gown and accessories, and those for bridal attendants in keeping with your type of wedding, your over-all scheme, your budget, and whether the gowns will be handmade or purchased.

• Start a master list of persons to be invited to the wedding, including those suggested by you both and your families. Make a plan for thinning if the list becomes too long to be accommodated. Develop a system for checking duplicates.

TWO TO THREE MONTHS BEFORE THE WEDDING

• Order invitations from your stationer or engraver according to the model and the script desired. Order in round numbers in lots of fifty or one hundred, allowing more than the total of lists compiled to date. Calculate the percentage of acceptances you can reasonably expect, and so estimate the number of invitations it will be feasible to send.

• Arrange for announcements (to those not being invited to the wedding) according to the same plan of estimating numbers as for invitations.

• Order informals for acknowledging your wedding gifts at this time if you prefer these to other simple suitable note paper. The number should approximate that of the size of the invitation list.

• Explore possibilities for where you will live, making whatever tentative arrangements are possible. If you are fortunate in having a definite place into which you will move, it is not too soon to plan for its furnishing and to start getting it in order.

ONE TO TWO MONTHS BEFORE THE WEDDING

• Bride goes to a good gynecologist for her premarital examination according to the suggestions outlined in Chapter Five. She follows through on his (or her) recommendations before the wedding, including a return for routine blood tests a week or two preceding the wedding date.

• Groom gets his complete premarital examination, making appointment for blood tests.

• Address the invitations in preparation for mailing three to four weeks before the wedding. The outside envelopes may be picked up before the engraving is finished if you wish. The envelopes are addressed in pen and ink in a legible hand by the bride with whatever help is offered by members of her family, the groom and perhaps members of his family. One bride made a party of it with both families gathered around the dining room table, address books at hand, following a pleasant informal meal in joint-family style.

• Decide on your honeymoon plans considering the special interests of you both and the function of the honeymoon (see Chapter Eight). Make advance reservations for accommodations and travel.

• Select "going away" outfits and trousseau, including appropriate accessories.

• Check your luggage needs.

• Express interest in what both mothers will wear to the wedding, giving what suggestions and help seem to be indicated.

THREE TO FOUR WEEKS BEFORE THE WEDDING

• Mail the wedding invitations (*not* the announcements, yet). First class postage is expected. Air mail is indicated only for relatives and friends in far distant places.

• Order the wedding cake and make final arrangements for the wedding breakfast and/or the reception. Estimate the number to be served with final figure promised as replies come in, just before the wedding (two or three days to a week is usual).

• Select the photographer and discuss with him what kinds of pictures you will want, and make definite appointments with him.

• Check on the legal requirements for marriage in your state.

• Arrange for out-of-town guests.

• Bride gets a permanent if she needs one, and makes appointments ahead for the day before the wedding, or at a time that seems best.

• Select and order your flowers for the wedding.

• Arrange for decorations needed for the wedding, the wedding breakfast, and the reception.

• Register your preferences at the wedding bureau of the store where your friends and family will most likely shop for your gifts.

• Plan for the way in which you will acknowledge your gifts as they arrive, and how they will be displayed.

THE WEEK OR TWO BEFORE THE WEDDING

• Final check with your doctors, routine blood tests preliminary to getting the license.

• Go together for your marriage license.

• Arrange transportation for the wedding party.

• Make final preparations for the rehearsal and for presenting gifts to the wedding party. The rehearsal is usually the day before the wedding. A simple party in connection with the rehearsal is an acceptable time for bestowing gifts upon members of the wedding party. Caution: Do not attempt too elaborate an affair the night before the wedding. You'll want to be rested and fresh then.

• Groom gets hair cut; bride gets hair done and whatever else that will make her feel lovely.

• Allow plenty of time for dressing and last minute details on your wedding day.

The Wedding Planned on Short Notice

• Set the date and decide the type of wedding, clearing the time with the minister and both families.

• See your doctor(s) for a complete premarital examination and the blood tests required in your state.

• Make arrangements for what you both and the other members of the wedding party will wear.

• Write invitation notes and order announcements.

• Arrange for wedding cake, refreshments, flowers, and photographer.

• Get your marriage license.

• Keep calm, share the responsibilities, enjoy every minute of it . . . it's your wedding!

Wedding Costs

Wedding costs fluctuate with the times. When prices are generally high, then everything used for the wedding costs more than when price levels are low. But even then, wedding costs vary tremendously. Your wedding may be as economical or as expensive as you make it. Modern brides are spending far more for their weddings than their mothers dreamed of a generation ago. The average bride today spends $250 for her gown and accessories, alone. In addition to the actual wedding costs is the vast array of things that the bride buys or is given, to the tune of some $4,000 in purchasing power per marriage.[1]

Even when price levels are high, a wedding does not need to be an extravagant item in your budget. The items that tend to make the wedding expensive are largely those having to do with "show." By choosing simple wedding costumes and decorations and keeping refreshments within line, a wedding may be very lovely and still of moderate cost. Or, if money is no object, an elaborate wedding can cost many thousands of dollars.

According to convention wedding costs are assumed by both the bride and her family and the groom and his in the manner outlined below. Although this represents the general custom in the United States, it need not be interpreted rigidly. As in other aspects of wedding procedure it is well to know the traditional conventions so that you may know from what you depart when you plan your own wedding.

HOW CUSTOM DIVIDES WEDDING COSTS

The Bride or Her Family Pays for . . .

- $ Wedding gown and veil
- $ Bride's personal trousseau
- $ Wedding reception, breakfast, or dinner
- $ Transportation to church and reception
- $ Wedding decorations and music
- $ Invitations and announcements
- $ Gifts for the groom and the bride's attendants

[1] Alexandra S. Potts, "Brides: The Nation's Billion Dollar Babies," *Public Relations Board Newsletter*, Vol. 7, No. 9, June 1961, pp. 3, 4; and Robert Wacker, Jr., "Our Wild Extravagance . . . The Great Big Wedding," *McCall's*, January 1960, pp. 50, 51, 117, 118.

$ Bride's bouquet and mothers' flowers

$ Bride's "going away" corsage

$ Wedding trip

$ Wedding ring

$ Minister's fee

$ Marriage license

$ Gifts for the bride, best man, and ushers

The Marriage Ceremony

Virtually all groups, primitive and civilized alike, have a special ceremony marking the transition from the courtship to married life. In our
own history we had for hundreds of years two ceremonies: the betrothal,
which was a business arrangement between the families to take care of
property arrangements, and the wedding ceremony, which came somewhat later and carried the mark of finality.

The wedding ceremony was originally performed by the father
among the Hebrews, the Greeks, and the Romans; but as the early
Christian church became powerful, the priest's blessing was added to
the ceremony. As the church concerned itself more and more with
marriage, witnesses were added, and all marriages were performed by the
clergy. With the Reformation the Protestants came to regard marriage
as a civil contract, and the state undertook the responsibility of super-
vising the ceremony in Protestant countries. In Europe today it is not
uncommon to be married by a civil court and then to repeat the ceremony at a church wedding. In America we have delegated to the clergy
the civil authority to perform marriages, giving them thereby both civil
and religious sanction over marriage.

The functions of the marriage ceremony today are:

1 To impress on the couple and all relatives and friends the changed status
of the pair, both legally and psychologically.

2 To announce the new status; to give public support and stability to the relation emphasized by the titles *Mr.* and *Mrs.* and by the assumption of the
husband's family name by the wife.

3 To give legal protection to the wife and to the children born of the union:
to place the responsibility for their care and support with the pair and not
with the state.

4 To glorify and sanctify the relation (religious marriage), giving it divine
blessing and approval — God approves.

Wedding Services. Weddings in the many churches of the various faiths differ widely. Not only the procedures prescribed by the particular church but the training and beliefs of the individual minister and the preferences of the couple play a part in determining the nature of the wedding ceremony. An occasional couple write a part of their own ceremony, incorporating their own convictions and commitment with the traditional vows. Some ministers have developed their own introductory statements that precede the usual vows in the wedding ceremony. The following is used by permission as illustrative.

WEDDING CEREMONY

Address to the Congregation

There is an ancient story which contains a profound insight: It is not good for man to be alone. We rightly approach a wedding ceremony with reverence and with awe. For marriage has welled up out of the depths of personal and social need. In it the fundamental impulses of the individual and the race, biological, personal and social, come to an overt focus. The ceremony itself is the public avowal of a new relationship, the most basic which can exist among men. It signifies that two people stand at one point along the unending stream of human development, a point at which countless others have stood before and countless more will stand in ages which are to come. Yet it is for the human race, as for them, unique in the totality of timeless aeons. The centuries of the past have looked forward to this occasion. Those of the future should have good cause to regard it with respect and gratitude.

It is meet and proper that so awe-inspiring an occasion, when Eternity emerges as a visible point in the present, should be celebrated with dignity and solemnity. All races, tribes and cultures, from the most primitive to the most advanced, have made of this step an occasion for rejoicing and an expression through ceremony and rite of profound social concern. So today, society expresses its legitimate and inescapable interest. For a wedding is more than the joining of two persons to each other. It is the closing of a link in the endless chain of human relationships, a link which binds the present to the past and out of which the future can most advantageously emerge.

The wedding is properly a religious ceremony. For in marriage, basic forces which determine human destiny find their richest and most creative expression. The noblest sentiments and highest ideals of the human soul stand by in expectant concern for their future. The God who sustains all which is, ultimately presides.

Address to the Couple

For you, this ceremony will mean entrance into new relationships which will affect many aspects of your lives. Your legal status will be altered in important respects. The merger of names will symbolize an extensive change in your social status and relationships. Changed personal relationships, some of which may prove onerous, will remind you that things are no longer as they were.

It will mean for you a new security in your personal lives. For marriage is an oasis of refreshment and renewal in an often arid world, a point of stability amid the bewildering and often alarming changes of a rapidly shifting social scene. Your marriage will mean that each of you will have one whom you know and can respond to as a whole personality. In all the welter of mass humanity and whirling shifts of friendships, you can find stability. Marriage will mean for you that intimacy which is necessary for the best satisfaction of the deepest needs of your souls. You will find a new security in acceptance, a security which is freely yours without the need for pretense and dissimulation. For you there will always be one situation in which you can be as you really are, without risk of rejection. Marriage means in part, the weaving of a rope of relationships upon which each of you can put the full strain of your own worst, without fear that it will break.

You will find a new security and richness of love. Among the greatest needs of all is a two-way flow of affection. Marriage will increase and enrich this for you, unimpeded by conventions and unspoiled by fear of its loss. Such married love is above and beyond all other forms of human love. In it alone are intermingled the depth, intimacy, and permanence essential for your greatest satisfaction and growth.

Your wedding means a recognition and acceptance of new social obligations. To marry is to enter into partnership in a building enterprise. It means the construction of a social relationship which inevitably involves others. To marry is not only to establish a center of emotional security for yourselves. It is to create a basic unit of society. And in so doing you find your own greatest fulfillment.

The vows which you are about to take pledge you to fidelity, one to the other. This does not merely mean fidelity to taboos, or even to a person. The man and woman who live together secure in each other's love are being faithful to far more than each other. They are being faithful to a social situation which can produce people who can live without fear, who are sufficiently mature emotionally as neither to seek nor to need dictatorship and aggression. They are being faithful to the basic foundations of the social structure in which all are formed and nourished. They are being faithful to the provisions which society makes for the protection and the development of the deepest needs of persons. When you marry you do far more than to take unto yourself a spouse. You take a piece of the social future into your hands.

Then follow the usual vows and prayers.

THE WEDDING PARTY IN ORDER OF APPEARANCE
AT 3 PHASES OF THE WEDDING

Processional Usher escorts groom's parents to front pew right of center aisle
(Just before) T H E N
Bride's mother is seated by usher at left of center aisle (signal for the wedding march to begin)
N O W   T H E   P R O C E S S I O N
Ushers two by two
Bridesmaids two by two
Maid or matron of honor
Ring bearer — *if any* [2]
Flower girl — *if any* [2]
Bride on her father's right arm
(Groom, best man, and minister stand at the altar, facing the processional)

Recessional Bride on groom's right arm
Flower girl alone or with the ring bearer
Maid or matron of honor alone or with the best man [3]
Bridesmaids two by two or paired with ushers
Ushers two by two or with the bridesmaids
As soon as the wedding party has gone out, two ushers return at once for mothers of the bride and groom
The guests then depart

Receiving Line Bride's mother
(Left to right) Groom's father [4]
Groom's mother
Bride's father
Bride
Groom
Maid or matron of honor
Bridesmaids (if preferred they may mingle with the guests, as the ushers and the best man do)

[2] If children are in the wedding party, they should be rehearsed carefully once or twice before the ceremony, at the place of the wedding.

[3] The best man may go directly to the vestry for the groom's hat and coat, and his own, joining the wedding party at the door, if this seems more convenient in what comes next.

[4] The bride's father may stand beside his wife, then the groom's mother and father, then the bride and groom. This more modern form keeps the principal couples together and is sometimes more pleasant and graceful for the receiving line.

Special Cases

There are many special situations in which the usual forms and rules do not seem to apply. Let us consider just a few of them.

Two Faiths — Two Ceremonies. When members of two faiths marry, their wedding has to be worked out to meet the requirements of their respective churches as well as their personal preferences. If a Catholic is to have his or her marriage recognized by the Roman Catholic church, it must be performed by a Catholic priest according to the rules of the church. Some faithful Jews feel married only when it has been done by the rabbi.

One Baptist bride called her pastor on the evening of her wedding day and begged him to "marry us again, for I just don't feel right being married only by his rabbi." This minister replied that it was hardly necessary to be married again, since they were already married, but that he would be willing to *reaffirm* their marriage and give it his blessing as a Christian clergyman. This pleased the bride, was satisfactory to the groom, and violated nothing in either's religion.

Some couples marrying across religious faiths plan for such a dual-wedding service in which all members of both families as well as the dictates of both churches will be satisfied. It seems hardly necessary to remind you that such things are best discussed and agreed upon early in the relationship, with plans laid well in advance so that all concerned know what to expect.

Double Weddings. Two couples (usually sisters or brothers) may marry without other attendants, each serving as the other's witnesses. Or the double wedding may have all the pomp and splendor of the huge church wedding, *times two!* In the latter case, the older bride and her attendants enter first, then the younger bride and her attendants, with the recessional in the same formation with each couple leading its own bridal party. If the brides are sisters, one invitation may be issued for their double wedding, in which case the older sister's name appears first.

Divorce, a Complicating Factor. If the bride's parents are divorced, the invitations may be issued by her mother, with her present husband as host, if she has remarried. In this case, the bride's father may give her away if she wishes, after which he steps back to the pew behind her mother. Whether or not he remains for the reception is best decided by discussion well ahead of time. Except in most unusual cases, the absent parent is invited to the wedding, and members of the family behave without bitterness toward each other.

The mature bride whose parents are divorced may issue her own invitations and announcements and walk down the aisle either alone, or on the arm of a favorite uncle or other older male relative.

Similarly, if the bride is herself a divorcée, she may issue her own invitations, and the couple may announce their own marriage. If the bride is a very young divorcée, her parents may announce her marriage as usual. The remarriage of a divorced woman is usually not formal, or in a white gown and veil. It may be held in a chapel, home, or garden, with one attendant (not a child by a former marriage).

Orphaned and Widowed Brides. The bride who is an orphan may have a formal wedding if she wishes, by asking some older woman to be her sponsor, and walking down the aisle on the arm of some favorite older male relative or close family friend.

The remarriage of a widow is usually simple and informal, and not in white wedding gown and veil, which is the symbol of first marriage. Her own children may attend her if she wishes. She may write personal notes as invitations and announcements, using her full name.

Sickness and Death in Wedding Plans. An invalid mother, grandmother, or sister may attend even a formal church wedding in a wheel chair, or the wedding may be planned at home where she is. Bride, groom, or any of the bridal attendants may participate in any wedding in a wheel chair or on crutches if need be. In the case of a close member of the family being suddenly stricken ill just before the wedding, the ceremony may be postponed by notifying the guests by wire, phone, or note.

When one of the parents of bride or groom dies suddenly, the wedding usually is postponed with some such wording as this: "Owing to the sudden death of Mrs. John James Jones, the marriage of her daughter Janice to Gerald Raymond Brown has been indefinitely postponed." This notice may be sent to the local papers, and to all guests already invited to the wedding. The marriage may proceed on the date planned but then it is a simple quiet wedding with only members of the immediate family present.

Broken Engagements. It is not only in Hollywood that something breaks up a couple before the wedding date; it happens in real life too. In such a case, there are two things to do at once: 1. cancel the wedding; and 2. return to the senders all wedding gifts. Guests already invited to the wedding must be notified that the wedding plans have been cancelled, whether or not they have sent gifts to the bride. Couples feeling embarrassed about cancelling their wedding should remember that it is far better to call off an unpromising marriage before it gets started than it is to carry each other into the anguish of an unhappy union. One of the functions of the engagement period is to sort out incompatible pairs.[5] It may take the wise guidance of a competent counselor to help the couple discover whether the break originates from something simple and superficial, or whether it stands for something basically wrong in the match.

Moving up the Date. In these days when so many things may happen to change things, it is sometimes necessary to advance the date of the wedding. A military leave is granted earlier than expected, a vacation date is advanced, an opportunity opens up, all sorts of things may call for an earlier date than the one originally planned. The procedure for meeting this type of case is simply to contact the guests and tell them where and when the rearranged wedding is to be. A simple wedding can be arranged at the last minute in the chapel at the military post, in the bride's home, in a club or garden, or even after one of the regular services of the church, if the couple are flexible in their planning. Indeed, this might serve as a motto for wedding plans generally: "Be Prepared for the Unexpected."

To be useful wedding plans should be based upon the values of those being married. If you realize that tradition has been upset many times, and that conventions serve but as guides, you can plan your wedding in ways that will be most meaningful to you and to those whom you love and want close to you on this your day of days.

Avoiding Commercialism in Your Wedding. You want your wedding to be nice. You know that it should be a lovely, dignified, and happy occasion for you all. Yet that does not mean that it must be expensive. Commercial establishments make weddings their business. They count on making money on the weddings they service, as of course they must

---

[5] See Chapter Five, "Getting Engaged."

if they are to stay in business. But that does not mean that you have to go along with all the expensive suggestions or elaborate plans that are offered you. This is your wedding and as such you have the say of what you shall or shall not have.

When the caterer suggests a full meal for your wedding guests, you may feel that it is worth what it will cost, or you may prefer to serve simple cake and punch in order to save the hundreds of dollars difference for something for your new home. When the florist begins to talk of potted palms and elaborate floral arrangements as well as expensive bouquets, you can go along if money is no object, or you can put your foot down on such temporary expense in terms of long-term values. So it is too with clothes, the rings, the photographs, the number of guests invited both to the wedding and to the reception, and finally how much you will spend on the honeymoon itself.

The bride who realizes that simple weddings can be quite as lovely as commercially staged ones has the courage to see to it that her wedding expresses what means most in terms not of dollars spent but of personal values. It makes little sense to go bankrupt putting on an expensive wedding that will be over in a matter of minutes when a little careful planning would save the money for a home for the years.

In the long run, it is not what you wear or eat at your wedding, but what you are that counts. As you put your emphasis on *being* rather than on *buying*, you are establishing a sound policy for the foundation of your home.

Readings

BLOOD, ROBERT O., JR., *Anticipating Your Marriage* (Glencoe, Illinois: The Free Press, 1955). Chapter 8, "Getting Married: The Wedding and Honeymoon," traces the roles of the various members of the family in the wedding, looks at the spirit of the occasion of the wedding and reviews what makes for the satisfying honeymoon.

BOSSARD, JAMES H. S., and ELEANOR S. BOLL, *Ritual in Family Living* (Philadelphia: University of Pennsylvania Press, 1950). An original study of the place of rituals in family life that might be studied to see the wedding in perspective.

BOWMAN, HENRY A., *Marriage for Moderns* (New York: McGraw-Hill Book Company, 1960 edition). This book contains an excellent chapter on the wedding and the honeymoon that any prospective bride and groom will find of practical help, and all others will see as full of interest.

FORCE, ELIZABETH S., *Your Family Today and Tomorrow* (New York: Harcourt Brace and Company, 1955). Chapter 12, "Getting Married —

Whose Business?" takes up many such topics as choosing the kind of wedding, hurried marriages, secret marriages, quiet marriages, and the honeymoon.

WOODS, MARJORIE BINFORD, *Your Wedding: How to Plan and Enjoy It* (New York: Bobbs-Merrill, new revised edition). All the practical details of what to do and how, that come up when a wedding is being planned, are helpfully discussed in this attractive book.

PART 2

BEING MARRIED

CHAPTER EIGHT

For Better, for Worse . . .

NEWLYWEDS

What type of honeymoon is best?

Are all the honeymoon intimacies easy to take?

Why do people talk about "settling down" as if it were so important?

Does marriage really make you different?

Is it true that unless you watch out love dies soon after you get married?

*T*HE WEDDING IS OVER. THE UNITY WHICH HAS BEEN BUILT UP DURing courtship and engagement has now been publicly recognized and ceremonialized. Now at last the roles of *husband* and *wife* which have been played in fantasy many times may be tried out. Once married, the man and the woman start on a journey from which it is difficult to turn back. In the chapters which follow our discussion will throw some light on the situations couples face in marriage, the skills and abilities needed, and the normality of trouble and frustration as a new family is launched into operation. Key ideas which merit attention include the following:

1 Marriage is a more complex way of living than single life and therefore is likely to aggravate rather than cure symptoms of immaturity such as restiveness, uncertainty, and unhappiness.

2 A key need of early marriage is to settle down and work out the routines of daily living.

3 As romantic love is replaced by conjugal love, the marriage becomes stabilized.

4 Conflict in marriage is normal and may be used constructively to hold the partnership together.

5 Happily married couples, in adult terms, are not necessarily couples who never quarrel but are those who have learned the techniques of resolving conflicts which arise.

6 Keeping the channels of communication clear is important for marriage solidarity.

The Honeymoon

In the early weeks of marriage young people are perhaps more impressionable than at any other time in their lives. Hope and expectation are keyed to concert pitch. Idealism is at its height. The newly married individuals continue the pattern of the engagement in ever increasing tempo, the pattern of widening the range of their mutual exploration of one another's personalities. These processes parallel, some will say overlay, deep anxieties about the undefined future and the realization that this relationship which is so precious has the capacity to hurt. All these conditions can bring about a delicately balanced state of the emotions in which small embarrassments are capable of having a devastating effect.

David Mace [1] expresses the situation well:

From one point of view, getting married could be represented as a rather terrifying experience. For something like a third of their life span two people have lived independent of each other — probably without even knowing of each other's existence. They have formed their own personal habits and learned to live their own private lives. Now, after a comparatively short acquaintance, they come together in the closest human intimacy, living together, sleeping together, yielding themselves up to each other. At the time, they don't think of this as an invasion of their privacy. Their strong desire for each other draws them together and they make their surrender eagerly. But for all that, the mutual unveiling of their bodies and minds can sometimes have profoundly disturbing and quite unexpected consequences. . . . To make these early adjustments as easy as possible we have wisely provided the institution of the honeymoon.

Full of excitement, thrills, and anticipation of delightful intimacies, the honeymoon is a continuation of the period of bliss characteristic of the engagement period. Two sources of emotion flow over in most marriages during the first weeks, the growing pleasures of the sex experi-

[1] David R. Mace, *Marriage: The Art of Lasting Love* (New York: Doubleday, 1952), pp. 46–47.

ences and the fears of the unknown and undefined future of the marriage. These are major components of romantic love. Indeed, the honeymoon marks the crest of the feelings identified as romantic love feelings. Thereafter the fear element, which has its source in the apprehension of the unknown and unpredictable problems of marriage, subsides unless activated by extramarital thrill-seeking or a new love affair. Romantic love feeds on the new and the unknown. As marriage settles down to a walking gait, romantic love is normally exchanged for a less exciting but more permanent combination of love feelings based on companionship and mutual interdependence, identified elsewhere as conjugal love.[2]

Conjugal love first appears in the companionable phase of the engagement relation and develops greatly during the early months of marriage. During the honeymoon the couple pick up souvenirs and buy furniture, which are quickly given a sentimental value. The snapshots of the honeymoon trip and the trails taken together are often reviewed. Thus the memories of the honeymoon make up some of the first tangible evidences of the conjugal love on which enduring marriages are based.

Planning the Honeymoon. The wedding journey is designed to meet specific needs and should not be postponed for several weeks or months until, for example, the bridegroom gets his vacation. The value of the honeymoon lies in the opportunities it gives the newlyweds to meet the first experiences of marriage away from people who know them, thus providing them a little time to get over the self-consciousness which comes with playing new and untried roles. Point number one in planning, then, is to set the wedding date at a time when a honeymoon is possible.

Although the plans for the honeymoon are for the most part jointly laid, the exact dates for the wedding and wedding journey are rightly set by the bride. The timing of the menstrual period and the irregularities which often accompany emotional stress are factors which need to receive attention in launching the marriage.

The engaged couple can add enjoyment to their first days of marriage if they depart from the trite honeymoon tours to Niagara Falls and Washington in favor of a trip which characterizes the individuality of

---

[2] See Chap. 12, "What Holds a Marriage Together."

their relationship. One couple who had met in Europe on a hosteling tour planned a similar tour by bicycle through New England. Another made their common passion for bird life the center of their plans for a week's outing at a bird sanctuary neither had visited before. A third couple spent most of their time in New York attending plays and operas when they weren't catching up on their sleep at a bohemian apartment off Washington Square. In this business of planning, the couple needs to realize that one man's meat may be another man's poison. A trout stream in the Rockies is no place for a couple of tenderfeet, the advertisement of the travel associations to the contrary. Life on a dude ranch can be very irritating if the couple doesn't know its cattle ponies. Point number two is to plan to do something on the honeymoon which both enjoy and can do reasonably well. There will be other occasions for the new and unusual when both parties are surer of themselves and are under less emotional tension.

The hazards to be avoided by the honeymooners are excessive costs and overfatigue. If the engagement has been one of planning and discussion, the honeymoon costs will have been worked out along with the budget of the first year's expenses. Placed in juxtaposition to the other costs of the year, the honeymoon will usually be estimated at a reasonable figure. Some estimate of the number of miles to be traveled and the number of things to be seen and done needs to be made. Trying to do too much in too little time will result in overfatigue and set the stage for quarrels when the couple is least able to cope with them.

Suppose we list a few do's and don'ts which might be reviewed by the couple anticipating marriage and a satisfying honeymoon:

1 Select a place where you can be completely alone and away from people who know you, and where privacy is assured.
2 Plan your trip to obviate overfatigue as much as possible.
3 Arrange for hotel or room reservations in advance.
4 Plan for time to loaf and sleep — newly married couples go to bed early and get up late.
5 Carry on with the planning and exploration talks of the engagement, discussing points on which you aren't able to find a basis for agreement as well as those on which you are.

Excitement of the Wedding Journey. The honeymoon customarily lasts a week or two and for obvious economic reasons rarely extends beyond a month. The wedding journey is an excellent introduction into marriage, providing as it does for a release of the tension which has piled up in the days before the wedding and for the maximum expression of idealism. The honeymoon also provides a point at which realities are allowed to intrude, as the pair prepares to return to familiar surroundings and mundane responsibilities. Fortunately the period of ecstasy does not continue long, for moving from one thrill and discovery to another is exhausting.

The adjustment in the first years is sometimes most difficult for those couples who have restricted their love activities too prudishly in the courtship and engagement period. They find themselves suddenly in marriage with all the barriers down and with all too little preparation for the expression of the excitement and attraction which arise in the intimacies. It is not uncommon for one or both parties to experience feelings of guilt or revulsion, to the mutual distress of both parties. For other couples who have anticipated great thrills in the first sex relations, there is sometimes disappointment — reality doesn't live up to the expectations. Said one such couple, "We were surprised that that was all there was to it; somehow we had expected more." The girl felt cheated, and the boy was hurt and worried that his wife wasn't thrilled. Both needed to realize that enjoyable sex response is a matter of learning, and that it grows with the years. They failed to grasp the fact that early sex relations are necessarily awkward, both because of their newness and because of the anxiety both feel toward the unknown. Where fear is present sex response is inhibited, and only after the couple have become thoroughly secure in their new role of husband and wife, of Mr. and Mrs., can they expect to attain the heights which the uninformed honeymooners feel is their right the first night.[3]

The honeymoon intimacies are taken almost as a matter of course by the couples who are able to recognize the sexual urges and expressions for what they are. They have studied what to expect, and after a certain amount of normal love play in the engagement period, the honeymoon presents to them an extended period of easily assimilated new ex-

[3] See Chap. 12, "What Holds a Marriage Together." In Stanley Brav's intriguing study of honeymoons nearly half of his respondents reported that they failed to achieve complete sexual harmony during their honeymoon, yet the majority considered their honeymoon a complete success. Sexual harmony was not considered essential to honeymoon success. See Stanley Brav, "Note on Honeymoons," *Marriage and Family Living*, Vol. 9 (Summer, 1947), p. 60.

periences. They are able to recognize and understand their own urges and make the most of them.

A fourth group of young people "make the most" of the honeymoon experiences, because they feel that the intoxication of early marriage is the most desirable part of marriage, that marriage should be one continual courtship in which love is kept aglow with constant thrills. This is the school which reflects most closely the Hollywood pattern of perpetual romance and which judges a marriage by the continuation of the burning thrills of love. If the love-light dies, a divorce ensues; and the light burns again only as new love appears, followed by another honeymoon, another trip to Reno, another honeymoon, and so on. These people take their fiction and movies too seriously and apparently know little or nothing about the studies of happily married men and women. Although the great majority settle down in time to more or less routine married living, there is usually an intervening period of disillusionment before they hit a normal stride. For these young people the psychiatrists would list coming to terms with reality as the most important single accomplishment of the first year of marriage.

Establishing an Etiquette of Intimacy

Still another area of interpersonal adjustment which the honeymoon makes possible involves the intimacies of personal hygiene. The early days of marriage could be greatly eased if young couples received more help about these matters, at least as much as about the intimacies of sex. They would be spared a good deal of distress if, as well as preparing themselves for sexual union, they recognized also the fact that in close intimacy of marriage men and women must learn a warm tender consideration for the little details of bodily hygiene which are part of the business of living. David Mace has pointed out that in the course of married life there are many lowly services which husband and wife must perform for each other. One of the important adjustments which must be made in the early weeks together is to get over any false modesty which the couple may feel about their own or each other's bodies.[4]

Why should couples, in this day and age of frankness and freedom of inhibitions about sex, find the intimacies of sensory details connected

---

[4] David Mace, *op. cit.*, p. 50.

with other bodily functions fraught with embarrassment and disgust reactions? The answer may not be obvious.

In America, the land of locked bathrooms and fully clothed people, of private bedrooms and dressing quarters, the child is often reared to adulthood carefully protected from the sensory details of the bodily functions of others. He is taught to disguise his intention of going to the toilet by asking if he may wash his hands. Girl children particularly are protected from vulgarity, as Americans define it. Added to and accentuating the problem is the universal tendency in the courtship and engagement period to idealize the other person, to endow the person with qualities of saintliness, and to shrink from the thought that the other person carries on the same bodily functions as common folk. While still holding these ideas, the carefully protected boy and girl marry and face for the first time the details of married living, with the doors of privacy torn off. The imaginary picture of the other person was nobler and kinder. The sensory details overwhelm the sensitive, sheltered girl and all too often produce reactions of disgust and revulsion.

Too much intimacy, too little privacy, in too short a period! Because of the way we have been reared, we must preserve some of the illusions for a time, at least. A minimum of privacy will need to be maintained indefinitely, just because Americans react to bodily functions of urination and excretion the way they do. This is difficult in overcrowded apartments with no private dressing quarters and with shared bathrooms, but every effort should be made to ease the transition gracefully from the more spacious parental home with its privacy to the more restricted accompaniments of married life. The informed couple will meet the challenge.[5]

Disillusionment and Settling Down

Disillusionment sounds like an ugly word, but it means, simply, "facing realities." G. V. Hamilton's study of two hundred married persons, A *Research in Marriage*, showed the illusions of the engagement and honeymoon period to have lasted well into the second year of marriage for most of his cases. Twenty-nine per cent stated that they had settled

[5] A searching analysis of the reactions of Americans to lack of privacy is given in Markoosha Fisher's *My Lives in Russia* (New York: Harper, 1944), pp. 59–76.

down to facing realities after one year, and 20 per cent after two years. The balance didn't know how long it took them to complete the process of disillusionment. Many couples claim to have had no difficulty in settling down after returning from the honeymoon, stating variously, "The process developed naturally," "We didn't expect marriage to be so very different and it wasn't," "It was a relief to find marriage so livable after all the ghastly accounts of divorce and separation," "We just kept on being good pals instead of going dramatic during the honeymoon, and we couldn't see anything to be disillusioned about." These couples started their period of disillusionment by facing realities in the courtship and engagement period, as their statements reveal, and made the transition into marriage with a minimum of anxiety.

Walking is the best gait for most people, but most honeymooners hit a tempo more akin to a gallop in the series of thrills sought and experienced. The change of pace which must come is called "settling down," and is a phase of disillusionment. Disillusionment includes not only the removal of blinders which have kept the lover from seeing the wart on the chin of the loved one, but also the mutual discovery that marriage doesn't change personalities. "We are still our old familiar, boring selves, and we thought we would be different when married. It looked as if we could change when we were engaged and on the honeymoon, but now. . . ."

Disillusionment is partly due to the discrepancy between what we have imagined marriage to be like, or been told it was like, or read it was like, and what we find it to be. Notice the discrepancy between the following stereotyped picture of the couple who lived happily ever after and the facts. It is the case of Mary Jane and Jim who were married and settled down in a cute little house with checked curtains at the windows. They are supposed to have had three years of happy married life, writes our ad writer for marriage:

Mary Jane, in a crisp house dress kept spotless and unfaded by Lux, has laid out breakfast — everything Beechnut but the eggs. Jim Junior is busily eating up his cereal for the fun of finding the Mickey Mouse at the bottom of the dish, thoughtfully supplied by the makers of Cream of Wheat. Jim Senior, spruce in an Arrow collar and fortified by a perfect night's rest under the auspices of the Simmons Bedding Company, is about to make his way to the office to earn the thirty-five dollars a week which somehow are to pay for the hundred-dollar radio, the Monel metal kitchen, the dapper little car, and the self-satisfied look that comes to those who have provided nicely for retirement at fifty-five. This intimate view of American home life is familiar to us all through the kindness of advertising mediums of every variety and haunting ubiquity. We are fortunate because without their aid we should never see such a pretty picture.

Let us peek in again without the rosy spectacles supplied by the nationally advertised brands. Mary Jane's frock for mornings at home looks a little frayed and faded. Her apron has definitely seen neither Lux nor a harsh washing soap for several days. She scrapes dispiritedly at the breakfast plates, slightly repulsive with congealed egg yolk and slimy cold bacon grease. For the fourteenth time she exhorts Junior to stop dawdling and eat his cereal. She is not, at the moment, enjoying her marriage very much. Why should she? Washing dishes day in and day out is not the same thing as canoeing in the moonlight with your heart's beloved. . . . Mary Jane is remembering five o'clock with Jim waiting at the corner, of dinner with dancing, of going to the movies, or a concert, or the theatre, or just a long ferry-boat ride. Of the difficult good-night kiss and the ecstatic knowledge that soon she would have Jim all the time for always. She is thinking rather wryly of how entrancing, how full of promise, this battered dishpan looked when it first emerged from pink tissue paper at the shower the girls gave her. She may even think, a little cynically, as she surveys the grey grease pocked surface of her dishwater, of the foaming pans of eternally virgin suds she expected from her perusal of the advertisements. Well, she's married now. She has her own house, her own dishpan, her husband, and her baby. All the time and for always. She doesn't even go to the movies any more because there is no one to stay with Junior. She speaks so crossly to the child now that his tears fall into the objectionable cereal. Why on earth won't Jim let her get Mrs. Oldacre in to stay evenings? He'll be earning more soon; Mr. Bayswater practically told him he would be put in charge of the branch office as soon as old Fuzzy retired. Five dollars a week savings — much good that does anyway. Mary Jane's thoughts about her husband become quite uncharitable. "If he only had the least understanding of the kind of life I have, but all he notices is Junior's shoes are scuffed out and he would not even try that Bavarian cream I fixed yesterday. It's all very well for him to think Jimmy Junior's cute when he sneaks out of bed — he doesn't have him all day and all night and nothing but Jimmy Junior."

Thus Mary Jane at nine o'clock of a Monday morning. At three P.M. the sight of Junior tugging a large packing box about the yard suddenly makes her heart turn over with delight and pride. What a duck he is. . . . She smiles all to herself with pleasure at the sunlight falling through the peach curtains on the blues and browns of her livingroom furniture. That recipe for apple pan dowdy — she'll try that for supper. Jim will be home in two hours and a half, home for a whole lovely evening. And Monday is Philadelphia orchestra night on the radio. For no reason at all life is abruptly good, very good.

Jim, meantime, is having his own problems, big and little. Mary Jane is a frequent pain in the neck to him. He likes his eggs with the whites firm and the yolks runny. Mary Jane gets them wrong every time — sometimes leathery, sometimes slimy. Why does she have to be so cranky with Junior, and why can't she keep him quiet mornings? She should know a man needs all the rest he can get. He has to give his best to the job — marriage is too expensive to loaf or to be tired. Mary doesn't understand that at all. He gave up his big chance in the Texas branch just for her, didn't he? But does she appreciate it? And yet Jim, too, has his hours of excitement and delight, of deep satisfaction in his wife and his son and his home and himself in the role of father in the family.[6]

How do you react to this latter view of marriage? It is more accurate than the version thrust upon us by the advertisers, but it is still only the top layer, the part we see, the common-sense interpretation of satisfactions and discords in the lives of Mary Jane and Jim. The roots of conflict lie much deeper in the personalities of sparring partners.

If the discrepancy between what you imagined marriage would be like and what it is in reality is as great as that presented above, don't feel marriage has cheated you. The first step toward permanent and satisfying marriage is disillusionment, the willingness to accept one's self and one's partner on the level of everyday living, to take the worse along with the better.

It should be pointed out that well-adjusted couples will recognize moments of rapture and the moments of disappointment, as well as the strong undercurrent of partnership in the run-of-the-mine emotions of daily life. The role of moods is important, some days we're up, some days down, some days romantic and some days realistic. Disillusionment, although primarily concerned with facing realities, includes finding a place for the delightful moments of the happier mood.

Setting up Housekeeping

In a play of recent years called 3 *Is a Family*, the young mother breaks down and weeps after her exasperated husband has criticized her inefficiency and mistakes in keeping the house straightened up, and her failures with the baby. "You must have patience with me; I know I'm inefficient, but you see, I've never been a mother before." The job was too big for her to handle all at once. She knew she was in a mess but

---

[6] Reprinted from *The Happy Family* by John Levy and Ruth Munroe, by permission of and special arrangement with Alfred A. Knopf, Inc.

"Remember! You said you loved me . . ."

was powerless to climb out of it. New jobs are like that, and marriage with its new household tasks takes some experience and planning.

Or take the poor bride in the cartoon on this page. Obviously, she did not manage her time correctly. She probably slept too late, took too long to get the groceries, left the chicken too long while she went to the store. She is counting on love to get her by! "If he loves me he will forgive and forget." If he is impatient and cross, she will claim he doesn't love her. But in a marriage based on companionship and conjugal love, the girl might say, "How would you like to pitch in and help me clean up? This job of being a wife is more difficult than I thought — and kiss me, dear, first!"

Both parties in a new marriage face adjustments to a level of living less well ordered and substantial than existed in the parental family. After all, it took their parents twenty to thirty years to provide their home with all its facilities and to organize their routines so faultlessly. The new husband may obtain an understanding of his wife's problems if he pitches in to help with the meal, setting the table and washing up the dishes afterward — as well he should. The new wife needs to realize she can't follow the same budget for her personal expenditures that she could under her father's high salary, and she should thank her lucky stars she has a wardrobe built up which will hold her over the first few years. These are only a few of the adjustments which occur in the shift from parental family living to the life of newlyweds.

Out of the clinical studies by psychiatrists of hundreds of housewives come these findings of value for new husbands: Personalities which require order, which require that a house be neat and spotless, that every chair have a special place and all clothes be put away, in other words, personalities which make wonderful housekeepers rarely make adaptable, understanding, patient wives. Rarely can a wife be both a perfect housekeeper and an understanding, flexible companion. The husband may get a not-so-good housekeeper who won't worry and fuss about him and the children. But the compulsion to keep order which makes for perfection in household management is incompatible with normal rough and tumble married living. Take your choice! A man may enjoy keeping things "shipshape" while on duty, but at home who wants to live under the eagle eye of an inspecting admiral?

Major Accomplishments of the First Year of Marriage

Courtship, engagement, and marriage can merge imperceptibly without jarring adjustments. A student's letter to one of the authors shows how normally and easily he and his wife achieved this merger:

> I didn't learn much about family in my first month of marriage, but I did learn a great deal about marriage. We moved into our own house, budgeted our time and expenditures; we consulted a physician about birth control methods and got a very good start on our adjustment to the new roles we had assumed. Nobody told us a great deal about how to manage our affairs and it seemed to come natural to us. . . . I am very happily married; I have a wonderful wife and mother for my children and two of the swellest, healthiest, most perfect kids that anybody could ask for.

If all marriages developed as naturally and normally as Bob's and Myrtle's above, there would be much less justification for formal education in marriage and family life. These young people changed the company they were frequenting and took on the roles and responsibilities of the new relation, just as they might shift tempo and dance steps on the dance floor. Ordinarily a person has to learn the steps in a new dance, but if he has watched carefully and is supple enough he can imitate the new step satisfactorily. In more stable communities young people have known each other since school days, and at maturity may slip quickly into the more intensified relationships of courtship and engagement with a pretty clear idea of the reactions they may expect from each other. They assume the responsibilities of marriage relatively easily because the examples of successfully married people are constantly before them. Married people, moreover, are available to check with as the marriage progresses.

In our discussion in this chapter we have blazed a trail for couples who do not have models of marriage so clearly accessible. The story tells of certain minimum expectations for couples in the first year of marriage. They have carried over into the honeymoon and first months of marriage the fascinating pattern of exploration and experimentation started in the engagement. They have learned how to live intimately together and may have achieved a satisfying sexual relationship. They have come to accept the realities of marriage with its routines and schedules and unromantic regularity. Romantic thrills are giving way to more companionable sentiments.

Our newlyweds have come to think of themselves as belonging to the married set and now feel comfortable in the roles of husband and wife, both at home and elsewhere. They are winning a status in the community as married folk and will soon be inducted into the circles of gardeners, marketing specialists, and canning artists. Some people may already have begun talking about the advantages of "having your babies while you are young."

Although there have been many quarrels and conflicts during the first year, the differences are being ironed out, and the friction has worn smooth the edges which seemed so easily irritated the first few months. The pair still has its differences but has come to know that quarreling is no longer any threat to its relationship, which in itself is a major accomplishment. Our new husband and wife have come to accept married life with its ups and downs and are prepared now to take the worse along with the better. The first year of marriage has been stimulating and satisfying. For the couple who worried about the pitfalls of marriage it is reassuring to know that marriage is sometimes full of fun!

Readings

CAVAN, RUTH S., *American Marriage, a Way of Life* (New York: Thomas Y. Crowell, 1959). Chapter 11 on the time and place for marriage and honeymoon offers good guides on these practical questions, while Chapter 12, "Learning to Live Together," covers the major adjustments of newlyweds.

DUVALL, EVELYN MILLIS, *Family Living* (New York: Macmillan, 1961). Chapter 14, "Early Marriage Adjustments," includes such topics as settling your differences, working wives, money management, recreation and in-laws in the new marriage.

FORCE, ELIZABETH S., *Your Family Today and Tomorrow* (New York: Harcourt Brace and Company, 1955). Chapter 13, "Learning to Be Mr. and Mrs.," includes such important questions as, "Have you married a stranger?" and "Are there recipes for happy marriages?"

LANDIS, JUDSON and MARY, *Personal Adjustment, Marriage and Family Living* (Englewood Cliffs, New Jersey: Prentice-Hall, Inc., 1955). Chapter 16, "What It Means to Be Married," reminds you that it takes time to make marriage adjustments — as studies by the authors detail in ways that you will find interesting and helpful.

LEVY, JOHN and RUTH MUNROE, *The Happy Family* (New York: Alfred A. Knopf, 1938). Probably written before you were born, Chapter 2, "Settling down to Marriage," is still one of the most insightful and fascinating treatments of early marriage adjustments in the English language.

MOORE, BERNICE MILBURN, and DOROTHY M. LEAHY, *You and Your Family* (Boston: D. C. Heath and Company, 1953 edition). Chapter 13, "It is a Man-Woman World," traces some of the ideas we have about what it means to be men and women and how they affect the relationships between a man and his wife in learning to be married.

CHAPTER NINE

Where Does the Money Go?

MONEY MATTERS IN MARRIAGE

How much money does it take to get married?

Do budgets have to cramp your style?

How about wives working?

Is insurance a must?

Does it take brains to shop?

Is it easy to borrow money?

How can you keep out of debt?

*M*ANY HONEST, RESPONSIBLE, HARD-WORKING PEOPLE WHO have good incomes cannot manage their personal finances successfully. Joe Bank who was earning $100 a week can hardly be regarded as a charity case. Neither was he dishonest. Yet he was in serious financial difficulties. He owed over $1000 and was getting deeper into debt all the time; yet he had had no unusual expenses, such as operations or illnesses. He was not now borrowing from a loan company. He had borrowed several times before, only to find his troubles increased. In desperation he admitted his own inability to get out by himself, and had gone for help to a company whose job it was to help people get out on their own power. There are many thousands like him: people who earn enough to live comfortably and well, but somehow cannot seem to make ends meet. The purpose of this chapter is to help, not only those in financial difficulties, but all who would like to live better on the incomes they have.

Can We Afford to Marry?

What income should we have before we marry? How much should we have in the bank? If we marry, will we be able to afford it? The only proper answer to this is that it depends upon how much you demand. A special report of the United States Bureau of the Census tells us what families actually did have to live on as of 1956. About a sixth of the nation's families (16%) had annual incomes of less than $2000, while over a third (37%) made more than this but less than $5000. Thus over half of the families in America got along on less than $5000 a year. Not quite 40 per cent had between $5000 and $10,000 annual income, and only 8 per cent had more than $10,000. The national economy's general inflationary tendency may be producing somewhat higher average incomes for families today. But rising costs, often increasing at a still greater rate, usually mean that most families will have some difficulty in making their incomes meet their customary requirements. Obviously most families will never have anything like the incomes which some people regard as necessary to support a family. Your ability to live on your income will be largely determined by what you demand rather than by the size of your income.

WHO MANAGES THE MONEY? *

	HUSBAND	WIFE	BOTH
Professional and business families	30%	26%	44%
White-collar workers	29	32	39
Farmers	37	16	47
Manual workers	24	42	34
All families (United States)	29	32	39

* Source American Institute of Public Opinion as quoted in Paul H. Landis, *Your Marriage and Family Living.* New York: McGraw-Hill, 1954, p. 234.

The question "Can we afford to marry?" then, must depend largely upon the prospective bride and groom for its answer. A discussion of the following questions may help in providing such an answer: How much income are you both accustomed to? Could you get along happily on less if necessary? What are your present and immediate responsibilities for the support of relatives? (Do not include the support which you may later be called upon to give to parents who may remain self-supporting for many years.)

In estimating your probable costs after marriage, figure that two can live as cheaply as *two*. What is it now costing both of you to live? If the prospective wife is living with her parents, estimate the money value of what she is now receiving from her family, such as room, board, medical and dental service, and perhaps an allowance, all of which she may lose after marriage. In confronting your financial problems, do not expect to start in where your parents are now, either.

About That Budget

Does the word "budget" scare you? A budget is only a plan to get the most from your income. Can. you afford this or that? How do you know unless your income is budgeted? Do you find it hard to make ends meet to pay all the bills? Do you wonder "where it has all gone"? Before you plan your budget, here are some facts you should bear in mind.

Expenses for various items will not be the same for each month or each year. In winter the fuel costs will run high, in spring and fall the clothing bills. Some years there will be extra expenses, such as a new car or a baby. Professor Bigelow points out that there is usually a family cost cycle which rises steadily through the years to a peak, and then declines sharply after the children have become self-supporting.[2] Changes in the financial condition of the country at large also profoundly affect family financial planning. Families vary also in their interests and desires. Some wish to spend more for one item, and some for another. In view of all these factors, then, it is hardly sound to say that a family should spend a certain proportion of its income for food, rent, clothing, or any other particular item. Each family must work out its own budget in the light of its income and desires. The following suggestions may prove of help in working out the budget:

1 List your monthly income.

2 List all *items of regular expense* which are predictable, such as rent, gas, light, telephone, installment payments, and insurance. Include groceries if you can estimate their cost with reasonable accuracy.

[2] See his chapter "Financing the Marriage" in Howard Becker and Reuben Hill, eds., *Family, Marriage, and Parenthood* (Boston: Heath, 1955).

3 List your probable expenses for other essentials, such as clothing, carfare, and laundry.

4 Allocate a personal allowance for each member of the family, including children old enough to spend money. (Such expenditures should be the private business of each individual, accountable to no one.) List each name with the amount of the allowance beside it.

5 Add all the above expenses together, and subtract the total from the monthly income. How much do you have left? Circle it in pencil. If you don't have a balance, your plane of living is too high!

6 Now comes the fun. Forget about how much you have left. Make a list of everything you want which you might conceivably afford. Spread yourselves. Include new furniture, dishes, silverware, washing machine, sporting goods, books, an exciting vacation, or anything within reason. Most of these you may not be able to get, but it is fun to write them down.

7 Go over this list carefully and arrange the items in order of preference. Yes, this is a good time for family squabbles, for differences of opinion and taste, but these might just as well come right out into the open. If you are not yet married and the girl friend cannot be present, arrange the items for yourself, with a family situation in mind.

8 Now go back over your so-called fixed necessities and see if they are as essential as you thought. You may decide to go without so much beer, cigarettes, or candy, and spend the money saved for a better vacation next summer, or for linoleum for the floor, or for a new suit. Cutting down on movies and entertainment might enable your wife to get the silver fox scarf she has always wanted, or you to get the fine tennis racket or set of golf clubs you have set your heart on. You will be surprised how many things which you thought you could not afford now become possible. Driblets added together often make a sizable sum. List in one column what you might leave out and in a second column what may now be included.

9 Now go back to point five. How much did you have left over after providing for the running expenses of the household? Add to it what you have saved from your driblets. Then take about three fourths of this total and plan to buy as many things on your list under point seven as you have money for.

10 Keep careful accounts, but do not be a fanatic on the subject. If you cannot remember where that dime went, forget it and go to the movies as you had planned.

11 Oh, yes, what about that other fourth of what you had left (point 9) after deducting all usual running expenses and buying what you wished? Save it. For what? For emergencies, such as sickness and hospital bills; for the education of the children; to give yourself a start on a home of your own; or just to start a bank account. But do not save it all.

For before next pay day you may run into something which you very
much want but which is not in the budget. If you can, get it. For if
your budget is too tight it will prove so uncomfortable that you may become disgusted and chuck the whole thing. Leave a little room for
moving about.

So you see, the budget is not a. Demon Chaperon always keeping
you from having what you want. It is a way of showing you how to get
what you want most, instead of losing much of your income in little
expenditures which leave you nothing to show for them. Almost any
family will find in a really sound budget a faithful servant. Do not let
it throw you. If you treat it well, it will give you a real raise in pay, and
after all, that is what budgets are for.

When You Have to Borrow

Many young couples find that unexpected illness, responsibilities for
parental families, new babies, and a host of other costly items have a
tendency to pile up so quickly that borrowing money becomes necessary to meet the bills. Spending beyond one's income just for routine
living is a complicating factor in family finances. This common experience is a result of many factors: 1. the bombardment of advertising;
2. the attempt to keep up with the Joneses or to live up to the standard
set by the vocational or social or neighborhood group with which the
new family is identified; 3. the realignment of a standard of living that
is involved when young people step out of homes that have been going
concerns for twenty years or more into a new household that doesn't
include even an eggbeater. So getting some kind of financial help from
outside is sometimes imperative.

It is almost as difficult to borrow money wisely as it is to earn it.
What are the possibilities?

1 **Friends.** If you suddenly find yourself without carfare or money to pay
the dinner check, borrowing from friends may be essential, but as a general practice avoid it like the plague. In the first place, you probably will
not be able to borrow enough to do much good in any real crisis; and secondly, you are very likely to lose your friends, because of your own embarrassment if for no other reason.

2 **Relatives.** Accepting a loan from members of the family is a matter so
dependent upon the nature of the relationship between borrower and

lender that no generalization is safe. Some young people do not feel comfortable in having to depend upon the family after they are on their own. Others approve of the various forms of family subsidy that are the modern equivalents of a dowry — showers, new home, bonds, allowances, etc.

3 **Advance on salary and wages.** This borrowing technique may help out if the crisis is temporary; otherwise it merely postpones the inevitable.

4 **Loan sharks.** These financiers make loans easy but may charge several hundred per cent interest before they are through with you. Never borrow from a loan company which asks you to pay a rate of interest several times as high as that of a legitimate loan company. If you get into the clutches of a loan shark, seek legal advice at once. If his interest rates are beyond the legal rate he cannot collect.

5 **Legitimate loan companies.** Available in most cities are loan companies which do not try to use tricky devices. Partly because of the high cost of collection, however, they charge about 2.5 to 3 per cent interest a month, or 30 to 36 per cent a year. Without in any way casting reflection upon such companies, we must recognize that this is a much higher rate of interest than most borrowers can afford to pay, or need to pay.

6 **Banks.** These institutions are designed primarily to loan to business enterprises, not to individuals for personal expenses. Usually they loan relatively small sums to individuals, and only if bonds or similar collateral is deposited with the bank in sufficient quantity to cover the loan. If you own bonds which you do not wish to sell, the bank may be the very best place to secure a loan at a relatively small rate of interest. If you do not own such securities, you may find that you will be unable to secure the loan.

7 **Credit unions.** There are now credit unions operating on a membership basis through labor unions, industries, and fraternal orders. The usual rate is 1 per cent a month, or 12 per cent a year, far lower than you are likely to pay elsewhere. By all means, before you borrow elsewhere, find out if there is a credit union connected with your place of employment or some other group to which you belong. If you must borrow, the credit union is best designed to meet your temporary need.

Giving Yourself a Raise in Pay

Obviously many people have serious money problems just because they do not earn enough. However, the financial difficulties of many middle class people arise mainly because they do not spend wisely the money which they receive. Some families are constantly bemoaning their poverty and longing for a raise in pay. But when the raise in pay does come, they find to their consternation that they are farther behind than they were before. The reason is that for every dollar of additional income they get, they raise their expenditures two dollars. No amount of additional income which they can ever hope to get can solve their problem. They must solve it themselves on the expenses end. Let us consider some suggestions for so doing.

Don't Throw Money out the Window. Here are some of the more common wasteful expenditures:

1 *Participating in confidence games and frauds.* You may never have bought fake oil stocks, but what about the panhandler on the corner whose take averages $30 a day? What about the numerous fake charities which abound? Did you pay a registration fee to that so-called employment agency? Or fall for the "free lot won with a lucky ticket" gag? Poor families which can ill afford the loss are annually mulcted of sums which run into millions. Approximately $200 per family is lost annually in such deals. Two hundred dollars would really help your budget.

2 *Gambling.* There is little bona fide gambling in the United States. Most of what is called gambling is really the donation of suckers to swindlers. Slot machines pay off from five to thirty cents on the dollar. Pools and bookie bets often give odds no better.

3 *Buying worthless products, especially drugs.* Do you pay good money for stuff in bottles guaranteed to take your unpleasant breath away, massacre bacteria, prevent colds, and warm up cold love affairs? Know, then, that most of these mouth washes, antiseptics, and patent medicines in general are of little value. If you want to lose weight, clear your skin, or treat an illness, you'll save money — and your health — by seeing your doctor first. One way of helping your budget is to look in your medicine cabinet.

4 *Buying things you don't want.* We all see things in stores which attract us. But when we get them home we wonder why we ever bought them. Anyone who goes through the stuff which he has bought but never used or cared about will get the idea. These white elephants, herds of them, cost money, lots of it. Cut them out and you can increase your income, considerably.

Get More and Better Goods for Less Money. You can, you know. Many products can be purchased for less money than the general public pays. Consider, for example, the following instance. Two little wives went to market. Mrs. Squander and Mrs. Canny went to the same shopping district on the same day. Each bought the articles and paid the prices indicated in the accompanying table.

No, you are wrong. Mrs. Squander did not get better goods. The last five items which each bought were identical in quality. In the sheets Mrs. Canny got the best buy, with a tensile strength of 71 and 72 pounds for warp and fill respectively. Those bought by Mrs. Squander had a tensile strength of 62 and 67. And tensile strength is probably the best indicator of wearing quality.

	MRS. SQUANDER PAID	MRS. CANNY PAID
6 percale sheet and pillow case sets	$24.54	$18.00
3 men's broadcloth shirts, 2 & 2 ply	14.00	8.00
3 nylon jersey slips, top quality	15.90	11.90
1 pair ladies casual shoes	11.40	8.10
1 bottle, 100 5 gr. aspirin tablets, USP	.50	.19
1 large bottle, make-up base	1.80	1.20
	$68.14	$47.39

With the remainder of her money, Mrs. Canny was able to get in addition:

1 chenille bedspread, good quality	$7.95
1 slip cover for chair	9.00
1 roll aluminum foil (large — heavy duty)	1.69
1 sponge mop	1.37
2 magazines at 35¢ each	.70
Grand Total	$68.10

Contrary to popular opinion, the best is *not* always the most expensive. Thousands of tests have shown that some products will last much longer than others which cost more. The less expensive articles are often the nicest, as well as the most durable. Price tells little about quality. Getting more and better goods for less money is one of the simplest ways of giving yourself a raise in pay. But, you say, how can I buy for less? How can I be Mrs. Canny in my shopping?

1 *Judge products on the basis of scientific tests, rather than sales or advertising claims.* The government does not buy jeeps on the basis of the pictures of pretty girls in advertisements. Neither do railroads buy rails because Betta Harake says they are the smoothest she ever rode on, or because a luscious radio voice describes them as "bright, shining,

smooth steel ribbons." Nor does the printer of popular magazines buy his paper on such a basis. They all depend upon specifications and tests. So should you. Since the consumer can hardly maintain his own testing laboratory, he must depend upon some such service as Consumers Union or Consumer's Research. Like clocks, their counsel is not always accurate, but taking their advice is far better than guessing. On the basis of such reports it becomes possible to buy with confidence nonadvertised brands which often sell at considerably lower prices than nationally advertised products. For example, a half-pound of a certain kind of baking chocolate selling for fifteen cents is the same quality as a nationally advertised brand selling for twenty-three cents. Not only soap flakes and similar products, but electric refrigerators, washing machines, radios, trailers, and tires could often be bought from chain stores or mail order houses for as much as 25 per cent less than nationally advertised brands of comparable quality and size. And the companies stand behind them, too.

2 *Purchase where you can secure good quality at a low price.* It may cost as much as seventy-five cents to assemble and deliver an order of groceries. Credit is expensive in both bookkeeping and losses. Such costs must necessarily be reflected in the prices charged for goods. The "name" of the store and personal service may also cause a further increase in prices, and consequently the mark-up of one store may be twice that of another. It is significant that the O.P.A. specifically permitted certain classes of grocery stores to charge higher ceiling prices than others. So if you want to give yourself a raise in pay, trade where the mark-up is low. The difference may be considerable.

3 *Take advantage of sales, especially seasonal sales.* Some supposed sales are frauds, but reputable houses do have bona fide sales at which goods, especially furniture and clothing, are offered at considerable discount. Saturday specials at chain stores often offer attractive opportunities for saving.

4 *Save money by paying cash.* With many products, especially radios and electrical equipment, some shops and stores will give a sizable discount to any cash customer who demands it. Regarding some merchandise it has been said that "only saps pay retail prices." It is usually cheaper to buy anything for cash. Bookkeeping and bad accounts are costly. The store which charges the same price for either cash or

credit really charges a higher price. If you do not have the cash, either borrow it or wait until you do have it.

5 *Consider buying secondhand items.* With some products, such as furniture, radios, or refrigerators, secondhand or discontinued models can sometimes be secured for half price. Perhaps you are prejudiced against secondhand goods. Remember, however, that new goods become secondhand after they have been in your house for only a few days. With products which have motors or mechanical equipment which will wear out, there is more risk. In any case, with a large purchase it may pay you to have some expert appraise the product for you, even if you must pay him a sizable fee. This precaution is especially important if you buy a house, new or old.

6 *Let the family become experts too.* Have each member of the family specialize in certain types of buying by reading up on the product and doing all the purchasing in that area. When contemplating a large investment, such as furniture, a refrigerator, or a car, special study should be given before buying.

7 *Keep what you have in good repair.* A stitch in time saves not only nine; it may save the whole garment. A little glue, a screw properly placed, may save the whole table or chair. Shiftlessness is by no means the only cause of poverty, but it is often a contributing factor. If you do not know how to make minor repairs, it will pay you to learn. Here again, specialization by each member of the family may prove economical.

Be Discriminating Regarding Luxuries. Many families of modest income could raise their standard of living considerably simply by eliminating one or more of the luxuries which consume so large a proportion of their earnings. Let us consider some of the more dispensable luxuries of the average couple.

1 *Entertaining and dining out.* Couples naturally want to do some entertaining. If this involves expensive food or liquor, the cost will run up. One couple dared to substitute simple sandwiches and carefully planned games for drinks, and got away with it. The saving may easily mean the difference between going into debt or keeping ahead of the game and being able to get something you have always wanted. Meals eaten out may cost a couple several dollars a week more than meals eaten in. It's all right if you want to spend your money that way. On

the other hand, don't complain about not being able to afford that new pair of shoes or that tennis racket which a very few weeks of economy at this point would make possible.

2 *Expensive apartments.* In most cities it is possible to secure commodious, comfortable apartments at a price considerably less than that charged for those with a swanky address. One couple who moved from their expensive place found that with the difference in rent they were able in the course of a single year to buy a good watch, an electric sewing machine, an extra radio, a fur scarf, two really good pieces of furniture, and a serviceable secondhand typewriter. What a simple way to raise your standard of living!

3 *The car.* A car is a desirable thing to own; it is a convenience, and sometimes a necessity. But for most people it is a luxury, since they could get along quite well with public transportation. If you are a mechanic, you may be able to operate a car at relatively small expense. Otherwise it can easily add several hundred dollars a year to your expenses. To determine its actual costs include gas and oil, licenses, insurance, depreciation, and interest on the investment of car and the garage. If you do not have a car, you will have a surprising sum available for other things.

4 *Proving you are better than the Joneses.* This is the most expensive luxury of all. Most people either feel inferior to others or wish to feel superior. It is too much work actually to become superior, or people may not have what it takes. So they try to compensate by paying more for what they buy. There are a few connoisseurs who really appreciate choice things and are willing to pay for them, but most people who pay high prices do so in order to make themselves feel important. A lady was considering two sets of dishes, one of which cost $100, and the other $150. She ordered the more expensive set without hesitation. She wanted the best, she said. After the dishes were delivered the store owner called up in distress. The clerk had made a mistake and mixed the price tags. Her dishes were the $100 set. Instead of getting her $50 back, she at once ordered the set which she had previously rejected. She was buying, not primarily dishes, but a feeling of personal importance.

This is a game at which you cannot win, for as soon as you find yourself able to outbuy everyone in your set, you move up the economic scale where the competition is keener, and you are right back where you were. If you doubled your income you would live and associate with people on a still more expensive level, and still could not keep up. Some people who get $3000 a month complain that they cannot live on their incomes. For most people there is and can be only one solution to their economic problems: learn to enjoy life in simple and inexpensive ways and stop trying to impress yourself and others by the prices which you pay. Many would find that if they learned to depend for their enjoyment upon themselves as family members who can have fun together rather than upon the things that money can buy, most of their economic problems would automatically be solved.

Production in the Home

Many people today do not include production within the home as part of their real income, nor do they consider how such income can be employed most effectively. Much production centers around the preparation and serving of food, and it is questionable whether this pays as such. We pointed out earlier that it might cost several times as much to eat out as to eat in, but this is true only if the family is already paying most of the preparation costs anyway. For example, if a five-room apartment renting for $100 a month includes a dining room and kitchen, the rental costs of preparing and serving food alone will amount to about $40. In addition, there is all the investment in equipment, including the refrigerator, stove, dining room and kitchen furniture, and dishes, plus the cost of gas and electricity used for food preparation and preservation. It is fair to say that the cost of serving food in the home must be estimated at about $2.00 a day, not including the cost of the food itself. Most of these costs go on whether food is served or not.

This is not, however, a complete picture, for the couple or family which lives in a room or two with no kitchen or dining facilities does not enjoy the same conveniences. The dining room, for example, is not merely a place for eating but also a work room, and makes the home more spacious. Furthermore, providing food in one's home brings satisfactions which eating out all the time cannot give. Thus, much of the overhead of the apartment which includes dining room, kitchen, and necessary equipment can be counted as necessary costs of satisfactory family living, just as you now regard the costs of the living room and its furnishings. Furthermore, the effort involved in the serving of meals is not necessarily unrewarding labor. Some people enjoy preparing food and decorating a table, just as they do dancing or playing tennis.

The preparation of food is not the only productive activity commonly carried on within the family. The making of clothing may in some families be considerable, and the repairing of furniture, clothing, or other equipment may have high economic value. Cleaning is another service of real value, as you will quickly discover if you pay to have it done. Since most women have more time in the home than men do, much of the responsibility for its productive activities falls upon them. If both husband and wife work outside the home, however, there is no reason why women should be expected to do more than their share. Women do not naturally cook and sew any better than men. Some of our best chefs and tailors are men. Conversely, the war has shown that women can become excellent mechanics. Any difference is due to the particular individual, not to the sex, and even individual differences are often due to past learnings and experiences. In this connection it should be noted that children can and should assume many productive tasks around the home, not only to make the household tasks less burdensome for others, but to develop the children as well and ready them to assume the responsibilities of a family when they marry.

Should Wives Continue to Work after Marriage?

Here is something to argue about. Before we line up in battle formation, let us objectively examine a few relevant facts. How did the issue come about in the first place? Years ago the productive tasks of the home were much greater than they are today. With childbearing and the lack of modern aids and conveniences, the work of most wives was probably greater than that of their husbands. Of them it was said, "Man works from sun to sun, but woman's work is never done." Gradually, however, the family bought more and more of the things which women used to make in the home: soap, clothes, and later bread and canned goods. Women bore fewer children and had more and more conveniences, such as vacuum cleaners and electrical kitchen equipment, to aid them. Since these purchases were made with the money earned by men, the burden on the husband became increasingly greater. He had to do what he did not have to do before: earn enough for two, as well as enough for the children. The woman's burden became increasingly lighter, and for some almost reached the vanishing point. In the earlier days, marriage was essentially an economic partnership. Neither husband nor wife supported the other, and even the children were supported only during the first few years. As time went on, however, and wives and children bought more and produced less, the increased burden on the husband became accepted as the normal and proper situation. In the middle and upper income groups, wives often became merely expensive luxuries. The extent of the support of a wife came for many men to be a test of their abilities. Far from resenting this situation, men often assumed the cost proudly as evidence of their earning power. Many came to resent violently the idea of their wives' working outside the home as a reflection upon their ability to provide support. This attitude is now changing, despite the anguished cries of those who cherish it. The idea that a man should support his wife, which is hardly more than a generation old, seems rapidly passing out. With this preliminary discussion, then, let us look at the situation as it seems to shape up today.

1 Some women are temperamentally so built that if they do not have a job of their own they either "blow up" or constantly meddle in the affairs of their husbands, and possibly those of other husbands as well. With them a real job outside the family meets a vital psychological need.

2 A few women have special talents and skills which ought not to be wasted. In this class belong some of our more talented teachers, authors, artists, and executives. Such women may take time out for children, but will and should remain employed for most of their productive years.

3 Wives of certain professional men, such as ministers, governmental officials, or big business executives, may find their full-time employment as helpers and hostesses for their husbands.

4 Wives of farmers usually have a full-time job where they are.

5 Many women are really employed extensively outside their homes, but are not so regarded because they are not paid. They are prominent in church work, P.T.A.'s, and various civic and community organizations and enterprises. A woman is not unemployed because she is not paid for her work.

6 Most wives have neither the strength nor the ability to carry on a very big job outside the home while their children still need careful supervision. Most wives in cities could carry on a real job, at least part time, before their children come and after they are grown.

7 Some women are so lacking in talents and interests that housekeeping, even without children, taxes their capacities to the utmost.

The wives of today who are employed, then, are doing essentially the same things their great-grandmothers did, except that now they are doing their jobs outside the home. During the first year or so of marriage the earning power of the husband is relatively low, while the expenses are relatively high. Usually all the furniture has to be bought, and the couple need to save up enough money for the first baby. During this period an increasing proportion of wives will insist upon carrying their share of the economic load. If the earnings of both husband and wife are used up for current living expenses, however, they face a real problem. A baby will mean that their expenses are considerably increased at the same time that their income may be cut almost in half. Many couples guard against this difficulty by living on the husband's income only and saving all that the wife earns. Putting some of the latter into home furnishings is one form of saving; the rest is banked. Then when the baby comes, their income for ordinary use remains the same, and they have a nest egg to take care of the extra expenses.

Some Hints on Insurance

Insurance is like marriage — no family should be without it. Yet to most people it is somewhat of a mystery. They may believe in insurance. But they have little understanding of *what* it is, *when* they should take it out, *how much* and *what kind* they should have, and *with whom* they should take it. Let us first consider the purpose of life insurance.

The primary purpose of life insurance is the protection of those who are financially dependent in some way upon the insured. We usually think of dependents as wife and children. The "dependent" may also be a creditor who has insured the life of a debtor so that in case of sudden death he can get his money back. A company may find its manager so valuable that they insure his life for a huge sum to protect themselves against a sudden deprivation of his direction. In any case, you do not take out life insurance because *you* need it, but because your dependents (of whatever type) need it.

When Should Life Insurance Be Taken Out? When you have dependents who need it, and not before. You would not take out automobile liability insurance before you have a car, or fire insurance on your "Dream Home" not yet built. Then do not take out life insurance before you have dependents, except in the case of G.I. insurance. This is so much cheaper than ordinary insurance that you should take it out while you can still get it, and hang on to it. Otherwise, wait until you have dependents. Don't be so silly as to think that if you take it out at a younger age, it will be cheaper. The rate will be lower, but you will be paying for more years, so the total cost will be greater. No insurance company can insure you for extra years, even the younger years, without additional cost.

The more dependents you have, the more insurance protection they need. Here we face a problem. As a man's family increases, so does their need for insurance. But as the children grow up and become independent, this need will decline. How can a family get high protection while the children are young, without saddling itself with a huge burden which will later be unnecessary? The answer is simple. Get the kind of insurance which gives you the greatest protection at the least cost, and automatically terminates when you no longer need it. This is term insurance. With some companies you can get this renewed each year without further examination, at an increasing rate. Or you can get it for a specific period, five, ten, or twenty years for the same rate each year the policy is in force.

The best family plan would be for the husband and wife to each take out a policy to protect each other, the husband taking out the larger amount. They should expect these policies to continue until death. In order to keep the payments equal, ordinary life seems the best. The children, however, do not need protection until the death of the father would normally occur. They need protection until they are old enough to take care of themselves. Therefore with each pregnancy the father would take out another twenty year term policy on himself. For the same money he can give his children twice the protection he could with ordinary life. Furthermore, when this protection is no longer needed, his costs will decline.

Should we insure the children themselves? If they have dependents, yes. If not, no. If you want to build up a fund to put them through college, buy government bonds. They will have a better chance to go to college if you insure yourself, not them.

How Much Insurance Should Be Carried? Statistics show that many families take out far more insurance than they can or will keep up.[3] Insurance that lapses or has to be surrendered is of no further value. People do not expect to let their insurance policies lapse when they take them out. But when economic conditions are not good, and a wage earner is out of work, insurance may be one of the first items that a family is forced to give up in order to ease its budget or obtain ready cash. During the Great Depression of the 1930's, people in the United States surrendered more insurance than they bought, not counting normal maturing of their policies. Even in relatively good years, Americans have given up a third as much as they bought of ordinary life insurance, and more than half as much as they purchased of the industrial policies. One study made in New York State covering ten years showed that over half of all ordinary life policies taken out were given up, and three fourths of all industrial insurance policies. So don't let an agent talk you into overloading. Better take a smaller amount and hang on to it. How much you should take will depend largely upon such considerations as:

1 The size of the family and the ages of the children.
2 The standard of living which the protected family expects.
3 What the wife could earn. A woman who is a permanent invalid needs more protection than one who is strong and healthy. The wife who has some training or skill, like nursing, stenography or a license to teach, needs less protection than one who would face widowhood without abilities or skills.
4 Other economic resources. In time, savings or the gradual accumulation of property may lessen the need for insurance protection. Include also any forms of social security, governmental or private, by which the family is protected.

What about Insurance as an Investment? This book is not written for wealthy people who may need huge policies in order to get cash with which to pay heavy inheritance taxes. For the ordinary family, the investments in insurance are for two purposes: to "level off" payments and to invest savings. The first kind is seen in the whole life policy. As people become older, their insurance costs rise. If the payments are

---

[3] See the *Life Insurance Fact Book,* published annually by the Institute of Life Insurance, 488 Madison Avenue, New York City 22, N.Y.

to remain the same throughout life, the company must "overcharge" people while they are young, so that they can "undercharge" them when they become old. The excess paid in the early years is saved by the insurance company and appears as the loan or cash surrender value of the policy. The interest on this saving is used to help pay the total costs of the policy. On the average the savings will be enough to pay off the entire policy by the time of death. This investment is actually a type of convenience to the policy holder, making it possible for him to meet the payments of later years without payments being prohibitively high.

Savings may be invested through the endowment policy. This is really a form of term insurance at about four times the cost. The excess is saved and invested by the company. If the person outlives the term of the policy its face value (say $1000) is returned in a lump sum. But if he dies before the policy expires his beneficiaries get only the same amount they would have received from a term policy. The company keeps the excess. If he had bought a term policy and saved the difference in cost, in case of prior death the beneficiaries would have received the thousand plus all the additional savings. These could amount to over $900. Endowment insurance is a "tails I lose" "heads I break even" proposition; not an intelligent proposition, even if you will probably live. It has one defense. Some people seem unable to save anything, even when their earnings are high. If they have to make payments on an endowment policy they may end up with savings which otherwise they would have squandered.

Apart from such compulsory saving, there are at least two possibilities for investment for the ordinary individual which are better than insurance. Government bonds are both more secure and more fluid. And if you want to guard against inflation, there are sound investment companies which will invest your money with as much care and skill as an insurance company.

Finally, remember that insurance agents are human beings. Most of them are not dishonest; neither are they saints. Their incomes depend upon the amount of insurance they sell. Don't expect them to recommend policies of other companies, even if they are cheaper and better for your needs. Expect of them what you would of any salesmen: that they will do their best to sell their products. When they sell protection they are often rendering a valuable service. When they try to sell their banking and investment services, their efforts are more questionable.

What Type of Policy Is Best? For those who can get it, G.I. insurance is the best insurance available. But most people will have to buy through regular companies. Some of these are ingenious at developing all kinds of "special" policies. But if you understand a few basic principles, you can easily reduce them to a few major types. For example, one policy provides for low payments during the first five years (when your earnings are presumably low) and substantial increase after that. This is likely to be a term policy which automatically becomes converted to whole life after five years.

Industrial insurance is not really a different kind of insurance, but rather a way of paying for insurance. Instead of making monthly or annual payments, you pay a collector who stops in each week to collect. Because of the costs of such collection, this is the most expensive type of insurance and should be avoided. Likewise, the limited payment policy is not a different kind of insurance, but merely a way of paying for whole-life insurance more rapidly, so that at the end of a specified period the interest on your reserve takes care of all future insurance costs, and you need pay no more in yourself. Group insurance is cheap, and valuable for those who, because of physical disabilities, cannot get any other kind. A group, such as the employees of a certain company, are insured as a whole. When you leave the employ of the company, your protection automatically ceases. In other words, it is term insurance, the term being the length of time you remain with the same firm.

We have suggested that insurance be used for protection only, and not for investment. There is one exception, the annuity policy. This is a type of social security operated by the insurance company instead of the government. If your retirement pension is not already adequately provided for, and you wish to be assured of an income for your old age, the annuity policies of insurance companies should be given serious consideration. The plan is for you to pay a certain amount each year into the fund. When you reach the retirement age as stated on the policy, the company either pays you a flat sum or a stipulated income for the rest of your life. If you die before the policy becomes due, the amount already accumulated is paid to your estate.

With Whom Should You Take Your Insurance? Some unscrupulous or uninformed people may try to tell you that in insurance you get just what you pay for, and that therefore it makes no difference with which company you take out your policy. This is simply not true. A comparison of ten large companies showed that the annual net cost per $1000 of ordinary life taken out at the age of eighteen varied from $4.90 to $7.50. Over a period of years such differences may amount to many hundreds of dollars, depending upon the amount of insurance taken out and the type of policy. In some states, including New York, savings banks sell certain types of policies at a cost much below the usual rate. Teachers and similar groups can often secure insurance from companies specially organized to serve them. All such possibilities should be carefully considered. Those who plan to take out any large amount of insurance might save considerably by going to an insurance advisory service (which has no insurance to sell) and paying a fee for competent guidance and advice.

Life insurance for most people is one of the most important and least understood expenditures a family makes. A well-rounded program of protection will, however, include such other types as health and accident insurance, whether or not there are dependents. Every family should have hospitalization insurance to cover every member, including the children. If a policy which also includes medical care is available, so much the better. Anyone who owns property which might burn, such as a house or furnishings in a home, should have adequate fire insurance protection. A car owner should have liability insurance, and probably fire and theft insurance. Since for these forms of insurance also the costs of reliable companies vary extensively, careful investigations should be made. The policies of mail-order houses and cooperatives often offer especially attractive buys.

Fitting Money Matters into the Total Picture

To the unmarried, sex may seem to be the really important factor in marriage. To those who have been married for some time and face a monthly array of bills, money may appear to be the really crucial issue. Actually the real significance of any individual factor like money is its relationship to the total picture. Money matters are related to all aspects of family life — they affect family life and it affects them.

"I told Charlie we'd have a perfect marriage
if we never mention money."

Obviously, any home worry affects the way a man does his job. If he leaves his home angry and resentful, his attitude will almost inevitably be reflected in his relations with his coworkers, the customers, or the boss. The man whose home is breaking up, or who fears that it may break up, cannot keep his mind on his work to the best advantage, all of which will ultimately affect his chances of promotion or even of keeping the job he has. On the other hand, a sense of happiness and security at home may considerably augment his earning power. It may well give him a goal for effort. He wants to show the little woman that when she married him she made no mistake. A new baby may call forth not only cigars but additional exertion. If at home he has found happiness and support, if his home experiences build him up psychologically, he actually is a better man and can earn more.

The effect of income on marital success is more involved than the effect of happiness on income. Certainly extreme destitution is poor soil in which to grow the fragrant flowers of marital happiness. The home of the simple Scotch peasant which Burns depicts in his "Cotter's Saturday Night" is stable, but one would hardly describe it as happy. The moral of the story, however, is sound: the most important consideration is not the amount of income, but the family attitude toward the total situation. This attitude is affected profoundly by two considerations: the security of the income, and the social standards by which it is measured. The cotter did not have much, but he was relatively secure in what he had. No world-wide economic forces threatened to move his economic earth, or cast the mountains of his livelihood into the midst of the sea of depression. Come what might, pestilence or famine, he would always have a job, an opportunity of directing his efforts in productive channels. He would never have to tramp the streets, day after day, looking for work which was not to be found, nor would he have to mope around the house or the tavern in hopeless despair. Furthermore, his standard of living, while low, was not lower than that of his neighbors, save that of the Laird, to which he did not even aspire.

Studies show that stability of income is far more important than amount of income. People need enough money to provide for basic physical necessities, but they can get along on very little provided they can be reasonably sure of that little. When they are never sure what they can depend upon from one year to the next, their morale is undermined, and their economic insecurity is reflected in greater marital unhappiness and conflict.

Another factor is personal and social expectation. A family with a $6000 income which insists on associating with a $12,000 income crowd will always feel poor and pinched. The wife may feel that she should have married better and the husband that he has failed. This situation may easily give rise to serious marital conflict. If, on the other hand, they are members of a $3000 crowd, the situation may be the reverse.

Money matters, then, can and do affect marriage profoundly. Their effects, however, depend primarily upon the intelligence with which they are understood and handled. No matter how large the income, money problems can become pegs upon which other difficulties and conflicts are hung and carefully preserved. On the other hand, a wise and ethical adjustment in other matters will reflect itself in greater money income and security, and sound financial relationships can make even small incomes strong enough to bear the load.

Readings

DUVALL, SYLVANUS MILNE, *Before You Marry* (New York: Association Press, 1959). Chapter 5, "Financing Your Marriage," deals with such questions as: How much does it cost to marry? Should a wife work outside the home? What do you know about savings and investment? Have you considered a long range housing program?

LANDIS, JUDSON and MARY, *Youth and Marriage: A Student Manual* (Englewood Cliffs, New Jersey: Prentice-Hall, Inc., 1957). Units 16, 17 and 18 have to do with "Finances and Adjustment in Marriage," "Getting Your Money's Worth," and "Buying Life Insurance."

LANDIS, PAUL H., *Your Marriage and Family Living* (New York: McGraw-Hill Book Company, 1954 edition). Chapter 14, "Getting together on Money Matters," includes a sample budget and other aspects of financial planning for marriage.

MONEY MANAGEMENT INSTITUTE, *Money Management Library* (Chicago: Household Finance Corporation). A series of twelve pamphlets on various aspects of money management for the individual and the family.

MOORE, BERNICE MILBURN, and DOROTHY M. LEAHY, *You and Your Family* (Boston, D. C. Heath and Company, 1953 edition). Chapter 15, "It Takes an Income to Run a Family," has an excellent section on the meaning of financial security and how a couple can achieve it.

MORGAN, WILLIAM and MILDRED, *Thinking Together about Marriage and Family* (New York: Association Press, 1955). This entire guide to study about marriage will be of interest, but see especially Topic 13, "Making Money Matters into Family Assets."

COMMON CONFLICTS

Is it true that the way to hold marriage together is to bear and forbear?

Shouldn't the course of true love run smooth?

Can fighting be fun?

How can unpleasant fighting be stopped?

What kind of help is there for the discordant?

*H*AD ROMEO AND JULIET LIVED TOGETHER LONG ENOUGH, THEY probably would have had their disagreements like everyone else. Whenever two individuals undertake a close and continuous association, inevitable occasions arise when there is a clash of wills. The closer the association and the freer the personalities, the more vigorous this clash may be. Since marriage is the most intimate and the most demanding of all adult human relationships, this element of conflict is an inescapable part of its nature.

Conflict is Normal

Two tasks that are productive of conflict face the newly-wed. The first is concerned with establishing a common set of workable routines, a mutually acceptable way of living, and a new set of family policies out of the two systems carried over from the parental families of the betrothed. The second task involves two egos struggling for individual survival as the marriage moves to bring about incorporation of both in a common joint personality. Conflict serves a useful function in setting the optimum distance and nearness personalities can take in a new marriage. Much of the "fussing" at one another which occurs in the first years reflects these two processes of accommodation of ways of living and a healthy resistance to self-destruction.

Every marital union is, to a certain degree, a mixed marriage. The two parties bring from their parental families different wants and variant ideas of what's funny and what's important. Every time a decision is reached in a young marriage, some of these differences are likely to come to light. Only by grinding the gears a bit at the start is it possible to learn how to mesh them correctly. Consensus of opinion can only follow exchange of differing views.

Susan and Jim are a couple whose conflicts should have occurred early in marriage rather than late for the good health of the relationship. They were seventeen and nineteen respectively when they married, just out of high school. Susan was especially eager to make the marriage a success.

Jim and his four brothers had been reared by his widowed father without experience in the needs and wants of women in a family. He was never exposed to the orderliness, neatness, and regularity of housekeeping procedures so prized by the good housewife. He professed ignorance of the costs of permanents, sheer stockings, and household articles. To complicate matters even more, Jim had been reared to feel that the man should be the head of the house and control the purse strings.

Susan appears to have overlooked these differences between them during the engagement, and early marriage found her ill prepared to cope with the situation. Instead of forthrightly battling out the issues when Jim came late for meals or sometimes didn't eat at all, as had been the pattern in his parental home, Susan adapted herself to her husband's unorthodox behavior. After the children arrived, it became increasingly difficult to manage financially with what Jim gave her.

Susan made no moves to battle for joint handling of the family finances. She held back the angry words with the intention of preserving harmony. Tensions built up in the financial area and, as so often happens, spilled over into the recreational area, and finally affected their sexual relations which heretofore had been mutually enjoyable.

Jim now admits to Susan's pastor, to whom she has appealed for help, that his marriage has gone sour. Yet he is baffled by it all: they have had only one or two serious squabbles after six years of marriage.

Six years is too long to go without a quarrel. There were basic differences here that begged attention before settling down to the routines of living. A good fight might have cleared the air, defined the issues, and ventilated the house of some of the unresolved tensions before they cracked the relationship. Conflict has a dual function: the solution of issues and the release of the resentment and tensions which arise in every relationship.

Withholding Circumscribes the Relationship

Consistently repressed tensions are hard on the relationship. They tend to circumscribe and narrow the topics of conversation in a marriage, and to delimit the areas of activity together. In the case of Jim and Susan, family entertainment, family finances, and sex relationships were rarely discussed because of the strain both felt when these matters came up. Tensions disturb the normal functioning of the family because they accumulate and spread and become associated with other areas of living.

The second area of married life in which conflict serves a useful purpose is in setting the boundaries of ego protection and ego involvement. There is a marked tendency in the ecstasy of the honeymoon and early months of marriage to establish a closeness of association which becomes burdensome, especially when erotic discoveries have ceased to suffuse the relationship with pleasure. Quarrels destroy these burdensome patterns and bring into being more tolerable customs. Where the early intimacy of marriage is not relaxed, it produces strain upon both and it rewards neither correspondingly — it is a sort of tax which makes everyone poor and enriches no one proportionately — and the conflicts which redefine this situation are therefore highly useful.

Married couples seek by experience to find the optimum nearness that they can tolerate. Like porcupines who approach one another for warmth yet are repelled by the other's barbs, the married couple must achieve that distance which is optimum for warmth without being too ego involving. Clearly this can be achieved only through conflict of a sort. Ultimately the couple must feel for themselves the reality of each other's emotional resistances and take the measure of each other's capacity for mutual accommodation.

Sometimes restrained discussion is advocated as a better alternative to quarreling. But the danger is that cold discussion arrives only at

"That's all I have to say on the subject, my dear.
The argument is closed."

an *intellectual* solution which fails to do justice to the *emotional* elements in the conflict. If research and clinical evidence are valid, it is best that these emotional elements be expressed. Marriage partners can come to terms on a basis of reality only when they have *felt* the heat of each other's hostile feelings. A marriage should be organized to include the expression of both positive and negative emotions if it is to be a communicating and satisfying relationship.

Changing Feelings about Marital Conflict

"Marriage isn't what it used to be," you may have heard as people discussed the liberation of the wife and child from the traditions of the patriarchal family and the transformation of the father from a dominating figure to a companionable partner in family life. Many of these re-markable changes have occurred in the past generation, but most people are not sufficiently out of the woods of transition with respect to freedom of discussion to accept discord and disharmony in marriage as evidence of growth. As participants in the transition we are uncertain about the desirability of quarreling, and many of us will feel conscience-stricken after "indulging," as we call it, in a marital spat. Let's draw the lines clearly between the two schools of thought and see the direction in which we seem to be heading.

First, let us look at the school of marriage whose traditions linger with us yet, the patriarchal system of thought which flowered in Puritan New England. Out of this period came our hundreds of maxims glorifying marital bliss, family harmony at all costs, and so on. It was an adult-centered world, in which children were to be seen and not heard, where the wife and mother was passive, patient, benign, and long-suffering. Peace and quiet in the home were evidence of the power and absolute authority of the father. Quarreling of any variety was evidence, on the other hand, of the breakdown of patriarchal authority and was to be quelled without delay. Writers and public speakers of the period supported the father in his position by repeating platitudes for the edification of children and their mothers. We use some of them today: "Forgive and forget," "Bear and forbear," "Let bygones be bygones," "Speak when spoken to," "God bless our happy home," "Home, sweet home," "Turn the other cheek," "A soft answer turneth away wrath."

The harmony of the patriarchal household was purchased at a high price in frustration and dulled sensibilities. Actually there existed much of what might be called covert conflict, deep resentment at the high-handedness of the authority which enforced harmony at such cost. It is probably safe to say that there has been less increase in marital conflict since Puritan days than one would suppose. The conflict has merely changed from covert, undercover resentment and discord to open conflict. Families in those days couldn't afford to waste their energies, they thought, fighting among themselves, and they attempted to bury the differences which cropped up within the family rather than air and settle them once and for all. It was important to preserve front both within the family and without. Indeed it was a matter of family pride and a mark of class to preserve harmony in the home.

We are burdened today with the vestiges of the self-righteous, sweetness-and-light mode of thinking. The hundreds of couples who come to marital guidance clinics regularly to gain relief from guilty feelings of unworthiness because they quarrel at home are living proof of this assertion. Moreover, the emergence of a democratic, person-centered family with its accent on the sacredness of personality has not cleared away the debris of broken patriarchal traditions. It will take a little time. Meantime, children in democratic homes will be given assurance that quarreling is not something to fear or condemn, but something to understand. Some of the guilt and unworthiness may be made to disappear with our generation!

The Mental Hygiene of Conflict

Mental hygiene, which was ushered in with the democratic, personality-oriented family, accepts a certain amount of overt conflict as normal. Much of the conflict merely indicates the presence of differences which occur as a couple explore new areas or attempt new tasks. Gradually the friction wears the protruding parts smooth, and a consensus is reached. Thereafter conflict is less likely to occur in that specific area, but it may and should bob up again and again as long as the family continues to meet new and different problems.

The modern couple will expect that in marriage they have a place of security and intimacy where they are free to behave like human beings with the normal variety of emotions. The workaday world, organized as it is, does not permit the frank expression of resentment, vanity, jealousy, and selfish ambition along with tenderness and love, all of which exist in the normal person. The individual must control his annoyances and his affections, he must often act like something more than human to get along in our complex industrial society. If he flies off the handle at his boss he may lose his job. There needs to be some place, however, where the individual can give vent to his annoyances and be himself, and that place seems to be in marriage. If there is that kind of cantankerousness in a marriage, the couple should chalk it down as proof that their marriage is performing one of its main functions — providing a place to let off steam and re-establish emotional balance. If a marriage is so fragile that it must be maintained by the same kind of artificial manners that keeps an office force functioning, it is pretty precariously based. One insightful authority has stated in positive terms,

"One of the functions of marriage is to weave a rope of relationship strong enough to hold each person at his worst."

As a couple enter marriage they face a number of adjustments, some of which are painful in the sense that it is painful to learn to ride a horse, to play a piano, or to develop any other complex skill. But new adjustments of marriage are more than learning new tasks: they also involve unlearning and revising old habits.

Many of the quarrels in marriage are helpful devices to dispel tensions engendered by unlearning of old habits and learning of new ones. Some arise out of the frustrations which the discipline of marriage exacts, and others arise quite naturally out of the unprepared-for intimacies of marriage. Much of conflict merely reflects the growing edges of a new relationship. It denotes growth and change rather than a passive acceptance of the new tasks on the part of either party. In the early stages much of the conflict consists of defining the issues and finding where the other stands on the many new problems they are facing.

Productive and Destructive Quarreling

Having taken the position that much of the conflict in marriage is normal and desirable, we must still distinguish between productive and destructive conflict. Destructive quarrels, to take one form of destructive conflict, are those which leave fewer assets in the relationship than it had before. Destructive quarreling is directed at the person and succeeds in destroying the illusions and fictions by which the person lives. It is a type of conflict which concentrates on the other's ego. It is of the belittling and punishing variety. Destructive quarrels lead to alienation as the love object is transformed into a hate object, and separation is thereby made possible. Destructive quarrels have at least one value. They succeed in sufficiently alienating incompatible couples so that engagements are broken, or if marriage has occurred, so that early divorce follows.

Productive quarrels may be differentiated by the fact that the marriage is made stronger through a redefinition of the situation causing the conflict. Productive quarreling is limited and directed at an issue, and it leads to a new and more complete understanding. Issues, problems, and conditions rather than the person himself tend to be the object of productive quarrels. Ideally, the quarrels tend to become fewer and less violent as the marriage progresses and basic routines and solutions to problems are established. The quarrel tends to become a discussion progressively delimited in the areas it covers.[1] Gradually the couple learn the techniques for handling conflict, so that for problem solving purposes at least it is not so violent nor so painful.

Another type of productive quarrel of the early years of marriage is that which relaxes the strain which builds up out of the unprepared-for intimacies of marriage. It gives the couple an opportunity and an excuse to desist from the intense honeymoon attachments and get a breath of air. Quarrels in the honeymoon and first year, moreover, serve to bring the parties face to face with the realities of their marriage. Some conflict helps to remove the blinders from their eyes and enables them to appreciate one another as persons rather than as imaginary incarnations of perfection. The reaction, "But you seemed so different, so much taller and romantic, when we were engaged . . . ," may bring pain of disillusionment but is a healthy experience. If romantic illusions have been built up it is a productive quarrel which brings the newlyweds down to earth. A husband can't live long in a rosy haze with an imaginary wife and remain mentally healthy.

One of the benefits of productive quarrels is that they reveal to the married couple how strong their relationship really is. Some men and women, deluded by the romantic notion that love must have left when monotony comes in, are surprised at the force of the love emotions which arise as a result of a quarrel. Quarreling thus helps to stabilize the marriage by reminding the couple, as they kiss and make up, of the depth of their love.

Dynamics of Conflict

What are the alternatives open to the couple who find themselves becoming panicky because of the frequency of their blow-ups? The more severe and deep-seated conflicts will require the attention of a competent psychiatrist. Quarreling which has departed from issues to concentrate on the person, which we have termed destructive conflict, becomes progressively severe after a few brutal truth sessions, and may be halted only by recourse to a highly skilled third party. Marital guid-

---

[1] Willard Waller and Reuben Hill, *The Family: A Dynamic Interpretation* (New York: Dryden Press, 1951), p. 310.

ance clinics accept just such cases, helping the couple accomplish, with the aid of the consultant, that which unaided they are unable to do for themselves.

| CHECK YOURSELF | Which of the following excerpts from quarrels suggest destructive and which productive quarreling? |

Destructive	Productive	
————	————	1 "You aren't fit to be a mother, leaving the baby all week with strangers."
————	————	2 "Why didn't someone tell me marriage would be like this, cooking and ironing and scrubbing all day?"
————	————	3 "You will never amount to anything and neither will we as long as we depend on you to support us, you loafer."
————	————	4 "This is the last time I'm waiting for you for supper; after this you'll get your own or come on time."
————	————	5 "You aren't the man I married. What did I ever see in you? Oh, I could just die. . . ."
————	————	6 "You sit home all day reading or go out to some catty dames' bridge club and leave the house like a pig pen."
————	————	7 "Get a cookbook, sister, get a book and start studying. This is the last lousy meal I'm eating here, understand?"
————	————	8 "Darling, you must put on your rubbers. You aren't so young as you were."

★ KEY Destructive: 1, 3, 5, 8 Productive: 2, 4, 6, 7 ★

Fortunately, not too many couples are burdened with conflicts which get so far out of hand. So much of conflict is normal and a part of living that it need not be the occasion for panic. The informed couple learn to recognize the source of their differences early and to relay to one another the message that excitement is brewing, without spoiling the fun by appearing too much in control of the situation. Let's look at the process a bit more in detail.

Most conflict situations find one party the aggressor and one the defendant. Married people need to know how to play both roles well to get the most out of the quarrel. They may have to change roles right in the middle to keep things moving to a satisfying climax in which tensions are fully released. There is sometimes what appears to be a bit of perverse interdependence, the aggressor needing the defendant, and after a while the defendant needing the aggressor, to carry the fight on. Both would feel cheated and disappointed if either party retired from the fray too soon.

The privilege of initiating the conflict is available to the party who develops the irritability first. He or she has a chip on the shoulder and is looking for trouble. The aggressor role includes, therefore, the insight to recognize in oneself feelings of malaise, uneasiness, or frustration and the willingness to do something about it. It includes the skill of identifying and forthrightly relaying to the partner the sore spots in one's make-up as they are touched in the sparring — "Ouch, that hurts." Obviously, it should also include the willingness to kiss and make up when the inner tension has subsided. Often the tension subsides without solving the problem which occasioned the outburst. But there is no hurry; the immediate need is to relieve the tension under which the aggressor seems to be operating. The original problem may lend itself to solution the next morning when things look rosier.

The marital sparring partner who plays the defendant role has a special responsibility. If the irritability of the aggressor seems due to hunger, sickness, fatigue, pregnancy, menstrual blues, or tensions aggravated by other physiological disfunction, the situation may call for listening it out, for reassurance and sympathy rather than active opposition. The person who has been emotionally wounded in his workaday contacts may need the same understanding and sympathy. Humiliations and personal defeats may be offset by the understanding interest of the partner. The partner needs to be sure of his ground, for there is nothing more infuriating to the person out to pick a fight than failure on the part of the defendant to respond to his aggressions. The need for response is all the keener in the person on an emotional spree.

In interpersonal relations much depends on the ability of the participants to anticipate the responses of the other. So much behavior consists of anticipated reactions that the skillful sparring partner must learn what the other expects and say, "He's asking for it; I'll give it to him." The sore spots alluded to above may sometimes be painful, and the partner may need to work around them in his verbal punching. For the wife to jeer at her husband's inability to make more money or to become president of the firm would be for most men a blow below the belt, because she aims at the area over which he has least control. Likewise for a man to taunt his wife about her inability to have children may be such a cruel jab that she will never quite recover. In time the sparring partner learns to anticipate the hidden weaknesses and finds where to aim his blows to get the maximum release of tension with a minimum damage to the personality. This discussion may sound farfetched to the student who has had no occasion to think it through, but every couple in conflict experience some of these reactions in some degree. Some participants become very skillful in their battling and recognize conflict for what it is, a tension-dispelling experience of real value.

Stages of Conflict. Unless the newly married have had a background of conflict in their respective parental families, they may be devastated by their first quarrels. In time they will come to recognize that conflict has a pattern and runs a course which is predictable. At least three stages are discernible.

1 At the beginning of the battle, the first stage, there is often petulant irritability and jittery nagging on the part of the wife, if she is the aggressor. If the husband is the aggressor, the symptoms of tension express themselves in emotionally toned growling, griping, and overcritical comments on the sloppy house, the overdone steak, or the bill from the hairdresser. The aggressor is readying himself to take out his accumulated frustrations on the partner, who takes it just so long and then begins to fight back.

2 The second stage is often the battle royal itself. It consists of laying the cards on the table, meeting accusation with accusation, arguing, cajoling, wisecracking. The second stage may be relatively short, a matter of minutes in fact, and again it may last in relatively nonviolent form for hours into the night, depending on the issues and the nature of the tensions which occasioned the conflict originally.

3 The third stage begins as the aggressor recognizes a let-up in his inner tensions and as he communicates that fact to the other by offers of conciliation and peace. The defendant may by this time have built up tensions himself and may be unwilling to kiss and make up, which may prolong the battle until both are relatively more relaxed. The participants often find this stage the most difficult to bring about. Pride, hurt feelings, and resentment hold over in unfinished conflicts, and although the battle may be over the war never really ends. Covert conflict all too frequently continues after the overt battling has subsided. More skilled couples prefer the third stage to any other, because it brings the release of tension and a glorious feeling that the world is right and marriage is "swell." For these

couples conflict is not something to fear, but something to utilize in order to strengthen their relationship when tensions and misunderstandings arise.

Ways of Handling Conflict

Opposition in marriage is universal and normal, but skillful handling of marital conflict must be learned. The channels of communication between husband and wife can be kept open during conflict only if they each use gestures of acceptance of the other as they differ. In the old West there was a saying, "Smile when you say that, pardner; them's fighting words!" In marriage, opposition is less likely to arouse animosity if the partner prefaces his assertions with a family gesture of acceptance. Heat in an argument, and animosity directed against the person are joined in some conflicts, but they need not be threatening if the combatant is secure, knows he is loved, and that the love is not conditional, dependent upon his agreeing with the spouse.

There is real danger for those who have studied a little psychology, or a little psychiatry, and who attempt to apply the psychiatric labels to the partner under stress. It is rarely helpful, for instance, to say in the heat of the battle, "You are being hostile," or, "You are acting paranoid," or, "You are being regressive," and so on.

An obvious requirement for successfully handling conflicts in marriage is previous experience with conflict in one's parental family or with one's peers. There needs to be a deep held conviction that problems can be solved and that consensus is possible. A happy by-product of observation of successful quarreling in one's parental family is the absence of fear when conflict looms in later marriage. People who are afraid of combat are often the first to get hurt.

Proud should be the family which has reared its children to be tough-minded, invulnerable to the glancing blows of inept opponents. Thin-skinned, sensitive people find it difficult to focus on the problem, tend to take opposition personally so that it is difficult to carry through a productive conflict which sticks to issues.

There are still other ways of handling tensions than the forthright methods described above. In the film, *Who's Boss*, the husband warns his wife upon arrival that he has had a hard day and may prove irritable during the evening by *twirling his hat*, and his wife has a signal just as voiceless; she *wears her apron astern*. With this advance notice, the partner less fatigued can take some responsibility for providing a sounding board for the day's tensions. The wife may decide to "feed the beast" at least a snack, if supper is going to be late, knowing that hunger complicates any tensions which may have arisen. The husband may whisk the children out from under foot, knowing that preparing a hot meal requires supercoordination that demanding children can upset.[2]

Some married partners who perceive conflict ahead attempt to battle out their tensions first on the wood pile, or with a golf club, or bowling. The wife may scrub the floors or pound Sibelius out on the piano. When they return to face each other the original conflict is probably still unresolved but they are better prepared to deal with it, now that the feelings of unpleasantness have subsided. This is a species of running away, to fight another day. But the problem is ultimately tackled!

Some individuals are teamed in marriage with partners unable to play any of these combatant roles. They are conflict shy, avoid trouble at all costs, and resort to substitutive activity to keep their marriage on an even keel. Daydreaming, rationalization, deprecation, martyrdom, illness, and idealization are some of the mechanisms employed to escape from the reality of the marriage. The conflict is handled by avoiding it, by the wife or husband becoming too ill to face it. Martyrdom is closely allied to illness as a way out of facing the conflict. The martyred partner glories in the hurts and troubles which afflict her (it may be the husband) and thus avoids the real basis for conflict. Not uncommon in workaday America is the man (or woman) who escapes the pain of discordant marriage by plunging into work and spending all his time at it. The daydreamer manages, on the other hand, to forget marriage entirely, or sufficiently so not to be bothered about real life situations. In fantasy she creates a substitute husband who is kinder and more romantic than the real one. Rationalization, deprecation, and idealization are all mental mechanisms which enable the person to make the best of an unsatisfactory situation without really facing it squarely. We say, "Other people are worse off than we," or "I don't think I deserve anything better; after all I'm just a working man," or "She's a good mother for the children." The obvious difficulty with these substitutive adjustments is that they tend to mask the real issues. Even though

---

[2] For a more detailed discussion see Evelyn Millis Duvall, and Reuben Hill, *Being Married* (Boston: D. C. Heath and Company, 1960), Chapter 14 "Coping with Conflict."

they start as temporary expedients in the trial and error adjustments of early marriage, the marriage structure may be based permanently on a substitutive basis.

Marital Counseling as a Means of Meeting Progressive Conflict

Marital counseling services are available in a number of large cities for couples whose marriage conflicts prove too much for them. The case of Charles and Edna demonstrates the possibilities of professional counseling services for cases of progressive domestic discord.

Charlie is a young physician just getting a good start in building up a practice in a small Midwestern city. Three years ago he married Edna, who sang in the choir of the Methodist church. In their courtship and engagement period they did all the things young lovers do, from discussing the kind of furniture they liked to the number of children they would have. Their marriage has been a happy one on the whole. Their year-and-a-half-old son is a darling whom they both adore. The practice is building up so well that they are making regular payments on a little bungalow at the edge of town. Everything should be wonderful. They love each other, have their little home, their baby, and the promise of the kind of future they both have looked forward to all their lives. The one problem that has disturbed them both greatly has been their frequent and heated quarreling. Spats seemed to start up over nothing. But once they were started Edna found herself getting so mad she just couldn't contain herself, while Charlie shut up like a clam, and after he had stood just so much slammed out of the door, not to return for several hours. Edna felt that if Charlie loved her, he would be willing to stay and talk it out and make some rules so that they wouldn't fight over the same thing again. He felt that she was being unreasonable most of the time and that she should be able to control her temper better. The situation became so acute that several months ago they went to see their minister about it. He was an up-and-coming young pastor with a good training in helping people out of trouble, and after listening to both sides of the case, suggested that they go to the not too distant city and visit the marriage and family counseling agency here. He told the couple what they might expect from such a service and said that he was suggesting that they go to such a center in much the same way as he would recommend a good hospital or doctor if some troublesome physical difficulty didn't respond to home remedies.

Two week ends later the couple were found chatting pleasantly with the counselor. She assured them that she wasn't going to pry into anything that either of them didn't want to tell her, but that sometimes it helped to talk out bothersome problems with a person who was not tied up emotionally in the situation. She helped them both to see that she was not a Mrs. Ellery Queen who could unravel human mysteries in the first twenty minutes, but that her training might help her to suggest to both of them just where to look for the real reasons for their trouble. The counselor indicated that by working together, some suggestions for meeting the situation might emerge. The couple seemed relieved to find that the counselor was not assuming a know-it-all attitude and that she seemed to be the sort of friendly person who could be trusted to like you, whatever you told her. She looked as if she would hear your story without being shocked or making too much of it.

Each described the situation as he saw it. The wife got so excited as she relived the last quarrel that she started to cry. Then feeling better, she leaned toward the counselor, saying earnestly, "You see how much this matters to me. If only we could get to the bottom of it all, I'd be the happiest girl alive." She was encouraged by the counselor's reflection that it was just that motivation to do something about it that was the most important step toward an effective solution.

After several individual interviews and a simple personality study of each, the couple came in again for a joint conference. At that time they were each helped to share with the other the insights they had gained concerning their problems and to look at them together. It was slow going the first time, a new way of approaching the problem for both of them. By the third and fourth session with the counselor they were much more at ease, and had begun to talk in terms of what they would do now that they were returning home.

Within three months they were both more comfortable with the whole idea of their quarreling, and neither of them became panicky when one started. As time went on, the quarrels grew less frequent and lasted for shorter periods. Each developed some understanding of what it was in their early experiences which made them feel so differently when a conflict situation emerged. Both began to develop some skill in handling themselves and in understanding the other when the fur

"Oh, it's nothing to worry about. Every marriage requires
an adjustment period."

began to bristle. Of course they still squabble, and they probably always will. But they can take it now, and are comforted by the recognition that there is less of it to have to take.

The baby sister who recently arrived has added to their sense of being a family, and to the growing satisfactions of their life together. As young Doc put it himself, "No one could have told me a year ago that marriage could be like this. Why, with all the education I had, I never had the foggiest idea that you could be as scientific about your feelings as you can about a tonsillectomy. I want some books to read. This has all been an eye opener to me."

Yes, it's an eye opener to many folks. Listening to the Mr. Agonys on the radio and reading the lovelorn columns in the daily papers give many people the idea that asking for help on a personal or family tangle is childish. Many are afraid that the problem will be taken out of their hands and that they will be told what to do without having a part in the decision. Others are skeptical about the type of person who acts as a counselor. Still others hesitate to tell their personal problems to a stranger who may not keep their confidences. All of these fears and reluctances are perfectly justified. There is a certain sanctity about our emotional and married lives; we don't want things spread all over town. It is this respect for the persons and for their confidences that is characteristic of a good counseling service and of a well-trained counselor. This is the big difference between the shoddy quackery that we are all afraid of and the reliable, modest, helpful counseling service which is becoming more widely available.

Criteria for judging a good counseling service are fairly simple to enumerate. Briefly summarized they are as follows:

A GOOD MARRIAGE COUNSELING SERVICE

1 Doesn't promise quick results or make snap judgments.
2 Doesn't diagnose until after a careful study has been made.
3 Keeps all information confidential.
4 May charge nominal fees which are frankly discussed.
5 May call in other trained specialists to help.
6 Uses only trained professional workers from reputable colleges specializing in such fields as social work, human development, psychiatry, and related areas. (At least a master's degree in the specialized area is the usual professional standard.)
7 Is affiliated with such reliable bodies as local councils of social agencies, and nationally with such professional organizations as the National Conference of Social Work, and the National Council on Family Relations.
8 Does not advertise or try to drum up business, relying instead on slowly building up a clientele of satisfied users through referrals from other agencies and professional persons.
9 May have a membership and a board of directors of reliable citizens who take the responsibility for supporting and interpreting the program to the community.

What, then, have we said about marital conflict? First, much conflict is normal. It performs a valuable function in maintaining emotional balance through the release of tensions accumulated in a workaday world. Second, much of conflict in early marriage is understandable as the outcome of merging two different sets of family habits into a new pattern — a painful process which is speeded up by overt conflict and definition of the issues. This type of conflict tends to be progressively delimiting in the area it covers as the marriage continues and

serves a valuable problem solving function. Third, in distinguishing between productive and destructive quarreling, the former was shown to
be limited, and directed at issues, problems, and conditions rather than
at the person. Destructive quarreling concentrates on the ego of the
participants and destroys the fundamentals on which the marriage is
based.

In line with the newer thinking concerning the nature of personality
needs, this chapter has advocated more honesty in the husband and
wife relationship. This involves facing issues squarely and mastering the arts of conflict in rough and tumble discussion. It is not so much
the conflict in marriage which is to be deplored as the inability to face
the issues and battle them through. Conflict has a dual function: the
solution of issues, and the release of the resentment and tensions which
arise in every relationship.

Every couple needs to learn the techniques of handling conflict situations. Thousands of informed, mature married couples are reporting
the feasibility of the approaches to conflict described in this chapter.
To aid others less fortunately endowed, the inexperienced, the immature, and the progressively discordant couples who are unable to handle
the complexities of normal conflict in marriage, there are fortunately an
increasing number of reputable marital counseling agencies close at
hand.

Readings

BLOOD, ROBERT O., *Anticipating Your Marriage* (Glencoe, Illinois: The Free
    Press, 1955). Chapter 10, "Solving Marriage Problems," analyzes where
    marriage problems come from, and step by step suggestions are given for
    working them through constructively.

CAVAN, RUTH S., *American Marriage, a Way of Life* (New York: Thomas Y.
    Crowell Company, 1959). Chapter 16, "Finding One's Place at Home
    and at Work," is particularly helpful in pointing out the inevitable dif-
    ferences between husbands and wives, how they feel about their mar-
    riages, with implications of what they can do about their differences.

DUVALL, EVELYN M., and REUBEN HILL, *Being Married* (Boston: D. C. Heath
    and Company, 1960). Chapter 14 "Coping with Conflict," contains
    some particularly helpful material on what husbands and wives do when
    they differ, as well as a full discussion of ways of resolving conflict.

LOCKE, HARVEY J., *Predicting Adjustment in Marriage*: A Comparison of a
    Divorced and a Happily Married Group (New York: Henry Holt and
    Company, 1951). Chapter 4, "Marital Disagreements and Conflicts,"
    summarizes the research findings about disagreements in marriage, who
    gives in, what each doesn't like and how they feel about each other.

MACE, DAVID R., *Marriage: The Art of Lasting Love* (Garden City, New York: Doubleday & Company, 1952). Chapter 4, "How to Handle Quarrels," is a helpful treatment of the right way and the wrong way of handling quarrels in marriage.

MAGOUN, F. ALEXANDER, *Love and Marriage* (New York: Harper & Brothers, 1956). Chapter 11, "Emotional Adjustments," treats of the need for readjustment that marriage necessitates for husband and wife, what they disagree about, and how their conflicts can be resolved.

WALLER, WILLARD, and REUBEN HILL, *The Family: A Dynamic Interpretation* (New York: Dryden Press, 1951). Chapters 13 and 14, "Married-Pair Living," and "Bases of Marriage Conflict," are meaty chapters for the mature student.

CHAPTER ELEVEN

"I've got some money saved from my newspaper route we can use, Dad."

WHEN CRISES COME

Does sudden poverty make or break a family?

Is desertion a poor man's divorce?

What is meant by "death education"?

What is the immediate reaction to death of a loved one?

How can you handle the case of the "other woman"?

What are the marks of recovery from a family crisis?

*T*O FIND YOURSELF BROKE WITH A FAMILY TO SUPPORT AND NO JOB in sight is tough; to take the death of a family member in stride is more difficult still; to adjust to the faithlessness of husband or wife requires insight and understanding; and to face possible desertion or divorce is beyond the powers of most young people. Yet these are the crises virtually all families face at some time. Death, the crisis least talked about of all, will normally hit the average family not once but several times. Sudden poverty hovers constantly over all but the wealthiest of families under an industrial economy which has produced cycles of inflation, depressions, and widespread unemployment every five years since 1790. These are hard blows to take but they are part of living — families must be prepared not so much to avoid them as to regard them as challenges. Indeed, there is no avoiding trouble if you want to have the satisfactions of living in a real world. The question which should be raised is not, "How can I avoid family crises?" but, "How can I learn to take them?"

The first step in learning to take trouble in stride is to realize that other people the world over are facing similar problems — not, "Why does all this have to happen to us?" but, "I guess we're having our turn now." Another step in learning to take it is to recognize the normality of problems and conflict. Much of the anguish which follows a crisis arises from the shock of the unexpected and the fear that no recovery is possible. The shock of the blow is easier to absorb if one is relaxed and unafraid of the pain which is bound to follow. Some families are so well prepared for trouble they grow under it. Their preparation for crises began back in courtship and early marriage, and even before.

In the early years of marriage the husband-wife relation stabilizes, with each taking roles with prescribed duties, many of which continue after children arrive. Later, with the children, the family heads work out solutions to the problems of daily living. Members learn the answers to most questions, and they express it neatly — "This is the way we do it at our house," or, "I was brought up to think this way." Conflicts are settled and decisions made regarding vacations, birthday parties, and school difficulties. Well-organized families have the resources for meeting these problems without too much distress and readjustment.

When the family meets a situation for which there is no ready solution from past experience and no immediate answer forthcoming from family members, then the family is said to face a *crisis*. Sudden poverty, infidelity, divorce, desertion, and bereavement are good examples of disruptions which throw most families into temporary confusion. Some families may be permanently disabled, particularly if the remaining members are unable to absorb the duties of the persons incapacitated by the crisis. Other families are drawn closer together by the threat to their unity and survive the crisis stronger than ever.[1]

We have selected for discussion in this chapter crises that produce both demoralization (loss of morale and family unity) and dismemberment (loss of family member): sudden impoverishment, infidelity, desertion, alienation and divorce, and bereavement. The variety of family breakdowns is large and worthy of our attention as we enter the discussion of family crises.

What conditions must a family maintain to withstand the buffeting of circumstances in this turbulent country of ours? The family mem-

---

[1] It appears that middle-class families may have more troubles but weather them more successfully than working class families according to Earl L. Koos, "Class Differences in Family Reactions to Crises," *Marriage and Family Living* (Summer, 1950), pp. 77–78.

A CLASSIFICATION OF FAMILY BREAKDOWNS [2]

Dismemberment only	Loss of child
	Loss of spouse
	Orphanhood
	Hospitalization
	War separation
Demoralization only	Nonsupport
	Progressive dissension
	Infidelity
	Sense of disgrace — reputation loss
Accession only	Unwanted pregnancy
	Deserter returns
	Stepmother, stepfather additions
	Some war reunions
	Some adoptions
Demoralization plus	Illegitimacy
dismemberment or	Runaway situations
accession	Desertion
	Divorce
	Imprisonment
	Suicide or homicide

bers must be physically fit and healthy; they must have adequate mental resources to cope with complexities and unpredictables; they must be adaptable and flexible; they must have achieved a workable adjustment to one another as members of a group and must be proud of their family membership; and they need to have an income from some source adequate to maintain a normal standard of living. In addition, to remain healthy, the family needs the support of neighbors and friends and of community agencies like the church and the school. Lacking any of these attributes, a family may muddle through for a period of years without breaking up. But in the face of a crippling crisis such a family will become badly disorganized, and dismemberment or demoralization will take place.

[2] Expanded by Reuben Hill in *Families under Stress* (New York: Harper, 1949), p. 10, from a classification originally suggested by Thomas D. Eliot, "Handling Family Strains and Shocks," in Howard Becker and Reuben Hill (eds.), *Family, Marriage, and Parenthood* (Boston: Heath, 1948), p. 617, n.

Down on Your Luck

Sudden impoverishment is one of the crises which has been studied most completely, and there is considerable agreement concerning its effects on the family. One of the surprising findings from the depression of 1929–36 was the ability of many families to absorb the shock of impoverishment without demoralization or great personal disorganization.[3] The reactions of the family when the breadwinner is laid off and the income ceases must be seen against the backdrop of associations within the family and the family's earlier reactions to crises. As children are added to the family, methods of adjustment develop and become habitual. Father traditionally earns the money and spends most of his day away from home. Mother runs the domestic end of the household, supplying services and supervision of the children, who are primarily consumers with minimum responsibilities and who are accustomed to depend on parents for the satisfaction of their major wants. There comes a crash on the market — people are thrown out of work. The loss of father's job and the subsequent loss of income disrupt this habitual arrangement. It leaves father with time on his hands at home, exercising unaccustomed supervision of children, and it places other members of the family in situations for which they have no accustomed responses.

One of the best descriptions of the nature of the crisis of impoverishment is drawn from a study of one hundred Chicago families:

The development of a crisis often involves disorganization, that is, a breakdown in the organization of the family or person. The depression, as a crisis, may effect wide-spread disorganization, for the influence of the economic aspect of the family is so pervasive that lowered income may affect every realm of family life. The family may have to abandon certain objectives, such as buying a home or educating the children: it may be unable to conform to certain social and community standards in which it has always taken pride, such as the prompt payment of rent and bills or the maintenance of a certain type of home: it may be disturbed by the shifting of the dominant role, perhaps from the father to the mother or to a son or daughter. Not only is the family organization shaken, but the members of the family most affected also may become personally disorganized over the loss of accustomed activities, a lowering of status, or a failure to meet responsi-

[3] Ruth S. Cavan and Katherine H. Ranck, *The Family and the Depression* (Chicago: University of Chicago Press, 1938), pp. viii–ix.

bilities. This disorganization may be evidenced by worry, nervous breakdowns, excessive fears, or demoralization.

A crisis and the disorganization that accompanies it are highly charged with emotion, a reaction to be expected when habits become ineffective and new modes of response must be found and adopted. In the case of the depression the emotion tends to be fear — fear of loss of status, of loss of money reserves, of failure to have needed food and clothing, of the necessity to go on relief. When re-employment is not found, worry, discouragement, and depression follow. Some people become resentful or angry, but most of them are simply afraid of a moneyless existence for which they have no habitual conduct and no philosophy. For many people the condition of unemployment continues over many months, even over several years. It is almost impossible, however, for a highly charged emotional state to continue over a long period of time. Therefore, the period of unemployment cannot be considered as a static period. The situation, as it appears during the first shock of unemployment, is not the situation as it would be described six months or a year later. The unemployment may still exist, the income may still be low: but the experience of a person who has been unemployed for a year is not the experience of a person who has just been told that he has no job. At some point the disorganization reaches a climax and the extreme tension lessens. This turning point is psychological; it may not coincide with the time at which employment is lost. Self-confidence and financial resources may postpone the peak of the crisis until an indefinite number of months after the time when unemployment begins. Perhaps the disorganization may be said to culminate when the family accepts the fact that it can no longer continue its old mode of life, when it admits that it can no longer control the situation by its old procedures. Such a realization usually brings with it severe emotional reactions which have perhaps been manifesting themselves in minor form during the period when the disorganization was developing. This period of acute emotional stress is usually terminated either by an adjustment to the situation or by the development of pathological reactions. If an adjustment to the new circumstances occurs, new roles are assigned, new functions defined, a new status accepted. This adjustment may take the same form as the old family organization, so that after the period of disorganization the old roles, functions, and status are readily resumed; or the adjustment may involve roles of a lower status, curtailed functions, and lowered community status. In the case of a break or failure to adjust, the family may disintegrate through separation of its members or the person may escape through mental illness or suicide. In any case, there is a tendency for the period of extreme disorganization to reach an end, either through reorganization or disintegration of the group or personality.

. . . another factor must be considered: the habitual ways in which families and members of families have met earlier changes and crises. A crisis, because it sweeps away the customary ways of living, tends to expose the resources or deficiencies of the family or person. The family that, in the past, has faced a difficult situation squarely, evaluated it, and made adjustments to it may be expected to react in this way to the depression, even though there may be an initial period of disorganization. The family that, in the past, has refused to face issues or has evaded difficult situations may be expected to evade facing the changes in family life brought by unemployment or decreased income. It seems clear from the present study that only rarely did the crisis cause the development of any totally new reactions. Rather, the crisis caused an exaggeration of previously existing family and personal habits. The man who occasionally drank began to drink to excess. The family that was harmoniously organized became more unified and the members more loyal. Reactions to the depression therefore cannot be stated categorically; the depression as a family and personal crisis must be viewed in the light of previous methods of meeting difficulties used by the family or its members.[4]

Although no studies have yet been published on the subject, it would not be surprising to find that the impact of rapid fluctuations of income upward in war-boom prosperity days was fully as disorganizing for some families as the sudden impoverishment experienced by millions in the depression of 1929–36. In both instances the family is faced with a disruptive occurrence in which the old customs of the group and the old attitudes and habits of the family members are no longer consistent with the new situation brought about by the crisis.

Desertion: A Breather from Marriage

Closely allied with impoverishment and internal dissension is the crisis of desertion, which afflicts approximately 330,000 families a year.[5] It has been sometimes called the "poor man's divorce," because it occurs so frequently among the economically impoverished. As a forerunner of divorce, desertion is also relatively common in the upper classes. Still it is not divorce, because it has no legal status whatsoever. "It is the ruthless and lawless evasion of responsibilities, whereas divorce is at

---

[4] Cavan and Ranck, op. cit., pp. 5–8.

[5] Jacob T. Zukerman estimates one million women and children are today the victims of family desertion; see his discussion, "A Socio-Legal Approach to Family Desertion," Marriage and Family Living (Summer, 1950), p. 83. As of September, 1956, roughly 50 per cent of the 606,717 families receiving federal-state support under the Aid to Dependent Children program were those in which father was absent from the home and not supporting the children. See William M. Kephart, The Family (Boston: Houghton Mifflin, 1961), p. 548.

least legal and recourse to it is playing the game in the open, by the rules." [6] It differs from separation in that the latter includes some arrangement, voluntary or compulsory, for support of the deserted.

Of all the crises, desertion is the most devastating on the morale of the family because of the difficulty in bringing about any program of stabilization. Reorganization of the family around the remaining members may be postponed indefinitely pending the return of the deserter. Realistic solutions are rejected in favor of wishful hope or cowering fear, depending on the attitudes toward the absent one. Moreover, if the deserter does return there is always the fear, or hope, that he may abandon the family again in the face of difficulty. Desertion represents an escape of a sort, not unlike drinking or neurotic illness, which is conveniently used by the offender both as a club or power device to control the family and as a means of release when family responsibilities become too confining.

Men desert in significantly larger numbers than women. It is considered socially much more criminal for mothers to desert their children than for fathers to do so. The desertion in many cases appears to be timed to avoid the economic responsibilities which pyramid as new dependents are added to the family. Social agencies report periodic desertion of husbands just before the birth of a new baby. The men sometimes return when the agency has paid the bills and the economic situation is stabilized. It is rare that a case can be so simply explained. Indeed, in most cases there exist in the family before desertion bitter dissension and deep emotional tensions.[7] The immediate economic pressures aggravate a situation which is already tense and which may precipitate action causing the man to flee. Because the deserter so often returns, desertion has been called a vacation from marriage, a "breather," during which each party has the chance to think the matter over.[8]

Although desertion may be the solution to a personal problem for the deserter, it leaves all the complications of a family crisis in its wake. The family members, after the first desertion at least, are unable to find

---

[6] Ray E. Baber, *Marriage and the Family* (New York: McGraw-Hill, 2nd Edition, 1953), p. 495.

[7] Almost 70 per cent of desertions studied by Zukerman occurred in the first ten years of marriage, *op. cit.*, p. 84.

[8] Ruth S. Cavan, *The Family* (New York: Crowell, 1942), p. 287.

any ready-made solution to their difficulties. Added to the economic embarrassment occasioned by loss of support is the threat to family pride and to family integrity. The children feel a psychological let-down and will interpret the father's departure as rejection, particularly if they loved him. The mother may rightly interpret it as a reflection on her personal attractiveness. The seeds for demoralization are sown with every member of the family. The deserted family is ripe for dis-organization, and is often unable to bring about a reorganization be-cause of the refusal to admit that the situation is permanent. Thou-sands eke out a living at a submarginal level for several weeks or months or years before reporting to a welfare agency, hoping against hope that a reunion will be possible to restore things as they were.

Infidelity

One of the least understood yet most discussed crises in family life is marital infidelity. Like desertion it represents a solution of a personal problem for one member while creating a family crisis for the others.

Few crises are filled with more insecurity and sense of loss in a mar-riage than that involved when "the other woman" or her male counter-part breaks the sense of unity so important to marital solidarity. The fear of faithlessness haunts many married people and is especially under-standable when the members of a pair are separated for long periods of time. The triangle rarely fits into a family circle. Even when popular opinion tended to be lenient in allowing a man to sow his wild oats, to have his fling, to go gaily through his dangerous forties and his treacher-ous fifties, his "poor little wife" was pitied as deeply as though she had been bereaved. Friends and neighbors watched to see how she was taking it. Her loss was accentuated by a keen sense of inadequacy and shame, for hadn't she failed to hold her man?

With the explosion of the myth that "men are built that way," con-stancy has tended to be more widely expected of husbands. But the emancipation of women has been misinterpreted by some wives as li-cense and has made infidelity a double-edged sword that cuts both ways. Acceptance of woman's new freedom requires a whole new definition of our sex mores so that free interchange between people of both sexes may be possible socially, industrially, professionally, politically, intellectually, and financially without threatening the unique emotional sphere of the marriage relationship. This transition involves redefining what is "right" and what is "wrong" in many areas of common experience.

The check test below will enable you to test your own attitudes about situations that once would have been "wrong." Grandfather would

---

CHECK YOURSELF   Try out your own feelings about the following situations by checking *all right, it depends, questionable,* or *wrong* the conduct of the key person in the situation.

ALL RIGHT	IT DEPENDS
————	————
QUES-TIONABLE	WRONG
————	————

1 A *married secretary* works late to get out some important letters for her boss. He sends out for sandwiches which they eat together at her desk. No one else is in the office at the time except the cleaning woman.

ALL RIGHT	IT DEPENDS
————	————
QUES-TIONABLE	WRONG
————	————

2 A *married woman doctor* spends one night a week at a clinic in a poor section of town. It has been customary for some time for one of her colleagues (a married man physician) to drive her home when they are both through at the clinic.

ALL RIGHT	IT DEPENDS
————	————
QUES-TIONABLE	WRONG
————	————

3 A *woman* whose husband spends weeks at a time in Washington on business has taken in an older man as a roomer. No one else lives in the home except her year-old child.

ALL RIGHT	IT DEPENDS
————	————
QUES-TIONABLE	WRONG
————	————

4 A *married enlisted man* who hasn't been home in over a year is stationed near an urban servicemen's center. He has become acquainted with a hostess there, whose apartment he visited for dinner recently.

ALL RIGHT	IT DEPENDS
————	————
QUES-TIONABLE	WRONG
————	————

5 A *woman* whose husband is overseas met one of his old friends recently while lunching downtown. He accepted her invitation to stay and have lunch with her as they talked of her husband's work and interest. As he left her at the conclusion of the luncheon, he invited her to come out and see his family soon.

ALL RIGHT	IT DEPENDS
———	———
QUESTIONABLE	WRONG
———	———

6 A *man and a woman* (both married but not to each other) have jobs as inspectors that involve their traveling together a great deal by car. Frequently they are gone from home for days at a time. When away from home, they stay in hotels near the plant they are visiting. She registers under her own married name and occupies a separate room.

ALL RIGHT	IT DEPENDS
———	———
QUESTIONABLE	WRONG
———	———

7 A *singer* whose home is in Connecticut must spend two or three nights a week in town at her work. It is often necessary for her to work with her agent (a married man) and her accompanist (an attractive young bachelor) at her New York apartment in the evening. It is not always possible for her husband to be present on the nights she must remain in town.

ALL RIGHT	IT DEPENDS
———	———
QUESTIONABLE	WRONG
———	———

8 A *farmer's wife* is alone with the hired man in the house every Saturday night while her husband takes stock to market (an all night job).

ALL RIGHT	IT DEPENDS
———	———
QUESTIONABLE	WRONG
———	———

9 An unusually talented nurse is unable to continue her professional work now that she is married because *her husband* does not trust her with "all those good-looking young doctors."

ALL RIGHT	IT DEPENDS
———	———
QUESTIONABLE	WRONG
———	———

10 A *woman* whose husband handles legal cases for a large feminine clientele insists that there always be a third person present when her husband is on a case. She threatens to divorce him if she ever finds that he has been with a woman alone anywhere at any time.

---

undoubtedly check more of the situations as "questionable" or "wrong" than would members of our generation. The customs on which our codes of morality are based require a liberal use of insight into the consequences of behavior before applying them to specific situations like those above. Loyalty and fidelity are unusually hard to define in a world of changing values. Using the aids already given in the aforementioned chapter, however, one should be able to work out satisfactory answers to questions of marital fidelity.

If we interpret fidelity narrowly, as many people do, to make the appearance of evil equivalent to the thing itself, any situation which looks as though it might be compromising would be interpreted as infidelity. Chaperons were provided to supply complete surveillance in the dim past when infidelity was suspected in any situation in which extramarital sex experience might take place. Again, if we were to brand as evidence of infidelity all expressions of affection for anyone other than the spouse, we should also run into a dilemma. The normal person becomes genuinely fond of a great many friends and associates of both sexes. Is a person faithless who feels genuine affection for many fine people?

When we interpret loyalty, however, as mutual trust in each other and as faith in the marriage itself, neither the detective role called forth by the first definition nor the uncertainty inspired by the second is involved. The blow falls only if we find that our faith and trust have not been justified. It is only then that a crisis is said to occur. There is no crisis if there is no problem, or if the family members are equipped to meet whatever problem arises with their present resources.

Why, Then, Faithlessness? [9] Infidelity may almost always be seen as a symptom of unmet affectional need. The nature of the unmet need varies from couple to couple. Infidelity on the part of the husband may be an attempt to prove his manliness, or it may be a revolt against his conscience, or again a method of working out little-understood impulses stemming from childhood experiences. The other woman may represent a refuge from an overprotecting wife, or she may be a means of attacking the wife. Extramarital affairs grow out of the same attraction a forbidden piece of candy has for a hungry, undisciplined child — further proof of the importance of emotional maturity in marriage. Monogamous marriage requires that the participants be sufficiently mature to find in their relationship the satisfaction of their basic needs.

The Crisis of Infidelity. The act of infidelity by itself may be relatively unimportant to the stability of the marriage. It is the interpretation of the infidelity which the couple make that introduces panic into the rela-

---

[9] See Evelyn M. and S. M. Duvall, eds., *Sex Ways — in Fact and Faith* (New York: Association Press, 1961), Chap. 12, by LeMon Clark, M.D.

tion; what the participants see as the motive behind the defection is more important than the act itself. To some couples the slightest flirtation may prove calamitous, because it symbolizes much more than that to them. Others may tolerate without anxiety considerable swapping of partners and promiscuity in relations. A complicating factor in the interpretation of flirtations and unorthodox behavior with others is the health of the spouse. When he is bedridden, a man eyes his wife's recreational activities much more narrowly than when he is on his feet. Pregnant women are frequently suspectible to jealousy and read infidelity into situations where none exists. Jealousy is the product of insecurity and fear — the anxiety produced when one senses the possible loss of a love object. Unfortunately for the aggrieved person, jealousy may drive the mate into acts of infidelity which originally he may not have intended.

What to Do? A professional counselor can relieve the pain of the moment and can often deal with the underlying causes of the infidelity, the unmet needs and frustrations of the couple. Seeing infidelity as a symptom needing treatment is a more scientific answer to the question of what shall be done about it than has heretofore been given. Such a patient platitude as "give and forgive," or the self-righteous assumption that evidence of infidelity should always be promptly punished with separation and divorce, fails to meet the issues and introduces no satisfactory readjustment or reorganization to the marriage. Even when the other affair has gone so far that the salvage of the marriage is impossible, the abandoned mate may be helped by counseling to understand what has happened so that his or her resources may be mobilized for building life stronger from then on.

Alienation Crises

Quarrels occur in any marriage, as we have shown in the chapter on conflict. It is the mutually destructive type of quarrel which is most difficult to handle and which characterizes the progressive alienation of couples heading for divorce. If the process can be said to begin anywhere, it probably starts with the first brutal truth session in which both partners frankly expose their real feelings about the other. We have defined quarrels of this type as destructive because they concentrate on the person rather than on issues or conditions. They leave the relation with fewer assets than it had before. They attack the ego and reduce the self-respect by which persons live. Constructive quarrels, in contrast, make the marriage stronger through a redefinition of the situation causing the conflict. The destructive quarrels are progressive and succeed eventually in alienating couples to the point where separation is inevitable.

Affectional Responses Withheld. Disturbance shows up relatively early in the affectional response area. "Don't come near me until you're ready to say you're sorry," was Jane's response to Jim after their first explosive upset. The withholding of affectional response quite naturally broadens to include the sex life of the couple, in which antagonism is quickly reflected. There could well have been excellent sex adjustment to begin with, but through loss of understanding neither feels right about continuing intimate relations. Some people withhold affection to punish the mate just as they do to punish a child. Withholding of affection in marriage always evokes insecurity and anxiety, particularly for those individuals who have identified the good marriage entirely with continuous love intimacies. The familiar Hollywood pattern of early divorce is the only remedy that the over-romantic have devised to meet this situation. For most marriages the withholding of affection and sex intimacies is merely a first symptom of difficulty, to be followed by many more severe crises before divorce takes place.

Mention of the Possibility of Divorce. In the course of conflict there comes a great moment when mention is made of the possibility of divorce, the stage roughly equivalent to the declaration of love in the courtship process. Each member of the pair has thought of separation but neither has mentioned it, not knowing what the response would be.[10] One should differentiate between the banter of husband and wife in which the threat of divorce is used playfully and the more critical use of the threat among couples in serious conflict. The blow falls hardest on the one who is told. He is the one who must take the role of opposing the divorce and usually holds that role to the end. But there is an interdependence, which may seem to some perverted, each needing the other to continue the conflict, to work out the hostility. Both persons are really alienated, but one presses the fighting and one opposes the divorce. Each requires the continued participation of the other; indeed, each would be disappointed if the other stopped struggling. The

10 Waller, *The Family*, p. 514.

passive one suffers more intensely, but has the virtuous feeling of being right, while unconsciously desiring to break the relation.[11] The immediate effect of the mention of the possibility of divorce, then, is one of restraint from strife, but when the hostilities begin again the couple have become used to the idea of divorce, and definite steps are taken in that direction.

Others Find Out. At some point the fiction of solidarity is broken as the public is let in on the couple's troubles. The relationship changes, goes on a different basis. The expectation of success which was so important in holding the marriage together originally is replaced with the admission of failure. For many sensitive couples this is the master symptom of alienation: "People are talking about us." The couple have lost face and are no longer a pair in the eyes of the public. Invitations which include them both will decrease as friends refuse to take the risk of a row.

The public divides into two camps, friends who are for the wife and friends who are for the husband. They act as a wedge to divide the two. The more sympathy expressed to members of the pair separately, the more committed the couple becomes to separation. Take the following case:

I was first conscious of the fact that I did not want to go back to my wife, or that a part of me did not want to go back about two months after our break. I analyzed this, and thought that traced to the fact that I had introduced myself into this new community on a single-man basis, and people had sort of come to think of me as a separate individual, rather than as a married man. Then later I had talked to several people and I had wondered what they would think if I went back to this woman who had caused me so much trouble. They sympathized, of course, and that made it all the harder. Then later, people insinuated to me that I was such a fine fellow that it must have been my wife's fault. In telling the story of our break I had always been careful not to say anything against my wife, for two reasons: one that she is really a very nice person and the other that she might come to this new place and I didn't want people prejudiced against her when she did. But the very fact that I tried to be fair with her and take the blame myself made my friends all the more certain that whatever had happened had been her fault rather than mine.[12]

11 *Ibid.*, p. 520.
12 Willard Waller, *The Old Love and the New: Divorce and Readjustment* (New York: Liveright, 1930), pp. 131–132.

This case exemplifies well the role of the public in bringing about commitment to a permanent separation. The man's failure to identify himself as a married man further complicated the situation and accelerated the movement toward a complete break.

Breaking Up Housekeeping. The crisis of separation is one of the most severe because of the associations tied up with the home. Every piece of furniture symbolizes something, every piece brings back memories of common experiences. These belongings which must now be parcelled out and divided are reminders of days when. . . . The phase of separation which is probably most poignant is that of leaving the home to take up separate quarters. This act seems to signify more than anything else the lengths to which alienation has gone.

The severance of such a meaningful relationship is usually extremely painful. Although quarrels and conflict are useful in bringing out a decision that will stick, the couple should be able to say they tried hard to make their marriage go and to live up to the expectations of friends and well-wishers. Reconciliations which fail show the uselessness of continued compromises and force the conclusion that the marriage won't work and can't be made to work. The separation which comes with taking up separate quarters is a signal to friends and the public that the rift is serious. Usually both parties become committed permanently to the break, and they finally agree to divorce. The interval between separation and divorce is sometimes short, sometimes long, depending on the readiness and preparation of the parties.

Divorce. Divorce is a final severance, for which some preparation has to be made. It may take months before the actual work of reconstructing one's life can begin. The decree doesn't close the case, however; one doesn't divorce and live happily ever after. Indeed, the divorce court experience is described by some participants as being the most trying shock of the entire alienation process. Both members of the couple suffer through the procedure, with a feeling of numbness, of unreality, as if they were not really themselves but someone else looking on at the crazy scene.

After the divorce there is a period of mental conflict in which the individual attempts to reconstruct his world, often a period of depression, melancholia, and even suicidal attempts. Tensions build up which can be handled only with careful and skilled guidance. The divorced person should be watched for any evidence of depression and encouraged to seek counseling if symptoms appear.

Postdivorce Adjustments. Already during the alienation period preceding the divorce, personality adjustments are taking place. The many habits which hold marriages together, sex habits, response habits, food habits, work habits, all of these have to be broken and reoriented for the parties to face single life healthily. Everyone who has tried breaking a habit knows how painful the process is and how easy it is to fall back into the old routine again. Those who have gone on diets to keep a certain weight remember how insistently appetites cry out for foods to which they have become accustomed. The divorcing person faces the frustration of not one but several fundamental habits, and the separation is doubly painful if he must make that adjustment quickly. The habits of married living are much more fundamental than dancing or smoking or eating, and as they are broken, living loses its savor.

As the person is forced to turn within himself for satisfaction, the results are often curious. He becomes capable, or so he thinks, of doing grandiose things. A man revives dreams of boyhood and believes that in a short period he will become a great banker or writer. A woman after thirty years of being hemmed in by housewifely duties sees possibilities of attaining startling personal success. Now that the routines of married life no longer exist as hampering bonds, the person sees no bounds to his possible accomplishments.

Sour-grapes rationalizations [13] work overtime to convince the person he has done the right thing. Pleasant memories are repressed, and the illusions which supported the marriage are gradually replaced by cold, cruel reality. There is a certain grim conviction that the marriage could never have worked and that it was foolish to prolong it as long as it was prolonged.

Some helpful suggestions in reconstructing and readjusting the everyday life of the divorced warrants at least brief attention:

1 Talking the whole business out with someone who listens without praise or blame, who understands and helps but doesn't become involved; in sum, spending hours of counseling until the memories no longer bring numbing pain and can be faced with some objectivity.

[13] For a discussion of this mechanism, see pp. 17–18.

2 Developing new skills which have no associations with the marriage and which can show progress quickly, such as singing, painting, working at certain types of crafts; doing "something you have always wanted to do," in order to balance the accounts with something positive and satisfying.

3 Plunging into professional work with renewed vigor, but not to the exclusion of all social contacts.

4 Picking up social contacts; the person is his own best judge of the number and depth of new contacts he is emotionally able to take.

5 Reorienting oneself in terms of the rest of the universe, and working out a philosophy of life which gives purpose and zest to living.

Now, what have we said about the adjustments preceding and following divorce? The process is necessarily one of conflict, painful and divisive in its results. The timing of needs for sympathy and understanding is wrong; each is too absorbed in his own emotional difficulties to sympathize with the other, and a third party is turned to for sympathy. The process is long-drawn-out and somewhat painful, because the adjustment to the loss of a mate takes place in piecemeal fashion. To move faster in breaking habits of long standing brings danger of damage to personality and possible suicide. It is therefore dangerous to advise couples to divorce quickly.

The readjustment after the divorce consists in reconstructing life anew, developing new habits and new purposes which jibe with life as a single person. Assuming that the predivorce conflicts completely alienated the couple, the postdivorce period needs to be one of talking out problems which continue to arouse uncomfortable emotions and of picking up meaningful activities which will carry the parties back into normal social life.

Death as a Family Crisis

As it must come to every man. . . .

Of all the crises which afflict a family none is more sure to occur and none receives less advance preparation than death. Its discussion is discouraged in our society, and anyone who mentions seriously the possibility of death entering his family is shunned as a bit morbid. Death as a subject of conversation is almost as taboo today as was sex fifty years ago. Today we prepare our children for the shock of the birth of a brother or sister, for the newness of the first day at school, and, in the case of a girl, for her first menstruation, but to prepare children for death in the family is almost unheard of. There is no program of death education to cushion the shock of this universal crisis. Not only children, but adults as well, are shielded from the realities — mothers are not told when their children are dying — patients afflicted fatally are not prepared for the event that is a certainty. Until recently it was bad taste for picture magazines to show pictures of actual battle dead. In sum, there is virtually no preparation for the emotional shock that accompanies the death of a dear one. For that reason death is frequently a personal as well as a family crisis.

The importance of death as a personal crisis lies not primarily in the fact of dying or ceasing to exist biologically, but in the emotional shock which follows the break in the unity of the family. Two things happen to the member who is closely identified with his family: 1. he senses that the circle is broken and that the family is threatened with dissolution (What will ever happen to us, now that mother has gone?); 2. he senses that a part of himself as a person has been cut off, amputated, so to speak. The closer the identification with the deceased, the more distressing is the sense of personal loss.

The Shock Varies. The situation is eased considerably for family members who have left the parental home and have established families of their own. The emotional dependence which existed before their departure from their childhood home has been replaced by relative independence, and the sense of loss is diminished accordingly. The passing away of relatives, even brothers and sisters, brings less grief than the loss of parents with whom one is emotionally more closely identified. To make one further comparison, it might be safe to say that the mature independent adult normally senses greater pangs of grief at the loss of husband or wife or child than at the loss of a parent from whom he has won independence.

In general, death following a long-drawn-out illness brings less shock than sudden death for which no preparation can be made. Much of the mourning occurs in the period of illness as the relatives vacillate between acceptance of the loss of the loved one and wishful thinking that a cure can be found. Gradually, as the medical evidence piles up, the negative prognosis is accepted, and the parties assimilate the idea of permanently losing the afflicted one. As accommodation to the idea of losing part of one's self takes place, the afflicted one becomes an object of pity rather than a symbol of personal loss. It is at that point that the expression may be heard, "I hope his suffering will soon be over."

In time of war, bereavement is lightened to some extent by the public recognition achieved and by the realization that others face equal or worse crises. Although the hole that any one person leaves can never be completely filled, there is less of a break in family unity, because the other members have already made some adjustment to the absence of the member at the time he entered the armed services. The shock is lessened by the presence of neighbors and friends who offer understanding and genuine comfort. Moreover, death in wartime is given purpose and made meaningful both at home and in the war zones. In their adjustment, family members plunge into the common task with renewed determination to bring to fulfillment the goals for which *he* died.

On the other hand, bereavement in time of war is the less bearable because the victims are taken in the prime of life. The uncertainty of death in a "missing in action" notice leads family members to disbelieve later notices of death. For some people, only the rites of death serve as corroborators of fact, and the overseas death is hard to realize. When the body is not in evidence, it is easier to convert grief into disbelief.

To the person away from home who loses a member of his family the bereavement may be very difficult. He may feel for a time that the bottom has fallen out of life. He will miss the relief which comes in joining with relatives and friends in mourning. He finds that a part of himself as a person may no longer be responded to and that there is all too little help in healing the wound. Every opportunity should be taken to talk about the loved one with ministers, counselors, and others who are professionally trained to listen and understand. Letters home can draw off the overflow of emotions if one can express himself on paper and has the courage to let himself cry during the process whenever he feels like it. Weeping has already been mentioned as an effective tension-dispelling device. A person in mourning should allow himself the same privileges in the interest of recovery.

First Reactions. Even when anticipated, the actual death of a beloved person comes as a shock, and the first reaction is usually one of disbelief. A numbness comes over the bereaved and acts as a buffer to protect him from a shock that is too devastating to absorb all at once. It is quite common for persons to feel that the entire experience is a dream, unreal, and that they will awake to find things as they were.

The apparent calmness of the bereaved mourners immediately after receipt of the news is often a detachment cultivated to protect the self from the total reality. It may represent a repression of the news into the nether depths of the mind, where conflict may rage at great emotional expense to the individual. As realization intrudes upon consciousness, periods of uncontrolled abandon may appear, with weeping, cursing, self-blame, even self-injury. Accompanying these reactions is the longing for that part of the self which has been amputated: the beloved, now irrevocably departed, is relinquished with the greatest reluctance. The mind will play strange tricks on the bereaved — he will hear the voice of the departed, sense the presence of the other, and dream that they are together again. Clothing, mementos, locks of hair of the deceased, will be preserved as symbols to summon the presence of the departed. In extremity, the mourner may in his despondence be impelled to commit suicide to rejoin the other. These are first reactions which carry on after the rites of the funeral period are over. The routines of the mortuary, of funeral and burial, serve to dispel the illusions of disbelief and to channelize the emotions into approved lines. The rituals of funeral and burial are performed by professionals who take the responsibilities off the hands of the bereaved, yet give them the maximum opportunity for undisturbed grief.

In contrast to the well-defined routines of the funeral is the lack of definition for readjustment afterward. The professional undertaker retires from the scene, and no other professional person enters to aid the members of the family in the next phase of their readjustment. Each family is left more or less to shift for itself, with occasional help and advice from well-meaning relatives and friends. The family members are urged to resume normal activities as soon as possible — no time is allowed in our society for unnecessary show of grief, although it is not considered good taste for a widow or widower to remarry in less than a year's time after the funeral. Three days' sick leave are allowed the worker in civil service positions for funeral and mourning. He is expected back at work after that. Life must go on!

Trial and Error Adjustments. The first reactions to death are largely protective, designed to save the personality from serious damage. Eventually the bereaved seeks to assimilate the realities and makes trial and error attempts to pick up the threads of normal living. There are alternate periods of plunging into work and activity and of lassitude and depression. As time passes, periods of activity become longer and the periods of depression become shorter and less frequent. During the person's attempts to arrive at some pattern of stabilized behavior, he finds it necessary to force himself to respond to people, to children, and to his work. He resumes his duties with great effort at first, but gradually the routines are assumed and he rejoins the workaday world. There are also during this period frequent attempts to secure attention through wearing mourning symbols — the desire to tell of troubles to others is evident. There is much sharing of fate with children and friends.

Back in Life's Channel. As a reward for the many trial and error attempts at resuming normal activities, a new life organization will develop, and the bereaved will achieve the permanence and stability of settled living. The bereaved has accepted the death of the beloved and has made the experience a part of his personality, instead of walling it off and struggling against it. He is now able to resume relationships with others and may even substitute these relationships for those he had with the deceased. Religion is often a major source of support at this time, as we shall show in Chapter Fifteen.

One of the characteristics of the recovery is the emphasis upon participation in activities, upon entering into community services and other socially approved endeavors. If the deceased was active in any of these there is often an identification by the mourner in carrying on the work the other had started.

Successful recovery from bereavement means gradual relaxation of its tensions and frustrations in favor of some more satisfactory or at least tolerable patterns of behavior. The bereaved find someone else through whom they can satisfy their affectional needs: or they find religious beliefs which fully reconcile them; or they reabsorb their energies and redevote their affections in some life work as an alternate channel; or they assume the role of the deceased or project his personality by some conspicuous service in his name, or through creation of some appropriate and constructive memorial. Even gradual relaxing through forgetting . . . may produce successful recovery. . . .

. . . One may never feel a decision to take up life again: it is, in a sense, life which takes one up again. Mourning may never be absolutely finished, but it gradually approaches zero as a limit.[14]

CHECK YOURSELF   When condolences cease to arrive and the world moves on, there is apt to be a slump in the adjustment process. Which of the following are evidences of successful and which of unsuccessful recovery from bereavement?

Successful   Unsuccessful

———   ——— 1 Grief comes to be enjoyed for the attention it brings.
———   ——— 2 Energies and affections are reabsorbed in some life work.
———   ——— 3 The goals of the deceased are assumed in part by the bereaved.
———   ——— 4 Religion is abandoned because of failure to bring comfort.
———   ——— 5 Gradual relaxing occurs through forgetting.
———   ——— 6 Place at the table is set for the return of the deceased.
———   ——— 7 Ability is developed to talk about the deceased with warmth and appreciation unmixed with pain and self-pity.

★ KEY   Successful: 2, 3, 5, 7   Unsuccessful: 1, 4, 6

Ways of Meeting Family Crises

The family may be said to face a crisis when it meets a situation for which there is neither a ready solution from past experience nor an immediate answer forthcoming from family members. Individual families face the crises of sudden poverty, infidelity, desertion, and bereavement in many ways. By way of summary we show next, in greatly telescoped form, the steps which family members take in the tedious process of adjustment to any one of the major crises we have discussed: [15]

[14] Thomas D. Eliot, "Bereavement: Inevitable but Not Insurmountable," in Becker and Hill (eds.), *op. cit.*, p. 664.
[15] Modified and adapted from a chart developed by Eliot, "Handling Family Strains and Shocks," Becker and Hill (eds.), *op. cit.*, pp. 637–638.

First, comes the news of the event, followed by:

Second, prompt recognition of the facts or refusal to believe its actuality, failure to face facts, and

Third, prompt, realistic action in the emergency or escape mechanisms such as fainting, suicide, running away, drinking, tantrums, or violence;

Fourth, a period of rationalization, of fixing the blame, of clearing the self of responsibility, after the immediate situation has been met in some way, to protect the ego.

Fifth, a struggle to attain a livable balance, a trial and error search for solutions; depending on the previous ways of meeting crises the person will follow one or another of the major patterns of readjustment below:
   a. Escape: e.g., desertion, divorce, suicide, enlistment, dependency, delusions, drink, drugs, distractions, vice.
   b. Submission or defense: e.g., apathy, resignation, religion.
   c. Compensatory efforts within the existing and accessible resources of the family's members:
      1 Redoubled work.
      2 Substitution of new channels of income, affection, energy.
      3 Persuasion.
      4 Appeal to others for help: relatives, church, charity, clinics, relief, etc.

Sixth, attainment of a final adjustment and solution of problems by the intelligent use of new resources and the renewal of routines consistent with the new situation, enabling a new life organization to emerge — a re-establishment of stable habits, self-control, reorganized economic life, and normal social life — for those who do not find permanent adjustment in one of the phases of stage five.

Readings

DESPERT, J. LOUISE, *Children of Divorce* (Garden City, New York: Doubleday & Company, Inc., 1953). A famous child psychiatrist shows how children are affected by their parents' divorce and how the crisis may be tempered and weathered.

DUVALL, EVELYN MILLIS, *Family Living* (New York: The Macmillan Company, 1961). Chapter 20, "Strengthening American Families," discusses what stresses and strains can be anticipated at each stage of the family life cycle and what is recommended to prevent and to overcome family crises.

DUVALL, EVELYN and SYLVANUS, *Saving Your Marriage* (New York: Public Affairs Pamphlets, 1954). What to do when you have trouble in your marriage is the theme of this pamphlet designed to help couples understand where their problems lie and how to work them out successfully.

GROVES, ERNEST R., *Conserving Marriage and the Family* (New York: The Macmillan Company, 1944). One of the most realistic statements of the divorce problem as couples themselves face it in their own lives.

KOOS, EARL LOMON, *Marriage* (New York: Henry Holt and Company, 1953 edition). Chapters 15, 16 and 17 are an exceptionally complete review of the research on family troubles with sound guidance for how they are realistically met by actual families.

OSBORNE, ERNEST, *When You Lose a Loved One* (New York: Public Affairs Pamphlets, 1958). Professor Osborne sympathetically reviews the usual reactions to death, and talks about funeral arrangements, the place of mourning, the role of religion and ends with a helpful treatment of helping children cope with death.

CHAPTER TWELVE

Courtesy of Syd Hoff

"He's a dope, but he's mine!"

WHAT HOLDS A MARRIAGE TOGETHER?

Will love alone hold a marriage together?

What does sex symbolize in marriage?

What experiences test a marriage?

When is a marriage a partnership?

Why is it that happily married people come to think alike and talk alike?

*T*HIS CHAPTER CLOSES THE DISCUSSION OF WHAT IT MEANS TO BE MAR-ried. The accent in the chapters immediately preceding has been on the crises of marriage and family life, on the divisive forces which operate to break up and test marriage. This chapter emphasizes the forces and bonds which hold marriage together. It is dedicated to the proposition that successful marriages don't just happen, that marriage is what you make it. A happy union takes working at, and its accomplishment is the product of much sweat and toil in the art of getting along.

The Expectation of Success [1]

"We expect our marriage to work" is one of the strongest bonds tying a marriage together at the outset. This conviction supplies the motivation to stick together when the going is rough rather than to run home to mother. It impels the couple to work out the solutions to problems so they won't recur. Honeymooners with the expectation of success are already consciously addressing themselves to the task of building their

[1] We are indebted to Willard Waller for many of the ideas which appear in this chapter; see *The Family: A Dynamic Interpretation* (New York: Holt, Rinehart, Winston, 1951), pp. 322–335.

marriage so that it will work. They are saying, " We want to be good for one another and we want to be good parents. Show us how."

In spite of the high divorce rate in America, the standard held up for every couple is successful marriage. If a person can't make a success of marriage he is made to feel inadequate, and his failure is pointed out by members of society to young people about to be married. Along with the personal expectation of success goes the public's expectation of success. The individual couple may feel strongly the necessity of not letting down the friends who have wished them well. Making marriage work is often easier than facing the public with the admission of failure. One of the real forces in tying marriages together, then, is the expectation of success, the ideal of a happy marriage as the only possible outcome of the marriage, and the feeling that the public can't be let down by a break-up.

Friends are admonished in the "whom God hath joined together" formula to keep hands off the marriage and stay out of the sphere of marital interaction.[2] It is not good form to ask how the marriage is going or to inquire as to its health. The assumption in our society is that all marriages are happy until proved otherwise by appearance in a divorce court. It is doubtful if the net effect of this assumption of marital bliss is good, since it makes for hypocrisy and implies that conflict is abnormal and unusual, but the assumption is an additional force in holding many marriages together.

Social Life Organized for Married Pairs

A second reason for sticking together is the system of pairing young people off for social purposes. Most of our social life is organized around married couples or couples about to be married. The development of pair unity in the engagement period was furthered by the public's recognition that the couple did belong together shown by inviting them to social occasions as a pair. This acknowledgment caused the boy and girl to regard themselves differently and thus gave stability to the relationship. The years of married life add to this sense of "we" and further unify the couple. Together they explore the social circles (and are explored by them); together they make friends and choose the sets which they wish to join. Early in the marriage, if not in the en-

[2] *Ibid.*, p. 324.

gagement, a person learns to accept invitations tentatively until he can find out whether or not the other member of the pair is able to go. The public understands because it expects the couple to act as a unit.

Just because society in America is not organized for sexes separately as are some societies, the marital relationships are strengthened. Most of the entertaining in a community centers within the married set and is motivated by the "you invite us and we'll have to return the invitation later on" phenomenon, leaving almost no social activities for bachelors and spinsters and other nonmarried people. Moreover, to invite one member of a married pair and not the other is something of a breach of etiquette. The cards are stacked in favor of married couples sticking together if they want any social life. Two by two they go marching by.

The positive social pressures just described do hold couples together. In addition, the fear of public disapproval, of neighborhood gossip, and the fear of scandal are negative forces of which many couples are conscious. These socially imposed forces, however, are essentially *adhesive*, inasmuch as they are applied externally. They are most effective in a simple agrarian society where everybody knows everybody else, and are less effective within the social sets of the metropolitan centers. Of more importance today are the forces within the couples as individuals, forces which might be termed *cohesive* since they are based on the inner needs of the participants themselves. It is because marriage is welded together both by adhesive and cohesive forces, by external societal pressures and by internal desires and needs, that it is surviving the buffeting of social change in our day.

Marriage Satisfies Basic Adult Needs

One of the cohesive forces holding American marriages together is the power of the marital relationship to meet the basic affectional needs of its members.[3] The American family is built around the husband-wife relationship, and the power of that relation to satisfy the needs of the couple flavors the whole of family life. Children become accustomed to having their needs for affection, companionship, recognition, and response met in the parental family. Moreover, they are conditioned to

[3] The important role of satisfying the basic needs in marriage was anticipated in the discussion of the need for love in Chapter One, pp. 13-15.

expect that the phenomenon of love and affection will carry over into a family of their own making. With that expectation, the early courtship activities are surrounded by questions such as, "Does he love me?" "Is she good for me?" "Does he do anything for me?" or in sum, "Will he satisfy my hunger for affection and security permanently?" The history of the courtship is one of finding in the growing relation reciprocal satisfactions and increasing interdependence of one on the other to satisfy these imperious needs.

The adult is, after all, basically the child older grown. In marriage the child, now grown older, has transferred from the parent to the marriage partner his need to give and receive affection and security. The transfer takes place piecemeal, beginning with the first recognition of the capacity to love someone other than the parent, and continuing until the marriage is stabilized as the main source of affection and appreciation.[4]

To be wanted, to be understood, to be appreciated, to be loved, and to belong to someone are fundamental needs which parallel the needs to possess, to love, and to respond to someone. Uniquely met in the intimacies of the marriage relation, these needs should be listed among the main sources of cohesion holding marriages together in America today.

The Growth of Sympathy

As the marriage wears on and the couple come to take for granted the unreserved intimacies of wedded life, there is a growth of sympathy between the mates. The newlywed is all too often downcast when his wife is slightly displeased with him, but the experienced husband knows that she will get over it after a while. He has been all through this before and can predict the method of bringing the affair to a satisfactory conclusion. Here we see a value in some of the features of marriage which the Hollywood script writers have condemned in their "never let your marriage go to seed" attitude. It is disillusioning to a man to see his wife having breakfast in a housecoat with her hair in pins, and unpleasant for a wife to see her husband's unshaved face, but it is comforting to both to realize that such liberties do not seriously threaten the relationship. These are the jolly little coarsenesses which give to

4 See Chapter Two, pp. 28–44.

the marriage relation its unique strength.[5] Shady little sallies between them, the vulgarities which they alone think funny and which before marriage might have shocked them both, these indiscretions also hold a marriage together.

Gradually each member of a pair comes to share the mental states of the other, to live vicariously in the other, and to learn to predict the other. In this state of complete intimacy the members of the pair develop similar tastes and similar aspirations. The wife hears her husband's jokes hundreds of times but enjoys them because they are her jokes, and prods him to "tell that one about when we were in Chicago, dear."

In the growth of sympathy, the sharing of ideas often results in the sharing of depressions and predicting when they will come. Husband and wife learn to handle one another's blues as well as one another's temper tantrums. Each knows if he's put in the doghouse, the other will soon let him out.

Marriage solidarity develops immensely as members of the pair perceive the strength of the relationship. It is seen as they recognize, while fighting, that they care more about the marriage than they do about winning. It comes forcibly to their attention when a crisis like infidelity is met without the wife's running home to her parents as she would have done earlier in the marriage. It is seen in the willingness of the husband to tolerate shoddy household management or sterility of the wife with nary a hint at separation. The relationship has come to have a value in itself. All such incidents may not seem very romantic; indeed, some romantic-minded people would say such marriages had gone to seed. But family unity is built on just such foundations as these: "We have come to take each other for granted; we know we can count on one another"; " She'll see me through thick and thin. What a lucky man I am!"

Family Habits Create Solidarity

The married pair bring to marriage two separate systems of habits formed during life in their respective parental families as well as during the years away from the family. Consciously, at first, they must go about the task of adjusting the differences in the two systems. The

[5] Waller and Hill, *op. cit.*, p. 333.

wife must find out how strong her husband wants his coffee and when he must arise in the morning in order to get to work on time. The husband must learn that to his wife permanent waves are more important than golf equipment and that ashes on the rug are not to be tolerated. After a time the two systems are modified and become an interlocking habit system which is a great deal more stable than that of the single person could ever be; they rest upon the habit of adjusting to the situation created by the real or imaginary demands and expectations of others.

CHECK YOURSELF   Underline the correct alternatives in the following statements.

1 We have a (high, low) divorce rate in America accompanied by a (high, low) standard of success for marriage. (Because of, in spite of) the divorce rate, engaged couples feel they start with (high, only average) chances for happy marriage.

2 Life in American social circles is (as comfortable, not as comfortable) for bachelors and spinsters as it is for married people.

3 According to marriage authorities, it is not only (devastating, not devastating) to the marriage to come to dinner unkempt and unshaven occasionally but it (strengthens, weakens) the marriage permanently because it proves (how much, how little) the marriage means to the married pair.

★ KEY   1 high; high; in spite of; high.   2 not as comfortable.   3 not devastating; strengthens; how much.

Consider the following illustration of habits at work in a typical urban home:

. . . the husband used to laugh when the wife referred to ant-hills as ants' houses, but now he does not laugh any more; in fact he sometimes uses the expression himself. Each individual member of a family has made certain habit adjustments to the physical setting in which the family lives; each knows at just what height to insert the key in the lock of the front door and each has acquired the knack of giving a little twist to the key which makes the door open easily; each one is able to enter any of the rooms in the darkness and to find the switches for the lights without any difficulty; each knows where to sit on hot afternoons in August, and how to descend the rickety cellar stairs. And each one, likewise, has made a multitude of adjustments to the presence of others in the house. In the morning the father of the family gets up and starts the furnace. He walks carefully in order not to disturb the others, but there is no need of this, for the others have adjusted to his early morning noise and do not hear him. A little later the mother gets up and calls the children, perhaps a number of times, for they may have made an adjustment to her habitual technique and have shifted the responsibility entirely upon her; they have, perhaps, developed mother deafness. She then gets breakfast, sets the table, and calls the family. Father has been reading the paper, which is now split into sections. Each one eats his breakfast in his customary way; there is the usual interchange of pleasantries and the usual grumbling and complaining. Then ensues the morning crisis of getting the children off to school and helping father to catch the eight-thirty train, the struggle over the bathroom, the effort to find things, the examination of shirts to see whether they will do for another day, and all the myriad adjustments which arise from a civilization which demands neatness and promptness. Then all the members of the family but one leave the home, pausing a moment to say good-bye to mother and to pet the dog.[6]

This is just a small part of the family day and misses many of the habits of family living reflected in conversation and gestures. It does serve to illustrate, however, the intermeshing of social habits of family members. Once you become a part of a cooperative enterprise in which your behavior is habitually determined by the responses and helps of others, it is highly inconvenient to separate yourself. We will discuss this point more in detail when we come to the inertia to change which exists in all families.

As the pair become accustomed to each other and dependent upon one another for the sharing of family habits, they cease to operate in the family as individuals and come to take on a family personality. This is the reason married people in time come to talk alike, think alike, plan alike, and in some instances even to look alike. Back of the common gestures and facial expressions are common attitudes and beliefs. These habits serve as an additional source of solidarity in marriage.

Couples find that one of the techniques for making marriage work is to enter wholeheartedly into the business of building common habits. They may lose some of their premarriage individuality and independence, but they gain a more satisfying personality in the process.

Habits and Resistance to Change

In any marriage, after the initial adjustments to personal idiosyncrasies have been made and routines established, a level is reached at which the married pair feels comfortable. Decisions have been reached concern-

[6] *Ibid.*, pp. 328–329.

ing the division of duties, and the time schedule for each day has been committed to memory. The routines are fast becoming habits through repetition and the achievement of satisfying results. The major needs are being met, the major drives satisfied. The fact that habits are established makes experimentation less and less necessary. The couple are finding the grooves, and married life is gradually reaching an optimum level of interaction.

These routines act for the marriage as a gyroscope acts for a ship, pulling it back on an even keel when it is about to go over. It sometimes seems inevitable that a particular marriage should break up in divorce or desertion. Conflicts arise which seem impossible to resolve, but somehow equilibrium is restored, and things go on very much as before. Sometimes, too, a series of fortunate events makes it look as if a marriage were going to reach a level of impossible happiness — but that also passes.

An illustration may help to explain the tendency to stabilize marriage at a given level. When there is a "blow-up" each person is conscious of the cultural standards (that is, what is right in the situation) and of the fact that friends and families would disapprove if the truth were known. To add to their sense of guilt the couple may hear a sermon, or read a story, or hear a bit of gossip about a recently divorced couple which reminds them of the cultural norm. Discussion and reconciliation follow and the marriage is restored to its normal level. Thereafter the couple is tempted to let sleeping dogs lie. Ways are found for settling conflicts with a minimum of disturbance.[7]

Another explanation of marriage stabilization lies in an understandable reluctance to change a mutually satisfying relation in favor of something new or unknown. The collective habits of a married pair are solidly based on the needs and motives of both parties — or at least they were originally built up to satisfy the couple's needs. As long as these needs are satisfied there is inertia to change. Another kind of reluctance to change arises from the inability of either partner to know the mind of the other and the consequent difficulty of getting together on any ground other than that they now share.

In sum, one of the forces holding marriages together is the reluctance to give up "a good thing." The marriage may not be perfect, but to break habits is painful. They become vested interests, active in their

[7] Adapted from Waller, *op. cit.*, p. 331.

own perpetuation, as anyone knows who has tried to quit smoking or doodling.

Working toward a Common Goal

Dick is a medical student just beginning his four-year course and would like to get married, but he is afraid it is impossible for about six years. He has his M.D. to get first, followed by an internship and residence work. Marie suggests that there are things a girl would dislike more than working jointly with a man for an M.D. It would be *their* M.D., and they would share the experiences and sacrifices together, if they were married.

In the struggle to reach a common goal, a new feeling arises, a sense of having fought and bled together. Pride in common achievement, the sense of superiority which common accomplishments bring, or the feeling of struggling together against misfortune — such experiences are basic to marriage solidarity. They form a backlog to hold the marriage together in the crises which follow later in family life. The reference to "leaner" days, the technique of reminiscing together, reminders of the history of the relation, these can be called up when trouble arises on the home front.

In many a popular discussion of how times have changed it will be pointed out that the family has lost many of the old-time economic functions which made it a partnership. In the old-style family, making a living was a common enterprise which tied the family members together. Today it is more typical that the man earn and the woman spend the living. In the modern family, mutual interdependence arises largely out of husband and wife's sharing the budgeting and planning of expenditures, the joint consumption rather than the joint production of economic goods. In addition, it must be admitted that the division of familial duties between man and wife makes for interdependence, as any husband will find who is forced by circumstances to take over the task of managing the home while his wife is gone. One harried husband found, thanks to his rich parental family training, that he had been given some background for all except one of the wifely homemaking duties. Can you guess what it was? Braiding his daughter's hair! Even so, this husband's life was immeasurably brighter when his wife returned, and the balance of duties was established once again.

Another phase of partnership centers around buying furniture and setting up a home. The things you buy are often bought after much deliberation. You scrimped and saved for each stick of furniture. Each item brings to memory a multitude of associations which solidify marriage. In the divorce process the most painful step of all is breaking up housekeeping and distributing the furniture. The converse of breaking up housekeeping is the solidifying function of building a home by self-sacrifice and hard work. The good family person comes to talk about his accomplishments and his possessions as "ours": "*our* degree," "This is *our* chance," "When *we* bought this, Jane was just a baby," "*We* saved for six months for *our* coffee table."

Another evidence of partnership as a binding force in marriage is seen in the unselfish goals which a pair will set for themselves. Many marriages are initiated and grow as the participants strive to serve humanity in specific ways. The ideal of alleviating the lot of the sick and the lame, of leaving society the better for their marriage, unifies many modern couples. An age-old ideal is that of rearing healthy, useful children, and this appears to be positively related to marital happiness. Couples are drawn together and their marriage is given meaning as a partnership by the wider interests and services which they care about.

The Role of Love

Not to discuss the role of love in holding a marriage together would be an oversight. We have tried to show first that there are other forces working to this same end: the forces of public approval, the meeting of basic needs of affection and security, habits of living together, interests and intimate jokes in common, experiences in working toward a common goal, interdependence because of duties performed, and inertia to change, all of which have a part in maintaining the integrity of a marriage. It is difficult to know exactly what role love plays in the whole picture.

We are sure of one thing, that the romantic dogma has been a major source of premature break-ups through its brittle philosophy, "if you really loved me you wouldn't do this." Not helpful to marriage solidarity are the following romantic notions: that a marriage will ride through on love alone, that it doesn't take working at, and that true love always runs smoothly. Every marriage faces bumps and jolts —

to pretend otherwise is fantastic. The all too frequent example of the woman who runs out on a marriage before it really gets started just because her husband acts like a human being instead of a Prince Charming derives support from the romantic love philosophy. Marriages based mainly on romantic love are precariously set up, because they weaken as the emotion itself changes.

Conjugal love is quite another emotion. It grows as the marriage progresses, thrives on companionship, common experiences, and the number of happy episodes which are scattered through a rich marriage. Conjugal love builds on the familiar, the mementos, the souvenirs, and waxes stronger with each additional year of marriage. Unlike romantic love, conjugal love is impossible for newly acquainted young people, since it requires time to form and grows from continuous association. Romantic love is greatest where each party knows least about the other — you see, reality gets in the way of romance. This is the love that is blind.

As conjugal love comes to the fore in marriage the relationship is strengthened. Few marriages in America persist over any length of time without developing conjugal love sentiments, because they are based on companionship and common interests which intertwine the experiences of established marriages. In contrast, romantic love gradually disappears in the companionable marriage except for the lip service paid it in the exaggerated moments of bliss which occasionally occur throughout married life. Romantic love as a solidifying factor in marriage gives way to conjugal love, which is more mature and more compatible with the companionable features of contemporary marriages.

The Two Shall Be One

Married love, which we have called conjugal love, finds expression in many day-by-day experiences. None of these is more effective as a unifying force than regular, satisfying sex intercourse. The regular release of tension in coitus is extremely satisfying in the purely physical sense, and in addition it serves as an expression of fulfillment for the entire relationship.

Fred and Mabel are examples of happily married people. Fred comes home from a busy day at the plant full of the doings of his day. He tells Mabel about how grouchy the boss is, how green his new assist-

ant is, how much progress he is making on his new machine, what he
had for lunch, and what a funny duck he got to talking to on the way
home on the bus. This conversation takes up most of the dinner hour;
it leaves Fred relaxed at having spilled his day's experiences and gives
Mabel the feeling that she has been a part of Fred's day.

Mabel too has things to relate. She wants to share excerpts of the
letter she has just received from her folks. She is eager to discuss with
Fred what they will do with her mother when her father goes (this last
letter tells of another heart attack, and both Fred and Mabel know that
some day soon there will be one too many of them). Although they
don't reach a final decision, Mabel senses that Fred is back of her, whatever happens, and she feels a sudden burst of affection for her good old
dependable Fred right there while they are finishing dessert. She gets
confidence to confess that she has been running over her budget for the
month, which they talk over with some heat. They end up with an
understanding of the financial situation, and the atmosphere is cleared,
leaving them both relieved.

After supper they do the dishes together. Fred drops and breaks
the jelly dish. Mabel starts to fuss and then admits that she hated the
thing anyway. They got it last Christmas from Aunt Harriet, whom
she always has disliked. Fred grins and says he can't stand her either,
as he kisses the back of Mabel's neck. She leans against him for a moment and observes that this is one thing she likes about him: they both
dislike the same people.

Aunt Harriet gets a going over by both of them as they move into the
living room and turn on the radio. Their favorite mystery couple comes
on for a half hour, leaving them feeling as if they too had been out on
an adventure. Fred puts on some records that they both enjoy and
goes over his paper once more, and Mabel sews in front of the fire.
The clock strikes ten as the symphony hour comes on. They are both
tired but agree to stay up until the program is over. Mabel puts up her
sewing and stretches out on the sofa. Fred drops his paper and comes
over to sit beside her. As a favorite passage of music flows into the
room, Fred squeezes Mabel's hand and smiles into her eyes.

By bedtime there has developed a strong sense of belonging to each
other, a feeling of true unity. Sex intercourse then becomes not just a
physical release, but a symbol of the whole relationship. Into it flow
the meanings and the feeling tones of the broken jelly dish and the mu-

sic and Fred's boss and Mabel's mother and all the security that has come from working it all through together.

Next morning Fred gets up feeling like a million, and leaves for work with the conviction that it would take a dozen bosses to get him down today. Mabel goes out to shop with a tune on her lips, and in her mind a resolution to economize. Both face the new day with more poise, more peace, more strength and courage, because the two are one.

The accompanying diagram shows roughly what the sex relationship has meant to Fred and Mabel in symbolizing their sense of unity.

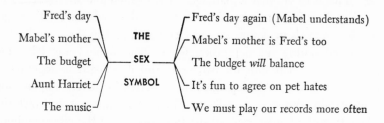

Making Marriage Fun

When the peace of the household has been broken and the offending party finds himself in the doghouse, he may utilize any number of devices to restore the *status quo*, one of the most effective being the use of humor. There is something funny about almost every marital crisis if the participants don't take themselves too seriously. A mate with a funnybone is an asset to any partnership and has saved many a marriage from cracking up.

Conciliatory devices become extremely handy to "save face" in a tense situation and are most often learned in the parental family in the process of growing up. In our culture we have developed a repertoire of techniques which most of us recognize when they are used on us, but which enable us to save face and make up if we really want to. These devices are no cure for fundamental alienation, but they tide over many a marriage in the early stages of conflict to the point where a workable balance is attainable. Every couple should be familiar with these techniques and should learn to use them to advantage. They are: 1. humor twists, such as punning, kidding, infantilisms; 2. storytelling; 3. compliments and flattery; 4. tension-dispelling devices, such as walking, swearing, crying; 5. appeals to the past history of the relationship;

6. displacing hostility onto a pet peeve common to both; 7. apologies, resolutions to improve, statements of plans for the future, etc.

Weathering the Storms

No marriage can be called a strong marriage at the outset. It is untried, untested; only after experiences with normal conflict and only after meeting such crises as war separations, depressions, unemployment, or serious illness can we be assured of the fundamental solidarity of a marriage. This is to say that a marriage is both tested and strengthened by the crises it has overcome. We have heard people say, "If we get through this crisis we know we can face anything together," and, "We got married during the depression when there weren't any jobs, and we lived on $50 a month for two years and it brought us together as nothing else could. We depended on ourselves for moral support, and our recreation consisted of walks to all the free museums and factories in the city and attendance at all the free concerts of the city symphony orchestra. We shall never be afraid of facing impoverishment, because we know from experience we can take it!"

Some of the forces we usually think of as making for break-ups also make for solidarity. It is a source of security to a married couple to have been through enough conflicts to learn how to handle them. The pair need no longer be afraid if tensions build up to a high pitch; a blow-up might clear the air. A good fight defines the issues, and leaves the combatants knowing that they are still loved and can get away with airing their differences. Over a period of time grievances accumulate and tension arises. There is a quarrel, and the grievances are expressed. Both persons experience a purging of their souls, and then settle back into the accustomed level of routine interaction. Crises, conflict, and illnesses, mastered and assimilated, act as forces to hold marriage together.

Why People Stay Married

Much has been written about marital conflict but relatively little about marital solidarity. The happily married pair have until recently kept their secrets locked up — only the alienated and the divorced have spilled for research workers. As far as we have gone in our discussion of marital solidarity, we are on firm ground, however. We have drawn largely from materials on well-adjusted families obtained from shrewd observers of family life and from the files of marital guidance clinics, which deal with both marital failures and marital successes.

What are the factors which hold marriages together in America today?

1 Couples begin marriage with the expectation of success, and this ideal of solidarity holds them together.

2 Much of social life is organized around married pairs — there is no satisfactory provision for the single person, unmarried, widowed, or divorced.

3 Couples find uniquely supplied in the marriage relationship the satisfaction of many basic adult needs: the desire for affection, companionship, security, recognition, response, and understanding.

4 Common interests, family jokes, and common experiences hold marriage together.

5 Marriage becomes a habit which is painful to break; the interdependence which develops because of duties performed solidifies marriage.

6 In the struggle for a common goal a new feeling of unity arises, a sense of having fought and bled together.

7 Conjugal love is a tying factor which grows as marriage progresses, thrives on companionship, common experiences, and the memory of things familiar.

8 The meeting of sexual needs comes to symbolize for the couple the sense of growing unity in the marriage relationship.

9 The use of tension-dispelling devices tides over many marriages in the early stages of conflict to the point where a workable balance is attainable.

10 Crises such as war separations, impoverishment, and serious illnesses test and may strengthen the untried marriage.

Readings

BEASLEY, CHRISTINE, Democracy in the Home (New York: Association Press, 1954). Questions like, "Is marriage a 50–50 proposition?" and "Who wears the pants in the family?" are discussed in this helpful and challenging book.

BLOOD, ROBERT O., JR., and DONALD M. WOLFE, Husbands and Wives (Glencoe, Illinois: The Free Press, 1960). Research report of how actual married couples work out their relationships in many areas of their lives as husbands and wives.

DUVALL, EVELYN MILLIS, In-Laws: Pro and Con (New York: Association Press, 1954). An exploratory study of in-law relationships with specific suggestions for working out harmonious relationships between the generations in the family.

ELLZEY, W. CLARK, *How to Keep Romance in Your Marriage* (New York: Association Press, 1954). A useful book that analyzes common misconceptions about romance that will last throughout life together.

LEVINE, LENA, M.D., *The Modern Book of Marriage* (New York: Bartholomew House, 1957). A practicing woman physician and marriage counselor compresses a wealth of experience and sympathetic advice into this practical guide to happiness in marriage.

MACE, DAVID R., *Marriage: The Art of Lasting Love* (Garden City, New York: Doubleday & Company, Inc., 1952). This book shows how marriage is a constantly changing adjustment between two people, and explains how you can take advantage of these changes and grow with them.

POPENOE, PAUL, *Marriage Is What You Make It* (New York: The Macmillan Company, 1950). This popular book written out of many years experience as a marriage counselor discusses some of the more effective ways of holding a marriage together with questions for checking your own competence and readiness throughout.

WOOD, LELAND FOSTER, *How Love Grows in Marriage* (New York: The Macmillan Company, 1950). A personal testimony of the progress and growth of love in marriage as it becomes more mature, more realistic and sturdier through the years.

PART

3

BECOMING A FAMILY

WHERE BABIES COME FROM

WHAT IT MEANS TO BE PARENTS

FAMILY LIFE AND RELIGIOUS LIVING

CHAPTER THIRTEEN

"Why didn't someone tell me?"

WHERE BABIES COME FROM

Will your children be just like you?

Just what happens during the period before birth?

Why can't some couples have babies?

How much does a baby owe to heredity?

*T*HERE ARE NO CHILDLESS FAMILIES, JUST CHILDLESS MARRIAGES, BE-cause it takes a baby to make a family out of a marriage. This chapter is devoted to the discussion of what it takes to bring a baby into the world, the process of embryonic growth from fertilized ovum to finished product. Each baby that is born has a history which starts long before its squeal is heard in the delivery room. To tell that story is our present assignment.

How Much Do You Know about Heredity?

In reviewing where babies come from we look first at the endowments each starts with, his inheritances. What do you know about heredity? Try yourself out on the following test by Dr. Amram Scheinfeld.[1] Mark each statement true or false. Check your answers with those of Dr. Scheinfeld, which follow immediately after the test. Give yourself ten points for each right answer. Then add up your score and see how you stand; 80 to 100 is excellent, 60 to 80 is good, 40 to 60 is average, 20 to 40 means that you will learn a lot from this chapter that you never knew before.

[1] Reprinted by special permission of the Curtis Publishing Company; see Amram Scheinfeld, "How Much Do You Know about Heredity?" *Ladies' Home Journal*, November, 1941, pp. 121–123.

_____ 1 A child's sex is determined by the father.

_____ 2 A son born to a man of seventy will be weaker than one he fathered at thirty.

_____ 3 A pregnant mother can in no way improve the future character of her child by keeping her thoughts pure, listening to good music, reading inspiring books, and so on.

_____ 4 The mother contributes more to her son's heredity than does the father.

_____ 5 Redheads are by nature more passionate than blondes.

_____ 6 In a blood transfusion, a mother's blood is safest for her child.

_____ 7 A Negro child may be born to an apparently white couple if one of them had a Negro ancestor.

_____ 8 Members of certain human races cannot reproduce if mated with members of a widely different race.

_____ 9 Women have just as much native intelligence as men.

_____ 10 There are no human "thoroughbred" families.

Here are the facts:

1 (*True.*) The human male produces two kinds of sperm which differ in a minute degree with respect to sex-determining properties. The egg produced by the mother is "neutral." Thus if one type of sperm (containing an "X" chromosome) fertilizes the egg, the result will be a girl; if the other type (containing a "Y" chromosome), a boy results.

2 (*False.*) Neither the age nor the condition of the father can change the nature of the chromosomes (hereditary factors) which he transmits to a child.

3 (*True.*) Any hereditary factors bearing on the child's character are in it the moment it is conceived. Not until after it is born can the mother influence the child's character for the better.

4 (*True.*) While their contributions to a child's heredity are in all other respects equal, the sex chromosome ("X") contributed by mother to son contains many additional "genes" not present in the sex chromosome ("Y") from the father. Thus, certain defects — such as hemophilia — are passed on to sons only by their mothers, because the genes for them occur only in the sex chromosome they get from her.

5 (*False.*) The hereditary factors producing hair coloring (and eye coloring as well) are not linked with those making for any specific type of personality. Any kind of coloring may go with any kind of temperament.

6 (*False.*) A mother's blood may often be as different from her child's and as dangerous to transfuse as that of some total stranger. Blood types are inherited through a combination of factors from both parents, and it is just as possible for a child and parent to have different blood types as to have different-colored eyes.

7 (*False.*) Only if both parents have Negro blood, and in a considerable degree, can a Negro baby appear. Stories to the contrary are either myths or cases of doubtful paternity.

8 (*False*.) All human beings belong to the same species, Homo sapiens, and are fertile with one another.

9 (*True*.) All intelligence tests now indicate that women have as much mental capacity as men, but that any intellectual inferiority on their part is due to less opportunity to develop themselves.

10 (*True*.) To produce human thoroughbreds, as in domestic animals, would have required the closest inbreeding between mothers and sons, fathers and daughters, brothers and sisters. As matters stand, all humans, even members of royalty, are biologically mongrels.

No One Else Just Like You! You are somebody very special. There never has been anyone like you. There isn't one chance in 300,000,000,-000,000 of there ever being another person just like you! Yet you were not a haphazard accident that could happen only once in the history of mankind. You were rather the result of a complete new deal of human characteristics. Every one of your children, and your grandchildren, and their children will be quite as unique — yet they will be your progeny and draw from the same general pool of inheritance that produced you. With Nature emphasizing uniqueness so strongly, how does she do it? What is the process by which you became you in the first place?

The fact that your father chose your mother (or the other way around) brought together two streams of heredity that had been branching out in similar twosomes since the beginning of time. And then out of the hundreds of human ova produced by your mother and the hundreds of millions of sperm available from your father, the fusion of the particular egg with the particular sperm that started you off was something that never could happen twice the same way.

You began with the union of one of your mother's human eggs which, though no bigger than a fraction of a dot on this paper, carried the full deal of her side of the family to you, and the microscopic sperm which brought you everything that had been dealt out for you from your father's side of the house. The microscopic miracle that carried all your characteristics and inherent tendencies in this union of two germ cells was an elaborate and highly exact arrangement of ultra-minute packets of hereditary determiners called *genes*. For each characteristic that was inherited there was a pair of genes (one from father, one from mother). The color of your eyes, the shape of your nose, the set-up of your body, the length of your fingers, the tendency to freckle or not, to sing on key or not, and to have twins or not, these and all of your other characteristics were to be found in potential form in the genes somewhere in the fertilized ovum which, in time, was to be you.

These genes are strung like beads on a string, each one exactly matching in position the parallel gene of every other germ cell, and separated at convenient lengths in tiny bodies called *chromosomes*. Military drill has nothing on chromosome formation. There are always the same number when they line up for review, each one in its place.

Deep in your reproductive organs is a cluster of cells that exist for the sole purpose of transmitting your particular line-up of genes and chromosomes to your children. These *germ cells* (produced in the ovaries of the girl and in the testes of the boy) coast along through childhood without much activity. At adolescence the ovaries and testes begin their business of turning out at regular intervals the germ cells that have the capacity of making a parent of you — an ovum every month in the girl, hundreds of millions of sperm every few days in the boy. Whether you marry or not, these germ cells are produced with a faithful regularity throughout your active adulthood. In germ cell production, instead of each chromosome splitting to form 48 new ones for each cell, each *pair of chromosomes* separates and one goes into each new cell, so that the final germ cell has just half of the original twenty-four pairs, twenty-four singles. Twenty-four singles from the mother plus twenty-four singles from the father equal twenty-four new pairs when they unite to form the beginnings of a new baby. Twenty-four pairs of chromosomes, each with its own gene determiners, now struggle for dominance. Some characteristics cover up others, in the same way that darker colors cover lighter ones on a canvas. A gene for dark hair, for instance, finding itself paired off with a gene for blond locks, has the right of way and wins the race for expression in the new individual. This tendency for some genes to win over others in the expression of characteristics is called *dominance* and works according to the well-known laws of heredity. The characteristic that is there but doesn't show in the new individual is said to be *recessive* (blond hair coloring in the illustration above is recessive . . . it doesn't show in this person, but paired off with another blond gene in the next generation might result in a true goldilocks). A monk by the name of Mendel, studying many generations of flowers in his garden during the last

This is what makes all the differences there are
between a woman and a man:

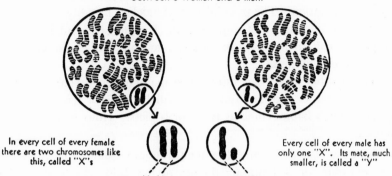

In every cell of every female
there are two chromosomes like
this, called "X"s

Every cell of every male has
only one "X". Its mate, much
smaller, is called a "Y"

X X   X Y

For reproduction, a female forms eggs, a male sperms,
to each of which they contribute only HALF their quota
of chromosomes, or just one from every pair

Since a female has TWO "X"s, each egg gets one
"X", so in this respect every egg is the same:

But as the male has only ONE "X", paired with
a "Y", he forms TWO kinds of sperms:

X

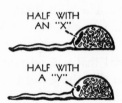

HALF WITH
AN "X"

HALF WITH
A "Y"

Thus: If an "X"-bearing sperm enters the egg,
the result is an individual with TWO "X"s

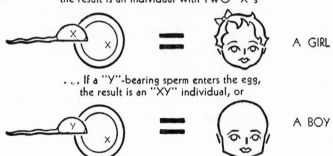

A GIRL

. . If a "Y"-bearing sperm enters the egg,
the result is an "XY" individual, or

A BOY

From Amram Scheinfeld, *You and Heredity* (Lippincott)

FIG. 1 How Sex Is Determined

century, discovered this tendency of some genes to cover the expression of others, and worked out the mathematical expectancy in each succeeding generation. The principles of Mendelian heredity are found to work in the inheritance of some human characteristics, but it is not as simple as that, so not even experts can reliably predict the characteristics of their children.[2]

Certain other aspects of inheritance may challenge you: What determines whether the new individual will be male or female? What happens when babies come as twins or triplets? How is skin color inherited?

Sex Determination. Careful perusal of Figure 1 shows that the father is responsible for determining the sex of his child. There are apparently two kinds of spermatozoa, and the sex of the child is determined by the type which enters the Fallopian tubes first and fertilizes the egg. There are hundreds of millions of sperm in each ejaculation of semen and it is pretty much a matter of chance which type of sperm reaches the egg first. Since a few more boys than girls are conceived, there would seem to be a slight advantage in favor of the male-determining sperm. The normal ratio of 105 boy babies to 100 girls at birth in the U.S.A. varies slightly with race and age of mothers,[3] but no one has been able to explain satisfactorily just why. Nor has any method emerged that will reliably select which type of sperm will fertilize the egg, so that the sex of the child-to-be remains a mystery until the baby is born.

Twinning. Twinning seems to run in families, and there has been a great deal of speculation on just how the tendency is inherited. No definitely reliable findings are available that will guarantee the production of twins — nor give insurance against their arrival in any given union! Like almost all of the other products of gene shuffling there is a new deal for each new child, and prediction of twins is difficult.

Figure 2 points to the following generalizations concerning twins: 1. there are two kinds of twins, identical and fraternal; 2. identical twins come from the *same* fertilized egg; 3. identical twins are always of the same sex and share the same heredity; 4. fraternal twins come

[2] Amram Scheinfeld, *The New You and Heredity* (Philadelphia: Lippincott, 1950).

[3] C. A. McMahan, "An Empirical Test of Three Hypotheses concerning the Human Sex Ratio at Birth in the United States, 1915–1948," *Milbank Memorial Fund Quarterly* (July, 1951), pp. 273–93.

IDENTICAL TWINS
Are products of

A single
sperm

and

A single
egg

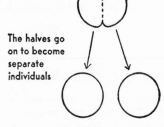

In an early stage
the embryo divides

The halves go
on to become
separate
individuals

Usually — but not always — identical
twins share the same placenta and
fetal sac

But regardless of how they develop,
they carry the same genes and are
therefore

Always of the same sex — two boys
or two girls

FRATERNAL TWINS
Are products of TWO different eggs fertilized by TWO different sperms

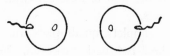

They have different genes and may
develop in different ways, usually—
but not always — having separate
placentas and separate fetal sacs

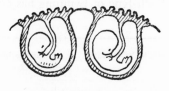

Also, as they are totally different in•
dividuals, they may be

Both
of the
same sex

Two boys

—or two girls

—Or a
mixed
pair

One
boy

One
girl

From Amram Scheinfeld, *You and Heredity* (Lippincott)

FIG. 2   How Twins Are Produced

from *two* different fertilized eggs, that is, two eggs and two sperm; 5. fraternal twins have no more in common in their heredity than other brothers and sisters, except that they have shared the mother's uterus; and 6. fraternal twins may be of the same sex or of different sexes.

Triplets, quadruplets, and quintuplets are formed by extensions of these two basic processes. For instance, triplets may be all fraternal (three fertilized ova), or all identical (one fertilized ovum with two divisions and separations), or partially identical and partially fraternal (one pair of identical twins and a fraternal third individual conceived and delivered together). The famous Dionne quintuplets are apparently identical. Often it is difficult without scientific assistance to tell which type of twinning has occurred.

CHECK YOURSELF   Fill in the blanks from your reading of twinning and your study of Figure 2.

1 The Joneses have just had twins, a boy and a girl. These twins must be _____.
2 Two boys, one blond and blue-eyed, the other dark and brown-eyed, were born of the same mother at the same time. They are probably _____ twins.
3 Two girls just exactly alike have been born of the same mother at the same time. They are not twins. Therefore they must be _____.
4 Twin girls marry twin boys. It is _____ that they will have twins.
5 Identical twins are always of the _____ sex.

★ **KEY**   1 Fraternal   2 Fraternal   3 Two of a set of triplets or more   4 Possible   5 Same

---

How Skin Color Is Inherited. The facts about skin color are not widely known. Especially is there public confusion about the inheritance of skin color in interracial unions. The materials presented in Figure 3 cover only two types of skin color genes, but there are probably more. Some of the facts on skin color inheritance implied from this chart are worthy of restatement: 1. two full-blooded Negroes could not have a white child; 2. two pure whites could not have a Negro baby; 3. two parents from mixed Negro-white stock *might have* a white child; 4. two parents from mixed Negro-white stock *could have* a dark-skinned child, even though they were relatively light-skinned themselves; 5. in respect to skin color, the mulatto is always of mixed

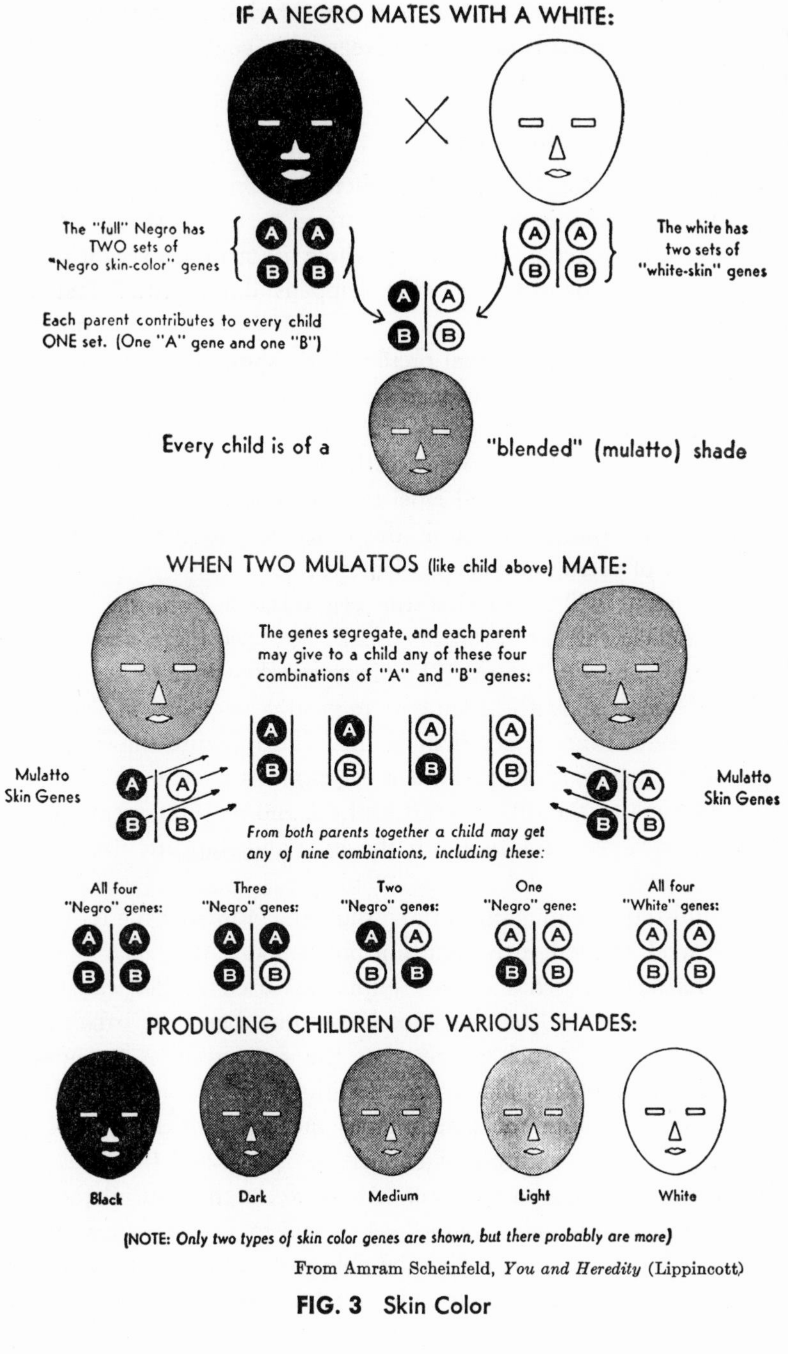

IF A NEGRO MATES WITH A WHITE:

The "full" Negro has TWO sets of "Negro skin-color" genes

The white has two sets of "white-skin" genes

Each parent contributes to every child ONE set. (One "A" gene and one "B")

Every child is of a "blended" (mulatto) shade

WHEN TWO MULATTOS (like child above) MATE:

The genes segregate, and each parent may give to a child any of these four combinations of "A" and "B" genes:

Mulatto Skin Genes

Mulatto Skin Genes

From both parents together a child may get any of nine combinations, including these:

All four "Negro" genes:	Three "Negro" genes:	Two "Negro" genes:	One "Negro" gene:	All four "White" genes:

PRODUCING CHILDREN OF VARIOUS SHADES:

Black   Dark   Medium   Light   White

(NOTE: Only two types of skin color genes are shown, but there probably are more)

From Amram Scheinfeld, *You and Heredity* (Lippincott)

FIG. 3 Skin Color

heredity, Negro and white; and 6. a true black-skinned child can occur only if *both* parents carry some Negro skin color genes.

The First Nine Months of Life

That period between the moment when the egg is fertilized and the
time when the baby is born is characterized by the most rapid growth
and the greatest differentiation of the whole life span, yet few of us have
the opportunity for studying what happens during these first nine
months of life.

The accompanying pictorial presentations show the development of
the baby from conception through birth.

Figure 4 shows a cross section of a uterus, a Fallopian tube, and an
ovary. To check his familiarity with the items shown in the chart, the
reader might try to locate and label the following: ovary, Graafian follicle (there are three or four in the ovary section), Fallopian tube,
uterus, body of uterus, and cervix of uterus.

The student will recall that the egg released from the ruptured
Graafian follicle enters the tube, is usually fertilized there, and journeys
down the tube into the uterus. The journey takes three to five days.

The elements shown in Figure 5 are greatly magnified in size. The
ovum is several times larger than in life. This picture shows thirteen
stages of development of one human egg from its place in the Graafian
follicle through to the tube, its fertilization, and its subsequent division
into many cells as it travels down the tube and implants itself in the
wall of the uterus.

The illustrations in figures 6 and 7 show the growth of the fetus from
the sixth week to the fourth month of pregnancy.

The fertilized egg has already implanted itself in the wall of the
uterus. The placenta has long since been formed and the baby's circulation established in such a way that the fetus receives its nourish-
ment from the mother's blood stream without coming into direct contact with it. The amniotic (membrane) sac has formed, in which the
baby floats in fluid (nature's own shock absorber), and the fetus itself
is now developing at a rapid pace. At six weeks the fetus already has
a definite shape, although it cannot yet be said to look very human! By
four weeks a careful student may be able to identify the arm and leg
buds, the spinal column which ends in a true-to-life tail, and the large

head with the beginnings of the eyes and mouth. By three and one half months (about fourteen weeks) the fetus is several inches long and is beginning to look like a real baby. Although it weighs only about two ounces, it is already complete with fingers and toes and a very shapely ear.

The two pictures in Figure 8 are arranged to show how the fetus is fed through the umbilical cord and the placenta in much the same way as a plant is nourished through its stem and root system. In the case of the fetus, the blood vessels of the mother and those of the baby lie close to each other within the placenta, and the exchange of food (from the mother's blood to the baby's) and waste (from the baby to the mother) takes place through the membranes of the blood vessels. The mother's blood does *not* enter the baby. Blood from the placenta is conveyed by blood vessels in the cord to the baby.

Figure 9 shows the baby in the uterus just before labor begins. The baby is full term and is ready to be born. Now it weighs seven and one half pounds, more or less, and is about twenty inches long. The baby is in the best position for birth with the head against the cervix. See if you can find the following landmarks of the mother's anatomy: the bladder (squeezed between the baby's head and the bone in front), the colon, the vagina, the pubic symphysis, the end of the mother's spinal column.

Figure 10 shows the cervix dilating (notice how much thinner it is than in Figure 9). The mother is now in labor. The *first stage of labor*, in which the cervix dilates enough to let the baby through, usually lasts about sixteen hours for a first baby (less for subsequent children) and is characterized by rhythmic pains that increase in intensity and frequency until the cervix is completely open. It is early in the first stage that the woman usually notifies her physician of labor pains. She will be ordered to the hospital when the interval between pains is from ten to fifteen minutes.

Figure 11 shows the cervix completely open. One thin portion of the cervix shows just at the baby's right ear lobe, the other high on the forehead. The mother is now in the *second stage of labor*, in which the pains come frequently and with great intensity. The pains now have a bearing-down quality as the uterine muscles attempt to expel the baby. This stage of labor lasts for an hour or two and is usually made endurable for the woman by anesthetic or analgesic.

In Figure 12 we see the baby's head already born and the doctor assisting in the birth of the shoulders. The uterine and abdominal muscles are contracting vigorously now. Note how the baby's shoulders turn to fit the size of the birth passage. Not all babies are born with head and shoulders first, although that is the most frequent position. The so-called breech presentation, buttocks first, is not an infrequent occurrence.

In Figure 13 we see the *third stage of labor*. The placenta is separating from the uterine wall and will soon be expelled along with the membranes and umbilical cord that is still attached to it. The other end of the cord has been tied and cut close to the baby's body. This expulsion of afterbirth and cord is the third stage of labor. It usually lasts only a few minutes and is felt by the mother as a series of pains similar to those which caused the birth of the baby. They bring about the final separation of the placenta from the uterine wall. The doctor examines the materials carefully to make sure that the placenta has been completely expelled after the birth of the baby, because of complications which might otherwise arise.

Abortions and Miscarriages

The emptying of the uterus before *full term* (nine months) is not uncommon, occurring in one out of every five pregnancies. The popular term *miscarriage* refers to the accidental or spontaneous emptying of the pregnant uterus, while an *abortion* is generally held to mean the act of artificially relieving the pregnant uterus of its contents. In medical language an abortion is the expulsion of the fetus and placenta for any cause between the time of conception and the twenty-eighth week of pregnancy. Between this period and full term, expulsion of the baby is called *premature labor*.

The cause of most miscarriages is unknown. Some may be due to defective germ plasm (bad eggs or sperms). Other causes are maternal diseases, such as chronic kidney disease or syphilis, and abnormalities, such as tumors of the uterus. Injuries and shock to the mother are not usually sufficient in themselves to precipitate a miscarriage.

Occasionally it is necessary for a physician to terminate a pregnancy to save a mother's life. This is called a *therapeutic abortion* and is done only under the most favorable conditions. It must be medically justified and officially authorized.[4] Unless carried out in a recognized hospital by a competent physician under the conditions just specified, interrupting a pregnancy by destroying the fetus is legally forbidden in most states, and known as *criminal abortion*. The dangers of *infection* and *hemorrhage* are great, since criminal abortions are usually performed under less than the best conditions by practitioners of questionable skill and training. Since there is no known medication which when taken by mouth will empty the uterus of its contents without grave danger to the woman, the abortionist must resort to surgical procedures. When these are performed without complete antiseptic safeguards they can be downright dangerous for the girl. If you or any of your friends are considering an abortion — stop! Talk it over with your family doctor. It's a privilege to have children, and there may be some other alternative that is much to be preferred.

The Rh Factor [5]

Since 1941, when it was first discovered, there have been hundreds of articles on the Rh factor in the blood. Many of these discuss the possible damage that may be done to the fetus in the mother whose Rh blood type is incompatible with that of the father.

Approximately 85 per cent of the white population of the United States have Rh positive blood. That is, they have blood containing one or more Rh factors. The other 15 per cent have Rh negative blood containing no Rh factor. Actually there are several varieties in the Rh family, but the above is roughly correct.

When both father and mother have the same Rh blood type there is no difficulty. Or if the mother is Rh positive, all goes well. But when an Rh positive man and an Rh negative woman have an Rh positive child, then *if* Rh positive blood cells from the fetal circulation escape into the mother's blood stream, they *may* stimulate the mother's blood to produce antibodies capable of destroying the Rh positive blood cells. The antibodies enter the fetal circulation and attack the baby's blood cells, producing *erythroblastosis*, or *hemolytic disease*. Some of the usual symptoms of this disease are jaundice, anemia, and general

[4] See Alan F. Guttmacher, *Babies by Choice or by Chance* (New York: Doubleday, 1959).

[5] From Evelyn Duvall, *Facts of Life and Love* (New York: Association Press 1956), pp. 77–79.

edema, or swelling, in the baby. Such babies may die as they near term, or soon after birth, or more often they will survive and be perfectly normal children.

Modern treatment of this disease has greatly increased the survival of babies that are afflicted. By 1955, only 10 per cent of the erythroblastotic babies were dying, in contrast to 30 per cent mortality as recently as in 1950, a remarkable record that should be reassuring to even the most anxious couple. One reason for this is that other conditions besides the Rh factor must be present in order for the disease to develop. For instance, this difficulty does not affect the first-born. It is after antibodies have been built up in the mother's blood by previous pregnancies that the baby may be affected. Secondly, there must be some leakage in the fetal and maternal circulations in the placenta in order for the red blood cells of the baby to reach the mother's blood stream. Usually the circulation of blood in the baby and in the mother is kept separate, each within its own blood vessels.

Pregnancy

Not every sex intercourse results in pregnancy. A couple may be married for some time before conditions are just right for conception to take place. Both sperm and egg must be right. The pathways that bring them together must be clear. And the timing of copulation must be such that the sperm reaches the egg while it is still in the tube (less than one full day's acceptance each month) in order for impregnation to take place.

Presumptive Signs. The woman may diagnose pregnancy herself by the appearance of a certain combination of symptoms. No symptom is conclusive by itself, but taken together they give her the basis for seeking definite confirmation in a medical examination.

The cessation of menstruation is usually the earliest and most important sign of pregnancy. When a healthy married woman who has been menstruating regularly suddenly misses a period, it is a good indication that pregnancy may have occurred. Occasionally a woman has one or two scanty menstrual periods after conception has taken place. More frequently, the menstrual period may be delayed by a variety of causes — change in climate, certain diseases, nervous tension, fear of or extreme desire for pregnancy.

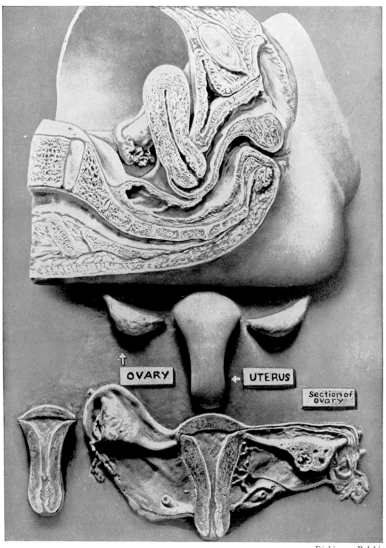

OVARY UTERUS Section of ovary

Dickinson-Belskie

FIG. 4 Cross Section of Uterus and Related Organs
Below: Before and After Pregnancy

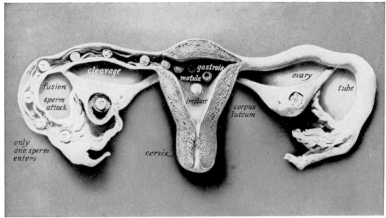

Dickinson-Belskie

FIG. 5 Travel of Egg: Ovulation to Nidation

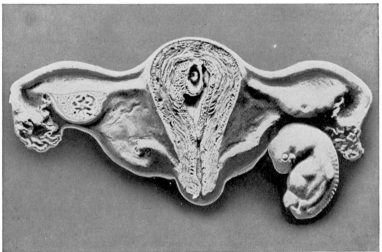

Dickinson-Belskie

FIG. 6 Fetus at Six Weeks

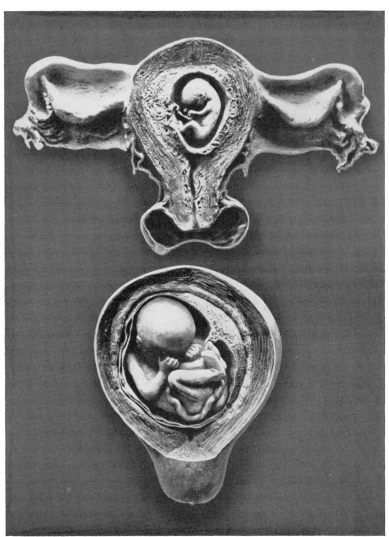

Dickinson-Belskie

FIG. 7 Fetus at 2½ Months and 3½ Months

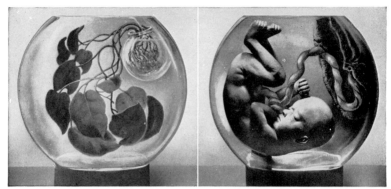

FIG. 8 Baby Grows Like the Plant

FIG. 9 Before Labor

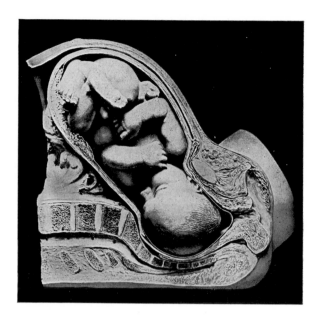

FIG. 10 Labor: Cervix Dilating and Bag of Waters

FIG. 11 Full Dilation, Cervix High, Head Deep in Pelvis

Photos by Dickinson-Belskie

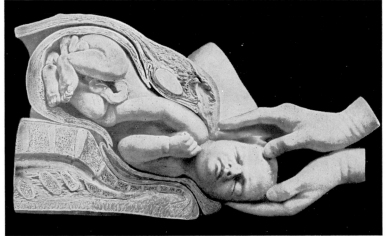

FIG. 12 Birth of Shoulders Rotation

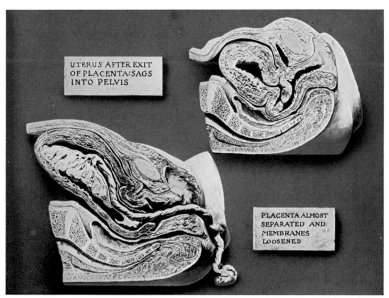

UTERUS AFTER EXIT
OF PLACENTA: SAGS
INTO PELVIS

PLACENTA ALMOST
SEPARATED AND
MEMBRANES
LOOSENED

FIG. 13 Third Stage of Labor

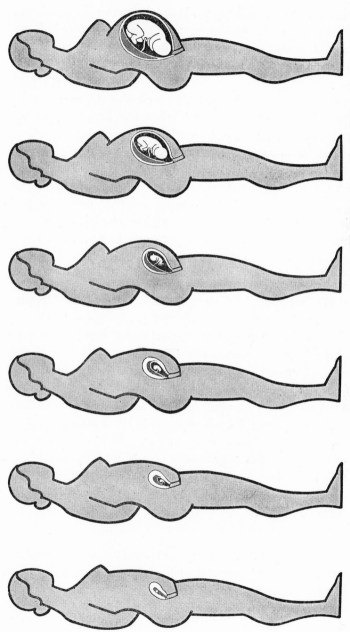

From *Life and Growth* by Alice V. Keliher (Appleton–Century)

PREGNANCY

Another symptom which appears in about two thirds of all women in early pregnancy is morning sickness. The pregnant woman will experience waves of nausea for a few hours in the morning, but even this symptom may be caused by other conditions and is only a presumptive sign of pregnancy.

A third symptom is a change in the breasts of the woman. Many women sense a fullness and tenderness of the breasts early in pregnancy, accompanied by a change in pigmentation of the nipple.

Frequency of urination is also an early presumptive sign of pregnancy. The tendency diminishes as the uterus rises in the pelvis and the bladder is no longer so closely associated with the enlarging uterus.

The married woman who experiences a missed menstrual period, who feels nauseated for a while in the morning, who is aware of changes in her breasts, and who feels the urge to urinate frequently may well presume that she is pregnant.

Pregnancy Tests. The woman may receive definite confirmation or denial of her condition from her physician, who will conduct certain tests before making a diagnosis. He will note changes in the uterus and changes in the coloring of the vaginal lining, and he may use one of several standard urine tests to establish the fact of pregnancy. These tests are based upon the changes in the hormonal excretions in the urine of the pregnant woman which affect noticeably the development of the sex apparatus or function in small animals, such as frogs, rats, mice, or rabbits. The great advantage of these tests is that they are remarkably reliable very early in pregnancy. They are well worth the extra cost if the wife needs to be sure of her condition early in pregnancy, e.g., if she is a professional woman under contract for twelve months. In most cases the urine tests are unnecessary for diagnosis; the experienced physician can usually detect pregnancy reliably by the other signs, but not as early, not before 8 weeks usually.

Positive Signs. As the pregnancy continues, many other confirming signs appear. Changes in the abdomen, the cervix, the vagina, and the uterus become apparent. By the middle of the pregnancy the fetal heart sounds may be heard. Fetal movements within the uterus may be felt from the fifth month on. X-ray pictures show the outlines of the fetal skeleton after the twentieth week and are positive proof of pregnancy.

When Will the Baby Come? As soon as the fact of pregnancy is established, the question inevitably arises as to just when the baby can be expected. Labor usually occurs about 280 days from the first day of the last menstruation. The rule in most frequent use is the following: determine the first day of the last menstruation, add seven days, and count ahead nine months. The date arrived at, however, is only approximate.

CHECK YOURSELF   Check every answer that is correct in the following list.

The first signs of pregnancy are:

_____ 1 Swelling of the abdomen   _____ 4 Bursting of the bag of waters
_____ 2 Lack of sexual desire   _____ 5 Changes in the breasts
_____ 3 A missed menstrual period   _____ 6 Movement of the baby in the womb

★ KEY   Only 3 and 5 are correct.

There may be a leeway of two weeks either way. As one obstetrician put it, "If I could know exactly when babies would arrive, I could take my vacations like a normal man, and I could catch up on my sleep. An obstetrician leads the life of a fire chief, constantly on call."

Maternal Care

Since maternal care became universal in America, having a baby is no longer the dangerous experience that it once was. The chief causes of maternal death are infection, hemorrhage, and toxemia, and can be avoided today by early diagnosis and regular supervision of the pregnancy and birth as well as of the post partum period. That is why there is such a striking decrease in maternal mortality associated with births in hospitals.

When Should Maternal Care Start? Ideally the couple should have gone to a physician for a thorough physical examination before marriage (remember the premarital conference described in Chapter Five). The physician would note at that time any remedial operation which might need to be performed before children should be conceived. If some time elapses between marriage and the time the couple is ready to conceive, another visit should be arranged with the physician. His go-ahead sign is based on a careful check-up paralleling the investigations which took place in the premarital examination. As soon as the woman suspects that she may be pregnant she should again put herself under the care of a reliable physician. After making a thorough physical examination from head to feet, he will take pelvic measurements to see if normal delivery or Caesarian section may be indicated by the position and size of the opening between the pelvic bones. Periodically through the pregnancy he will check the patient's blood, urine, rate of gain in weight, heart rate, and blood pressure. He will note the progress of the baby's growth even though his major concern is to keep track of the mother's health. These are factors which are all-important for the well-being of both the mother and the baby. Maternal care starts, then, before conception takes place and ends after the baby has been delivered and checked over, and the mother is back on her feet again.

You and Your Doctor

Selecting a doctor whose education, training, and experience will assure both mother and baby of the kind of care they need is not easy for the couple newly established in a strange town. Neighbors' recommendations over the back fence are not reliable. Far more adequate help may be secured by calling the best hospital in the community and getting its list of physicians who deliver babies. Cities that have family welfare agencies, maternal health societies, and medical societies will offer further sources of information. The couple unable to tap any of these local resources may write to the American Board of Obstetrics and Gynecology, 2105 Adelbert Road, Cleveland 6, Ohio, for a listing of doctors in or near their community that have been certified by that board. From such a list a choice may be made on the basis of convenience and personal preference.

Many smaller towns and most rural communities do not have obstetricians. A well-trained general practitioner can meet the obstetrical needs of most families successfully if he or she has the full cooperation of the couple. Pregnancy is a normal function requiring only regular supervision to keep the mother well.

The couple's confidence in the doctor is very important. If he performs his function well, he will need to know many intimate details of the couple's life together and will want to advise them about many of their daily habits, including eating, resting, recreation, vacations, sex relations, etc. The wife will need to trust her doctor implicitly so that she will eagerly follow his directions as her pregnancy progresses. It is helpful, however, to understand the reasons for the advice given by the physician. The husband must recognize that this relationship between his wife and the doctor does not exist to deprive him of his wife's full companionship, but to insure her health. Whenever possible, it is helpful for the husband to go with his wife on the first visit to the doctor, so that he may have a part in the general arrangements. At that time he may ask the doctor what the cost will be and agree on the payments to be made. The couple may want to ask about such things as:

1 The general condition of the wife and prognosis for the pregnancy.
2 The time when the baby may be expected.
3 Advice about diet, exercise, clothing, sex intercourse, bathing, rest, trips, etc.
4 Frequency of the wife's visits to the doctor during her pregnancy.
5 The hospital the physician takes his patients to, and how arrangements there are made.
6 Anesthetics that the doctor uses to relieve pain at birth.

One outstanding obstetrician gives his expectant mothers a little manual of directions in which he specifies the conditions under which he is to be called:

Notify Your Physician at Once in Case of:

1 Bleeding or brownish discharge from the vagina.
2 Cramps.
3 Excessive vomiting.
4 Severe pain in lower abdomen.
5 Headaches.
6 Disturbances of vision.
7 Swelling of feet and, particularly, of face and hands.
8 Scanty urine or bloody urine.
9 Persistent constipation.
10 Sore throat or cough.
11 Marked shortness of breath.
12 Chills and fever.
13 Sudden escape of fluid from vagina.
14 Anxieties, fears, and worries that persist.

Some of the general questions about the nature of pregnancy and childbirth may be discussed. The doctor will be glad to explain why a mother's experiences cannot affect her unborn child, why certain infrequent abnormalities and markings are unavoidable, why no one can accurately predict the sex of the child before its birth or determine its sex before conception, and why the mother's attitude and feelings are important for her health and well-being.

Does It Hurt to Have a Baby? Childbirth is usually painful. The pains which result from the contractions that open the cervix are sharp and increase in intensity and duration for several hours. The pains which mark the expulsive contractions of the uterus are intense, probably the most excruciating pain women ever experience. The knowledge that the pains are helping her bring forth her own baby helps the woman bear the suffering and to forget its agony soon after delivery. Although through the years ways of relieving the pain of childbirth have been sought, no completely satisfactory, safe, and universally applicable method has yet been found. Some of the newer methods such as caudal anesthesia, hypnosis, and even "natural childbirth" may hurt mother or child under certain conditions. The wise couple discusses the question with their doctor who makes the final decision.

Natural Childbirth. Childbirth is a normal, natural process. Some doctors [6] believe that much of the mother's labor pain is the result of muscular tension associated with fear. The expectant mother is trained for "natural childbirth" by instruction in what to expect (thus relieving unfounded anxieties), and by supervised exercise in the relaxation and control of pertinent muscle groups so that she may cooperate in the birth process more effectively.

Pregnancy Is a Family Affair

The man who said, "We are pregnant at our house," expressed the "we" feeling that is so important for both husband and wife during their period of expectancy. Pregnancy is a social condition quite as much as a biological state. It involves the adjustment of both the husband and the wife, their relatives, their children already born as well as

[6] Grantly Dick Read, *Children without Fear* (New York: Harper, 1944).

those yet to come. Yes, even more, pregnancy is of importance to the community and to the state. We find more and more laws introduced to assert the interest of the commonwealth in healthy, robust families.

Pregnancy and childbirth can be a strain on immature young folk, but the experience can be and usually is a happy adventure for emotionally and socially mature people. They show it in many ways. The husband who learns early how he may help will find that his role is not the anxious one portrayed in the cartoons of fathers nervously pacing waiting rooms. He may assume certain responsibilities of helping with the housework, plan recreational jaunts that are possible for his wife, make furniture for the new arrival, cooperate in maintaining the diet that the doctor has prescribed, and provide many other personal attentions that do much to ease the wife's burdens and to help him share more fully the experience.

More important than anything that the husband does is how he feels about the pregnancy and his expectant wife. If he is happy about it and proud of his wife, if he treats her as a real person and not as an invalid, he will be giving her the support she needs from him. The pregnant woman may become self-conscious about her figure and general awkwardness as the pregnancy continues and may need her husband's reassurance of his continuing love and admiration. Jealousies and oversensitiveness about her husband's activities outside the family are frequent and may be recognized as resulting from the restrictions imposed by her pregnancy. Even though his wife is not able to participate freely in the activities he enjoys, the mature man will show that he values her companionship. Her silhouette may not be what it once was, but their pride and pleasure in being "in a family way" compensate to both for some of the temporary cumbersomeness of the pregnancy.

Many couples openly enjoy their expectancy and take pleasure in thinking of themselves as parents-to-be. Men as well as women are eager to learn how babies are born and reared and cared for today. Classes for expectant parents are proving popular in many communities. Books on the subject of parenthood are read with new interest. Expectant parents are most receptive to teaching and find that study adds to their enjoyment of anticipation.

The husband who understands best his role during pregnancy is one who:

_____ 1 Completely ignores his wife.

_____ 2 Pokes fun at his wife's figure to make her laugh.

_____ 3 Plans with his wife for the coming child.

_____ 4 Is ashamed to take his wife out in public.

_____ 5 Reassures his wife that he doesn't mind. her changing silhouette and demonstrates his eagerness for the baby.

_____ 6 Treats his wife with solicitude as if she were ill.

_____ 7 Accepts pregnancy as a normal, natural function.

_____ 8 Impresses his wife with his lore of stories about mishaps and difficulties at birth.

_____ 9 Does what he can to make life pleasant and happy for both of them.

★ **KEY**   Correct: 3, 5, 7, 9

Having a Baby with Its Father Absent. It is sometimes necessary for the husband to be away from home during his wife's pregnancy. Unfortunate as this situation is, the mature couple can find much satisfaction in letters. Sharing the eagerness of anticipation, expressing the dreams of family reunion and the baby's future, choosing the baby's name, discussing detailed plans for the confinement and the care of the baby for the first few weeks until the mother is able to undertake its full care herself — all these bring a sense of partnership to the couple even though they are separated. The prospective mother can reassure her husband about her condition by relaying accounts of her trips to the doctor, telling him what the prognosis is, how she is spending her time, and how she looks forward to her husband's return and the baby's arrival so that they can all be a real family.

Infertility and Sterility

One out of every ten couples who want children are unable to have them. This inability to conceive is called *infertility*, which is treatable, or *sterility*, if the inability is permanent, and may be due to many causes. Sometimes the male sperms are not numerous enough or sufficiently active to reach and fertilize the egg. Rest, improved health, and medical treatment may correct the condition sufficiently for conception to take place. In the woman the cause may be 1) immature or infertile sex organs, 2) a tilted uterus, 3) obstructions of the cervix, 4) unfavorable vaginal secretions which affect the sperms' motility, 5) glandular deficiencies, or 6) closed tubes which make it impossible for the sperm and the egg to meet. *Infertility clinics* in our larger maternity hospitals are successfully treating many couples who desire their own children, with many responding favorably to treatment.

Test Tube Babies. Modern science is not yet able to grow babies in a test tube, but some advance has been made in helping couples who want babies to have them. Sometimes the treatment of the physician or of the infertility clinic is not enough to assure the couple of conception. When the man has insufficient or inadequate sperm, and remedial treatment does not correct his condition, the only way his wife may become pregnant is through impregnation with other sperm. The careful physician makes sure that the use of other sperm will be acceptable psychologically to both members of the couple, then selects a semen donor whose health and heredity are acceptable and compatible, and with a syringe deposits the semen donation in the upper end of the vagina, or directly into the uterus at the time of the month most favorable to conception. Legal tangles (the baby is not the husband's), religious, social, and psychological problems, and difficulties of matching donors to recipients without the knowledge of either keep artificial insemination from becoming widely accepted. It has promise, however, for the many couples who would otherwise be childless, and is mentioned in the recent literature as a possibility for some couples whose Rh blood types are incompatible and who have in previous pregnancies faced the frustration of miscarriage or fetal death.

Adopting Children

Not all marriages are blessed with children. Estimates indicate that roughly one marriage in ten is infertile for one reason or another. If the couple is truly ready for parenthood, emotionally mature enough to enjoy its privileges and responsibilities, and to accept the "chosen child" as their own, then adoption is a possibility.[7]

[7] Boss, Helen and Carl, *If You Adopt a Child* (New York: Holt, 1957).

Where to find a child available for adoption is a big question in many localities. It is not that there are not enough children needing homes. One child out of every eight in the United States is not living with both parents.[8] The number of babies born out of wedlock is increasing, as can be seen from the tabulation below, from the years 1940 through 1957. The second column lists the number of estimated illegitimate births each year in the United States. The third column indicates the illegitimacy rate — the number of illegitimate births per 1,000 unmarried females aged 15–44.[9]

YEAR	ESTIMATED NUMBER	RATE
1940	89,500	7.1
1945	117,400	10.0
1950	141,600	14.2
1957	201,700	20.9

Without proper controls all these babies form a potential black market in adoption. The "baby farm" offering babies for a price, or a "contribution" of several hundred to more than a thousand dollars, should be assiduously avoided. Such unscrupulous outfits rarely offer the vital records, birth certificates, and other controls that should come with adoption. The well-staffed state-licensed agency, public or private, places a child for adoption only after a thorough study has been made to safeguard the future of the child and the foster parents. Such an agency can be located through the state or local welfare department. *Adoption laws are built upon three important objectives.*[10]

1 To protect the child from unnecessary separation from parents who might give him a good home and loving care if sufficient help and guidance were available to them; from adoption by persons unfit to have responsibility for rearing a child; and from interference after he has been happily established in his adoptive home by his natural parents, who may have some legal claim because of defects in the adoptive procedure.

[8] Bureau of the Census, as quoted in Chart 13, *A Chart Book, op. cit.*
[9] From Clark E. Vincent, "Illegitimacy in the United States," Chapter 9 in Evelyn M. Duvall and Sylvanus M. Duvall, eds., *Sex Ways — in Fact and Faith* (New York: Association Press, 1961), pp. 139–151.
[10] Adapted from *Essentials of Adoption Law and Procedure*, Children's Bureau Publication Number 331 (Federal Security Agency, Washington, D.C., 1949), pp. 2, 3.

TOO MANY CHILDREN ARE ADOPTED WITHOUT ADEQUATE SAFEGUARDS!

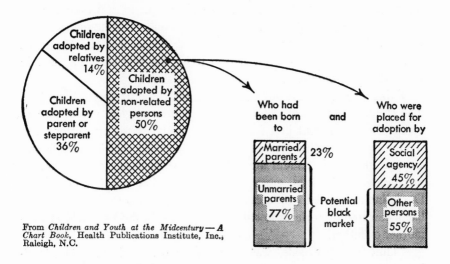

From *Children and Youth at the Midcentury — A Chart Book*, Health Publications Institute, Inc., Raleigh, N.C.

2 To protect the natural parents from hurried decisions to give up the child, made under strain and anxiety.

3 To protect the adopting parents from taking responsibility for children about whose heredity or capacity for physical and mental development they know nothing; and from later disturbance of their relationship to the child by natural parents whose legal rights had not been given full consideration.

Once the approved procedures for adoption have been followed, the parents may relax and bring up their chosen children as their own. Not all the answers in the heredity-environment controversy are in, but there is evidence that children tend to resemble their adoptive parents in many characteristics more closely than they do their biological parents. From what we know of personality development, we would expect this to be generally true. Surely one's "own baby" is not as carefully selected from the grab bag of genes as is the chosen baby at adoption! Parents mature enough to be ready to adopt a child take it as a privilege and a challenge, very much as emotionally mature parents have welcomed their babies from time immemorial.

Marrying a Ready-made Family

One way to become a parent is to marry one. In these days when re-marriage is common, it is not unusual for a man to find himself with not only a wife, but with a child or more as well, when he marries their mother. The stepmother so cruel and heartless in the fairy tale often turns out today to be a lovely person trying her best to win a place in the lives of the children of the man she married.

Being a stepparent is not easy. After all, the others were there first. The children may be expected to cling to their original parent and to accept the new parent in a full-fledged parental status only after he or she has proven worthy. Jealousy and sibling rivalry that in other homes are but irksome interludes are apt in the stepparent's eyes to be un-surmountable obstacles, green-eyed monsters that will not be tamed. Discipline ministered with a casual hand by the "real parent" may seem like a threatening form of hostility or rejection in the hand of the step-mother or father.

"Time is on your side" was never more true. Patience, understand-ing, and a willingness to wait and not force affection brings rewards of new family ties and renewed solidarity. Even teen-aged young people grow up and learn to love their stepparents; in fact that may be a good index of their growing maturity. As soon as parents and children seem ready, steps may be taken to adopt the stepchildren legally so that "your children" may be "our children" in the fullest, final sense.

Grandparents and the New Baby

Family solidarity at this time is often enhanced by the attention of the other relatives. Grandparents-to-be are especially interested in the new-comer. There is a sense of fulfillment in anticipating one's grand-children that even parenthood is said to miss. It is fortunate that the American trend toward excluding members of the extended family from the intimate father-mother-child constellation has been reversed with the increase in births under wartime conditions. Wisely managed, as-sorted grandparents are real assets to the new family. When help is hard to hire, a visiting grandmother who sees the new family through the birth and the confinement is a godsend. When new habits must be established around the new little family member, the going will be rough for the inexperienced parents. The perspective and the practical help of a grandmother who knows the way through the routine of bathing and feeding schedules is a real boon. When the new father and mother feel swamped with their new responsibilities, it is comforting to be able to lean for a bit on parents and to take advantage of their presence to slip out for an evening's fun as a couple once again.

THE WAY OUT [11]

If baby-sitters charge a lot,
  For services they render,
Call Grandma in to mind the tot,
  For she's the legal tender.

M. M. PARRISH

To be sure, grandparents do have limitations and should be used sparingly. Child training methods do change. But if grandma rocks the baby there are some child care specialists who will support her. The couple do want to feel that they are on their own and that they can manage their own family in their own way. But there are few in-law problems if the family members are well-adjusted persons. Modern grandmothers are as eager as their daughters and daughters-in-law to follow modern methods of child care. Together the two generations can greet the newcomer with a united front that promises well for his future.

Having babies is just about the most exciting and satisfying thing that can happen to a family. The more it is shared and enjoyed and enhanced by intelligent planning, the more satisfying it will become.

Readings

CARSON, RUTH, *Having a Baby* (New York: Public Affairs Committee, 1952). Prepared with the cooperation of the Maternity Center Association, this highly readable little pamphlet gives you accurate information on your role in having a baby.

CARSON, RUTH, *So You Want To Adopt a Baby* (New York: Public Affairs Committee, 1951). The adoption specialist of the Child Welfare League of America says that this pamphlet brings welcome answers to many of the questions that baffle couples who want to adopt a child.

GENNÉ, WILLIAM H., *Husbands and Pregnancy: A Handbook for Expectant Fathers* (New York: Association Press, 1956). A man-to-man look at

[11] From *The Saturday Evening Post*, April 28, 1951.

what to expect, what to do, what not to do, and what to understand to make pregnancy a happy family experience.

GUTTMACHER, ALAN F., M.D., *Pregnancy and Birth* (New York: Viking Press, 1957). A world famous obstetrician has written this detailed book for expectant parents, complete with an excellent index for ready reference on the question parents-to-be have on what it means to have a baby.

ROWLAND, LOYD W., *Pierre the Pelican Series* (Published by the Louisiana Association for Mental Health, 1528 Jackson Avenue, New Orleans 13, Louisiana). A series of letters to parents from the beginning of pregnancy to the child's sixth year, well written by outstanding authorities.

SCHEINFELD, AMRAM, *The New You and Heredity* (Philadelphia: J. B. Lippincott Company, 1950 edition). Popularly written book on human heredity in fascinating detail and with complete scientific accuracy, this may well become your basic reference in the field.

CHAPTER FOURTEEN

It's Fun to Be Parents

WHAT IT MEANS TO BE PARENTS

Do parents always have mixed feelings about their children?

What does a baby do to the husband and wife relationship?

Is adolescence always difficult?

Are there methods of discipline that really work?

Can parents be people too?

*E*VERY TIME A NEW BABY IS BORN THERE IS A BRAND NEW MOTHER and a brand new father. Each must learn his or her new role in the family. Each now has new privileges and new responsibilities. Previous relationships change as each member of the family adapts and adjusts to the newcomer. Even the family of many children realigns itself every time another baby enters the circle. This stretching of the family ties is satisfying and challenging. But it is strenuous too.

When the First Baby Comes

There are at least three stages in getting used to a new baby. The first is the flowers and pink ribbons stage. Mother is in her glory bedecked in her best bed jacket, with roses on her table and solicitous friends and family asking after her and the little newcomer. Father, who has felt like a fifth wheel during the long days of the pregnancy and the interminable hours of labor and birth, now comes into his own as exuberant herald to all the world of the miracle that has happened. He passes cigars to all the boys and showers this wonderful woman of his with tokens of his undying affection. Everybody is happy. The parents are thrilled. Life is wonderful — too wonderful to last.

Not long after mother and baby have returned from the hospital, the second stage of parent-child relations is apparent. The exuberance of the first flush of parenthood gives way under the weight of daily diapers, lusty cries at 2:00 A.M., and the cleaning woman who didn't come. The insistent demands of a hungry baby break into the tenderest moments of husband and wife. The mother's preoccupation with feedings and daily baths often seems to take precedence over diversions previously enjoyed by the couple. Let a friend suggest a movie or an evening out, and the chorus sounds from new mother and father alike, "What will we do with the baby?" Babies bring new responsibilities thick and fast, sometimes so fast that it takes quite a bit of readapting before things run smoothly around the little newcomer and his family.

Before very long the family has a helper or two. Aunt Molly is willing to come in and stay with the baby occasionally. Or a trustworthy baby-sitter has been found who allows the new mother and father an occasional evening out to themselves. The routines which at first seemed so exacting settle down into comfortable schedules. Baby gets used to its food and sleeps straight through the night without a whimper. Mother begins to feel more like herself now that she is around the house and doing her own work without getting too tired. It is fun wheeling baby to the store and back. Bath time has become a frolic for both mother and baby. Life is good again. The new family is really under way.

This characteristic cycle reappears in various forms again and again in the lifetime of the family. Enthusiasm and the sense of being in on a wonderful miracle of life occurs many times as parents take pride in their children. But the heavy weight of responsibility is constantly present; children *are* a responsibility. It takes many years to work through the ways and means of handling these obligations effectively and comfortably, but time is a great educator. And then comes the quiet satisfaction of being a family, the happy contentment so characteristic of parenthood.

Parents Are People

Parents are people first of all. Long before the arrival of their children, and long after the children have grown and gone, they will be people, persons in their own right. To hear some talk, one would think a mother and father were born and brought up as parents. Unfortunately, few gave much concern or time to the business of being parents before they found themselves with their own children to rear. No preparatory training period was required before children were allowed to come into the home. No license was necessary before practicing parenthood. Only the barest of biological essentials and social sanction were required.

Parents represent the last stand of the amateur. Every other trade and profession has developed standards, has required study and practice and licensing before releasing the student into his work. Before a girl can wave hair or tint nails she must have gone to school a specified number of hours, she must have apprenticed successfully under a qualified operator and she must have passed a state examination and become duly licensed. Nursing, social work, teaching, law, medicine, welding, mechanics, plumbers and plumber's helpers all must come up to standards appropriate to their successful performance. Only one profession remains untutored and untrained — the bearing and rearing of our children.[1]

There was a time when families were large. Then little girls learned how to take care of babies by helping care for younger brothers and sisters under the watchful eye of mother or big sister. There was a time when family ways were stable. Then girls learned to bake bread and make candles and churn butter and discipline children by watching and helping their mothers do these things, which they in turn would be expected to do when they grew up. Likewise, boys followed their fathers around the barn and shop and learned through years of apprenticing to play the roles they were to play later in their own homes. Now each generation finds itself in situations so strange that the learnings of childhood only partially carry over into adult usefulness. Families now spend more and more of their time in complex business transactions and community activities which remain mysteries to the children. Only the most fundamental tasks remain in the home — washing dishes, laundering, cooking, and bedmaking.

Parents have learned to be parents by being parents! Step by step as the children grow up the parents develop too; skills for handling situations are perfected; what to expect becomes clearer. By the time the

[1] For an uptodate review of parent education see Orville G. Brim, Jr., *Education for Child Rearing* (New York: Russell Sage Foundation, 1959).

children are grown, most parents have some pretty good ideas about what they would do differently if they could start all over again. But by that time their children are out starting in all over again, for themselves.

Parents start with their own particular concepts of what they may expect of a child. These ideas are gleaned from the expectations of the people with whom they have grown up. Although there are some common denominators, true for all levels of society, as to what constitutes a good child, most parents follow the demands and expectations of their particular set in their judgment of what must be expected of children. Recent studies at the University of Chicago indicate that there are significant differences between racial groupings, and particularly between the various socio-economic classes, in what is expected of children.[2]

These specific judgments of what a child should and should not do are gathered from neighbors and friends who exert pressure upon parents to exact behavior of one kind or another from their children. "What will the neighbors say if I let him . . . ?" is a powerful factor in the disciplining of many a child. These social pressures tend to strengthen and to modify the earlier learning of childhood as to what is appropriate and inappropriate behavior.

Parents tend to reproduce or to repudiate their own childhood training in the bringing up of children. It is a frequent experience for a parent to find himself involved in a situation almost identical with one he experienced as a child. He suddenly finds himself acting out the role his parent played. It may not be a pleasant role; it may not even be a comfortable one for him; but somehow, it suddenly appears full-blown in an actual situation.

Consider the case of Mrs. C. She is a modern mother, trying to bring up her child in a progressive manner. But one day in a burst of anger at her son's use of a vile phrase she found herself washing out his mouth with soap in exactly the way her mother had done when she had used unseemly language. Mrs. C. didn't believe in such harsh discipline. The methods which she was consciously putting into practice were more studied and less impulsive. But in the heat of the actual

2 W. Allison Davis and Robert Havighurst, *Father of the Man* (Boston: Houghton Mifflin, 1947); W. Lloyd Warner, Robert Havighurst, and Martin Loeb, *Who Shall Be Educated?* (New York: Harper, 1944); and Evelyn Millis Duvall, "Conceptions of Parenthood," *American Journal of Sociology* (November, 1946), pp. 193–203. See Chap. I, p. 6.

situation she reverted to what her mother had found effective. She was so identified with her own mother that in a crisis she reproduced her mother's method of discipline even though it was not her own!

At other times parents find themselves just as vigorously repudiating the patterns of their own parents. There is John Q., for instance. His father was a harsh man, quick to use the strap or hairbrush where it would do the most good, if any of his children disobeyed or defied him. John grew up vowing that he would never lay a hand on one of his own children. No matter what they do to provoke him, he insists on reasoning it out with them. Never once in his life has he raised his voice or his hand to his children. Because his father was harsh, he cannot be. Insightful parents learn to spot these compulsive responses and to understand their causes.

Parents Who Live through Their Children. Mothers and fathers who live vicariously through their children are doomed to disappointment. No one can live the life of another, not even of one's own child. But because of frustrations in their own youth, parents often insist on trying to find satisfaction through their children. Alice T. always wanted to

"You're so disobedient, stubborn, contrary . . . Mother's proud of you."

take violin lessons when she was a little girl. Her parents refused to allow this extra extravagance until she had mastered the piano. That day never arrived for her. Now she stands over her seven-year-old son insisting that he practice on his violin. He unfortunately doesn't share her enthusiasm for violin playing and is rebelling with all the fury of an active seven-year-old. So the mother is disappointed and despairing, while the son learns how to resist her efforts to live his life. Many parents are so eager that their children should enjoy all the satisfactions which they have been denied that they try to live through the child rather than with him.

Parents Who Grow Up with Their Children. The secret of successful parenthood seems to lie in the ability of the parents to keep on growing. Parents who continue to find joy in learning show by their enthusiasm and interest that learning is fun. By being the kind of people who live eagerly, they show their youngsters how worth while it all is.

Mary Ellen, like Alice T., always wanted to play the violin. She didn't get a chance until after she was married and had reared her three children past the diaper stage. Then she hunted up a first-rate teacher and began her musical education. She took her practicing seriously and was faithful in her lessons; she shared her little triumphs and failures with the family; she nodded understandingly when the children ran into snags with their lessons, for she knew what it was to unravel tangles. The children admired their mother's growing skill and co-operated actively in getting ready for the friends that she sometimes had in to play with her. When these little affairs grew into an informal chamber music group, the two older children begged to be admitted with their instruments. Today the whole family enjoys music together. Practicing is not a matter of parent-child tension but an accepted part of the whole pattern of family life.

Of course not every family finds its satisfaction in music. It may be books in some homes; or scientific explorations in others; or shop work and household decoration in another. But whatever the parents find absorbing, these things the children will find interesting. Yes, more than that, parents who continue to cultivate their interests are appreciated and enjoyed by their children as real people.

A father of five children put it neatly when he said, "It's more important that children admire their parents than it is for parents to admire their children." When parents continue to grow and to find life challenging, the children are led rather than driven into the good things of life. Discipline is relatively simple, because the parents are getting their own satisfactions for themselves, and because they are freer to understand and to deal with the children's problems as they arise. The development of the individuality of the child is assured when each member of the family is encouraged to develop his own interests at his own pace, without the stifling burden of having to satisfy the needs of another by the excellence of his performance.

How Parents Affect Children

Children are not chips off the old block. They are developing human beings with needs to satisfy and tasks to accomplish. Because parents are the people the child first knows and loves, because they are so all-powerful in satisfying his early hungers and funneling through to him the things he needs, the impressions they leave are lifelong. Just how this influence works in the life of any individual is seen only by careful study of his own particular life history. But certain aspects of parent-child interaction are so general that it may be helpful to consider them here.

Meeting Basic Needs. Present-day knowledge of the basic needs of children comes out of a rich background of years of insightful experience in learning how children grow and in learning what affects, for better and for worse, their development through the years. These findings have come relatively late in man's history. Many generations ago people generally knew that a horse which had been mistreated would probably be vicious. Centuries ago common people knew that living things required certain basic essentials of food, light, air, and favorable atmospheric conditions. When these elements necessary for growth were provided in proper amounts and at the times when they were needed, the organism, be it cow, corn, or human being, grew strong and sturdy, and thrived. When these essentials were lacking or delayed, the plant withered and died, the animal wasted away and became progressively unhappy, disagreeable, and listless. But it took the twentieth century to bring the scientific investigations and points of view which allow us to see children as dynamically growing, living organisms affected by understandable laws of growth which must be obeyed if life is to develop at its best.

These new findings have competed successfully with many theories and platitudes about child nature that have been handed down from generation to generation by people trying to make sense out of human conduct and development. The earlier efforts to understand youngsters were well-meaning but not well founded and have had to be repudiated or reformed in the light of more valid insights. Such time-honored sayings as the following are being revised:

- Spare the rod and spoil the child.
- Like father, like son.
- Chip off the old block.
- Children should be seen and not heard.
- Mother is always right.
- Cleanliness is next to godliness.
- A child is but a miniature adult . . . "little men," "little women."
- Just like his uncle Jim.
- A bad boy through and through.
- Treat a boy soft and you'll make a sissy out of him.
- You can't teach an old dog new tricks.
- Give a child an inch and he'll take an ell.
- Kill him with kindness.
- She's the spit an' image of her mother.
- Grandmothers always spoil children by being too good to them.
- If you are nice to a child, he'll take advantage of you.
- The school of hard knocks is the best teacher.
- Born under a lucky star.

Some of these principles are so unsound that their influence is seriously harmful. Many of these statements are just not true and clutter our thinking with fallacies that must soon give way to more valid findings. Some are but partially true, needing considerably more qualification and modification than is implied. They all need to be examined carefully and revised or rejected in terms of the more valid findings shown in the table on pp. 302–303. Most of us are in the stage of clearing up our thinking about ourselves and getting the basis for understanding our children that will help us supply their needs. Examination of this table shows the specific ways in which these human needs for security, love, response, and achievement may be met.

Discipline Makes a Difference. Discipline which promotes the development of the child has six characteristics: 1. it is firm, reliable, and kind; 2. it shows the child what others expect of him; 3. it encourages the child and promotes a feeling of faith in himself; 4. it strengthens the child's skills for better future performance; 5. it does not sever the child's sense of belonging to the group; and 6. it comes from mature. lovable adults worthy of being emulated.

All too often discipline is a means through which parents express their irritation and annoyance. Children often act in ways which annoy adults, it is true. The love of dirt and of noise and of endless exploration so characteristic of childhood is an affront to the values of adults. There is nevertheless little justification for calling scolding and punishment in such situations good discipline.

Haphazard techniques of discipline are likely to affect the child's feeling of personal worth, and his responses to other people may be adversely affected. Harsh, cruel punishment blocks and distorts the child's feelings for others and shakes his faith in himself. Discipline which alienates and isolates the child casts him outside the group and forbids him the privilege of being loved just when he needs it most! Lax and inconsistent treatment, on the other hand, fails to teach the growing youngster the necessary controls of society, so that he ends up like a ship without a rudder. To be effective, discipline must be administered by adults whose example is worthy of emulation and it should be firm and predictable. To treat a child otherwise is to play fast and loose with his emotions.

Terman's study reveals that firm, but not harsh, discipline accompanied by a close relationship with parents is related to later marriage success.[3] Marriage adjustments are but elaborations and modifications of the relationships built up in childhood.

Look at Alvin, for instance. He is the product of inconsistent discipline. He was the only child of an over-protective widowed mother. At times he felt overwhelmed by her heavy expectations. He spent most of his childhood dodging her passes and demands. He developed

[3] Lewis M. Terman and associates, *Psychological Factors in Marital Happiness* (New York: McGraw-Hill, 1938), pp. 228–231.

elaborate deceits and subterfuges. Then at other times he could get away with anything. He would just creep back into her arms for cuddling whenever one of his escapades had been discovered. His wife must now cope with the weaknesses resulting from the earlier inconsistent discipline. He keeps her frantic with worry, as he did his mother, as he flies from one affair to another, always returning with the little-boy winsomeness that was so effective in dealing with his mother's concern. He has carried over into his marriage the adjustment patterns he developed in his boyhood.

Sally developed quite a different attitude toward people in her childhood. Her parents were fond of her and in love with each other. She was brought up to know what was right and was given opportunities to perfect her skills in being a good girl. Her parents rejoiced in her growth and were understanding and sympathetic when she made mistakes. She and her father were fond of each other. She loved her mother and wanted to be like her when she grew up. By the time she was in her teens she was treated like a young adult in the household, and she thought of her father and mother as persons rather than just as parents. She married a man as emotionally mature as she, and her married life is the natural extension of the fine adjustment she made as a growing girl.

Discipline makes a difference!

EMOTIONAL SATISFACTIONS DESIRED BY HUMAN BEINGS *

AFFECTIONAL, WARM, SECURITY-GIVING SATISFACTIONS

For the infant they come mainly through

Affection. Being cuddled.† Given physical closeness, fondling, etc.

Response. Being attended to when in pain or uncomfortable. Being fussed over, talked to, given attention, etc.

Belongingness. Being cuddled and given physical closeness.†

For the young child they come mainly through

Affection. Continuing cuddling, etc. Verbal as well as tactual demonstrativeness.

Response. (Same as infant response.)

Belongingness. Acceptance by his mother (and closeness to her and later to father).† Having a safe family unit to belong to (i.e., parents harmonious, so that belongingness is not continually threatened).† Being given support when in trouble or doubt (in such a way as to let him feel he still belongs no matter what).†

For the adult they come mainly through

Affection. Tactual demonstrativeness. Verbal demonstrativeness. Being loved.

Response. Friendships — being liked for what one is rather than for what one does. Loyalty. Sympathy. Understanding. Consideration, etc.

Belongingness. Having a place in society at large, i.e., status (which involves likeness with others and differences).

FUNDAMENTAL SENSORY GRATIFICATIONS

For the infant they come mainly through

Sucking.† Cuddling.† General bodily comfort. (Hunger satisfied *without* a prolonged period of waiting.†)

For the young child they come mainly through

Sucking.† Pleasure and interest in elimination: messing.† Masturbation.† General bodily comfort.

For the adult they come mainly through

Satisfying sexual experiences. General bodily comfort.

SELF-ENLARGING, EGO-BUILDING, ADEQUACY-GIVING SATISFACTIONS

For the infant they come mainly through

Achievement. Gaining satisfying response by crying when in pain or when uncomfortable.† Progressively developing body activities.

Recognition. Being admired, having developments noted, etc.

For the young child they come mainly through

Achievement. Self-direction: maintaining independence in regulating own voluntary physiological activities, especially eating and defecation; exploring the environment with all sense modalities carrying through to immediate goals the impulses of the moment. Learning to talk and communicate (progressive symbolization). Being able to accomplish *comfortably* what his parents demand. Physical efficiency.

Recognition. (Same as infant recognition.) Having all accomplishments approved.

For the adult they come mainly through

Achievement. Vocational and/or avocational activities which can be successfully carried through to satisfying goals. Self-direction: being able to take responsibility and to make independent choices. Developing an individuality which one can think well of in spite of a realistic facing of weak spots.

Recognition. Having what one does appreciated and thought well of, admired, followed, etc.

* Adapted with permission from Lee E. Travis and Dorothy W. Baruch, *Personal Problems of Everyday Life* (New York: Appleton-Century, 1941), pp. 80–82.

† Items frequently frustrated in our culture.

CHECK YOURSELF   With the understanding of the basic needs of children gleaned
from the table on page 372, indicate what should be done in each
of the following situations. Mark the course of action you feel would most satisfactorily meet
the child's needs and help him to be stronger in a similar situation next time. Place a (1)
for the action which you feel is the *best* choice. Put a (2) for the courses of action which you
feel *might work*. Mark the statement with an (X) if you feel that the action might be *harmful,*
or *not effective.*

SITUATION 1. *Junior, aged six months, sucks his thumb.*

a _____ Tie his hands down to the mattress so he can't get his fingers to his mouth.
b _____ Let him have a little longer time at the bottle or breast.
c _____ Put a metal thumb guard on his thumb.
d _____ Splint his arm so that he can't bend his elbow.
e _____ Give him a piece of zwieback or toast to suck when he is tired or hungry.
f _____ Scold him severely every time you catch him with his thumb in his mouth.
g _____ Slap his hands every time they go near his mouth.
h _____ Ignore it. Most babies suck their thumbs. He'll outgrow it soon.
i _____ Cuddle him a bit when he is tired and restless.
j _____ Hold him in your arms when you feed him.
k _____ Put bitter aloes on his thumb.
l _____ Take up the matter with your doctor or child guidance specialist.
m _____ Ask your mother what she did.
n _____ Try a little of everything. Something is sure to work.

SITUATION 2. *Sally, aged fifteen, stayed out a whole hour later than she was supposed to last evening.*

a _____ Give her a good bawling out. She should know better.
b _____ Ignore it. She probably didn't realize the time.
c _____ Make her stay in every night this month as punishment.
d _____ Find out whom she was out with and forbid her from seeing him (or them)
again.
e _____ Buy her a good watch.
f _____ Try to find out why she was so late. Listen to her story.
g _____ See what she suggests for getting in on time after this.
h _____ Tell her she can't go out again in the evening until she's big enough to get
back on time.
i _____ Thrash her. You can't let girls roam the streets at all hours of the night.
j _____ Call up the young man who kept her out so long and give him a good talking to.
k _____ Discuss it calmly with her and work out some understanding about future
nights out.
l _____ Say nothing now, but next time she is ready to leave the house remind her
that you expect her in on time.
m _____ Give her an opportunity to help set the hour at which she feels she should
return.

SITUATION 3. *Nineteen-year-old son George, away at school, wants to marry the girl he has been going with the past two years.*

a _____ Absolutely forbid it. He's too young to know his own mind.

b _____ Pretend you don't care whether he does or not.

c _____ Go and visit the girl and get better acquainted with her.

d _____ Write George a letter giving him all the reasons why he should wait.

e _____ Wait until he gets home and then find out how he feels about it.

f _____ Let him do what he thinks best. He's old enough to know his own mind.

g _____ Go right down to visit him and put a finish to the whole affair.

h _____ Tell him if he marries now it will break his mother's heart.

i _____ Talk it over with a sympathetic counselor if it bothers you.

★ KEY

SITUATION 1. Harmful (X): a, c, d, f, g, k, n Might work (2): h, l, m Best choice (1): b, e, i, j

SITUATION 2. Harmful (X): a, c, d, h, i, j Might work (2): b, e, l Best choice (1): f, g, k, m

SITUATION 3. Harmful (X): a, b, g, h Might work (2): c, d, e, f Best choice (1): i

---

Sex Education Is Important Too. Little children learn by watching, imitating, and exploring. This is as true in learning about how their bodies are made and function as in any other area. To get the facts they desire about themselves and others, little children explore 1. by asking questions and talking about how their bodies work, 2. by watching and imitating adults, 3. by looking at the bodies of others, and 4. by feeling and rubbing genitalia. Now it happens, in our culture, that all four of these activities are considered taboo by some adults. Parents are sometimes uncomfortable at seeing little girls running about in abbreviated sunsuits and are shocked to see nursery school children looking at each other at toilet time. A great many parents and teachers have been so frightened by false stories of the evils of masturbation that they severely punish and shame little children who touch their genitalia. Too many adults still are embarrassed by the searching questions and interest of intelligent children naturally concerned about their origin, the functions of their bodies, and the happenings in human and animal families around them. Consequently many children are left at an early age with the impression that there is something dirty and shameful about the sex organs, and something wrong about sexual sensations. Adult embarrassment, uneasiness, and fear are transferred to the child almost without his being aware of it. As he grows older, sex references continue to bring feelings of guilt and shame. Dirty stories,

"Dad, will you bring me home a baby sister like Mom did?"

giggles, and other indirect outlets are found to take the place of the more normal, complete responses of sex love. Feelings of personal unworthiness make it difficult to fall in love with desirable love objects, and control of the powerful sex urges becomes difficult.

Parents who are more wholesomely conditioned and more aware of their own limitations clamor for guidance in the sex education of their children. Few topics are more popular in child study, parent education, and teacher training classes. Books like the following are basic.

SELECTED STARTER LIBRARY IN SEX EDUCATION

Books for Children

BIBBY, CYRIL, *How Life is Handed On* (New York: Emerson, 1947).

DE SCHWEINITZ, KARL, *Growing Up*, Revised Edition (New York: Macmillan, 1953).

CHILD STUDY ASSOCIATION OF AMERICA, *Facts of Life for Children* (New York: The Bobbs-Merrill Company, Inc., 1954).

GRUENBERG, SIDONIE M., *The Wonderful Story of How You Were Born* (Garden City: Hanover House, 1952).

LEVINE, MILTON, and J. H. SELIGMANN, *The Wonder of Life* (New York: Simon and Schuster, 1940).

STRAIN, FRANCES BRUCE, *Being Born* (New York: Appleton-Century, 1938).

Books for Young People

BECK, LESTER, *Human Growth* (New York: Harcourt, Brace, 1949).

DICKERSON, ROY, *So Youth May Know*, Revised Edition (New York: Association Press, 1948).

DUVALL, EVELYN MILLIS, *Facts of Life and Love for Teen-Agers* (New York: Association Press, 1956).

KELIHER, ALICE, *Life and Growth* (New York: Appleton-Century, 1938).

MUSEUM OF SCIENCE AND INDUSTRY, *The Miracle of Growth* (Urbana: University of Illinois Press, 1950).

Books for Parents and Teachers

BIESTER, LILLIAN; WILLIAM GRIFFITHS; and N. O. PEARCE, *Units in Personal Health and Human Relations* (Minneapolis: University of Minnesota Press, 1947).

ECKERT, RALPH G., *Sex Attitudes in the Home* (New York: Association Press, 1956).

KIRKENDALL, LESTER, *Sex Education as Human Relations* (New York: Inor Publishing, 1950).

STRAIN, FRANCES BRUCE, *New Patterns in Sex Teaching*, Revised Edition (New York: Appleton-Century-Crofts, 1951).

——, *Sex Guidance in Family Life Education* (New York: Macmillan, 1948).

——, *The Normal Sex Interests of Children* (New York: Appleton-Century-Crofts, 1948).

Gradually the old taboos are breaking down; parents and children alike are becoming comfortable about sex. The next generation of young people will not have to put up with obstacles now that the paths have been cleared.

Parent-Youth Interaction

The teen years are a time of strain in many a home. It is not unusual for young people to feel that their parents do not understand them. At the same time, parents are often bewildered, baffled, and worried about their teen-age sons and daughters.

Mothers and fathers who were close to their children when they were small are not always the ones who become the confidantes of their young people. The home that has built good lines of communication between parents and children through the years generally enjoys better relationships between the generations during the teens than does the home where the parents have always been too busy or preoccupied to be interested in their children's affairs. But even in the best of homes there is a pulling away from the parents as children become adolescent. There is a certain normal reticence that makes it hard to talk over with parents the very things that matter most to teen-agers.

Marvin Dubbé reports that of his sample of one hundred college freshmen men and women 99 per cent reported some difficulty in communicating with their parents. The high voltage subjects that prove to be the most difficult areas of parent-youth communication are 1. sex and petting, 2. misbehavior, 3. failures and defeats, 4. engagement, 5. health habits, and 6. beliefs. Dr. Dubbé appraises failure in parent-youth communication by saying, "For some the problems were few and slight and could be dismissed as negligible. But the evidence indicates that in 20 to 25 per cent of the young people, barriers of silence produced severe and lasting emotional injury." [4]

There are real reasons why youth cannot be as close to parents as they were as children. The major factor is that the teen years are a time for growing up and away from former dependence upon parents to mature autonomy. A young person feels that he must make his own decisions, choose his own friends, and live his own life free from interference. A teen-ager must stretch away from his parents if he or she is to find himself as a full-fledged person in his own right. There must be a period of finding one's stature as an independent human being before the interdependence of maturity brings the generations closer again as adults.

Every young person tackles certain developmental tasks [5] that must be accomplished if he or she is to emerge into mature adulthood. The developmental tasks of adolescence have been summarized in a text [6] for youth as:

[4] Marvin C. Dubbé, "What Young People Can't Talk over with Their Parents," *The National Parent-Teacher*, October 1957, p. 18.

[5] See Robert J. Havighurst, *Human Development and Education* (New York: Longmans, Green and Company, 1953) for a detailed description of developmental tasks throughout the life of the individual.

[6] Evelyn Millis Duvall, *Family Living* (New York: The Macmillan Company, 1961), especially Chapter 2, "Your Development as a Teen-Ager."

1 Coming to terms with your changing body
2 Getting along with others your age
3 Establishing independence from your parents
4 Achieving adult economic and social status
5 Developing a satisfying sense of who you are

While youth works at the developmental tasks of adolescence, parents are struggling to achieve theirs as middle-aged adults, and families with teen-agers are at work on their developmental tasks as whole families.[7] Issues arise when the developmental tasks of one generation conflict with those of the other. While a youth struggles to be free and independent, his parents recognize that they still have a great stake in his welfare, his decisions and his behavior as a teen-ager. As parents they have nurtured the young person from his earliest days and by now have an immense investment in him. They have gladly spent thousands of dollars and hundreds of thousands of hours in his care and nurturance. They want their children to grow up and become a credit to them. They realize the hazards youth faces in today's world and so naturally they worry about their young people who now make important decisions that will determine their future. The fact that times have changed since they themselves were young widens the gulf between the generations. As you remember from the listing "Ten Recent Trends in Courtship Customs," page 80, the dating and courting practices of your generation are not those that your parents and grandparents know from first hand experience. Some of the new ways of doing things frighten them with their potentials for danger. Other things you do are bewildering to parents who would like to understand you.

Parent-youth interaction can be improved as the two generations talk out what situations mean from both points of view. This can be done in the individual family as young people recognize that their parents have a right to know their plans such as where they are, with whom they are associating, and about what time they may be expected to return home. Parents reciprocate by respecting their young people's judgment, trusting them, and giving them their confidence. Agreeing on what is expected in specific situations helps keep things running smoothly in the family with young people. At the community level, the development of

[7] These are described in detail in Evelyn Millis Duvall, *Family Development* (Chicago: J. B. Lippincott Company, 1957), Chapters 11 and 12, "Families with Teenagers," and "Families as Launching Centers," pp. 289–388.

parent-youth codes in which both generations agree on what is expected of various age-grades through Junior and Senior High School in various types of social situations, have proven to be of great value.

Parent-youth codes usually include the items over which there is confusion and disagreement within a particular community, such as:

1 Hours (for school nights and week-ends, by grade levels)
2 Age at which dating may begin (group, double, and single dating)
3 Conditions under which "going steady" is approved
4 Parents' roles at teen-agers' parties
5 Use of the automobile
6 Teen-agers' earnings, allowances, and responsibility for money
7 Clothing appropriate for various occasions
8 Attitudes (mutual respect, trust, confidence, etc.)

Recognizing that parents are persons with rights and values to which they are entitled is important in getting along with one's parents. Some young people are so preoccupied with their own tasks of growing up that they ignore their parents' wishes and interests and run roughshod over their values to the discomfort of the whole family. As soon as young people become mature enough to treat their parents as human beings entitled to appreciation, honesty, and sincerity in their relationships, the major difficulties of the teen years are over.

One of the occupational hazards of parenthood is that one set of problems is worked through only to have another set appear. By the time parents have worked out some kind of adjustment with their teen-agers, the youngsters are no longer in their teens, but young adults off on their own, leaving mother and father in their empty nest, as you see in the following sketch.

When the Children Have Grown [8]

With a nervous twitch Mrs. Brown stirs the fire in the fireplace. "My, how quiet the house is tonight!" she murmurs to her husband as she settles herself with her knitting beside him.

Yes, it is quiet, too quiet. Mr. and Mrs. Brown are living in an

[8] Two thoughtful articles on the adjustments of parents in the empty-nest stage are available to the reader: Robert M. Dinkel, "Parent-Child Conflict in Minnesota Families," *American Sociological Review*, August, 1943, pp. 412–419; and Robert M. Dinkel, "Attitudes of Children toward Supporting Aged Parents," *American Sociological Review*, August, 1944, pp. 370–379.

empty nest. One by one the children have grown and gone off to college, to work, and to homes of their own. At first there was a peculiar pleasure in being a couple again. The Browns took to fixing up the house and yard, things they couldn't afford to do while there were clothes to buy and tuition to pay for. Now that the house is as they wanted it, it seems but an empty shell. Too bad that it couldn't have been this way when the children were here to enjoy it, that this leisure so anticipated a few years ago has such a taste of dry ashes! Yet that is life, as much a part of life as the bustling days of infancy or the turbulence of adolescence. So, what now, mom and dad?

Two things won't work. You can't follow your children. They have their own lives to live, their own adjustments, their own problems, their own families to raise. When crises come, the old folks will be welcome for a while. But healthy young folks want to be on their own. You can't live in the past without slipping out of today's realities. Memories warm for a while, but the embers die and the gray ashes are cold solace for an empty heart. Fingering old baby shoes and making scrapbooks of the children's past landmarks are week-end busywork, but such fare is pretty thin gruel for the hearty appetites developed through the years of family living.

The only way open is forward. You can't go back. You can't follow the youngsters. You can't stand still. You must go on. Now is the time when you who have been developing interests outside your children go on cultivating them as you always have done. Now there is time for all the things you've always wanted to do . . . to pick up that course, to train for this thing or that, to work for a cause or a movement, to open up a business or take a fling at art!

As we close this section on parenthood it seems fitting to quote from America's Pledge to Children at the Midcentury, a pledge to *all* children from the Midcentury White House Conference on Children and Youth:

PLEDGE TO CHILDREN

TO YOU, our children, who hold within you our most cherished hopes, we the members of the Midcentury White House Conference on Children and Youth, relying on your full response, make this pledge:

From your earliest infancy we give you our love, so that you may grow with trust in yourself and in others.

We will recognize your worth as a person and we will help you to strengthen your sense of belonging.

We will respect your right to be yourself and at the same time help you to understand the rights of others, so that you may experience cooperative living.

We will help you to develop initiative and imagination, so that you may have the opportunity freely to create.

We will encourage your curiosity and your pride in workmanship, so that you may have the satisfaction that comes from achievement.

We will provide the conditions for wholesome play that will add to your learning, to your social experience, and to your happiness.

We will illustrate by precept and example the value of integrity and the importance of moral courage.

We will encourage you always to seek the truth.

We will provide you with all opportunities possible to develop your own faith in God.

We will open the way for you to enjoy the arts and to use them for deepening your understanding of life.

We will work to rid ourselves of prejudice and discrimination, so that together we may achieve a truly democratic society.

We will work to lift the standard of living and to improve our economic practices, so that you may have the material basis for a full life.

We will provide you with rewarding educational opportunities, so that you may develop your talents and contribute to a better world.

We will protect you against exploitation and undue hazards and help you grow in health and strength.

We will work to conserve and improve family life and, as needed, to provide foster care according to your inherent rights.

We will intensify our search for new knowledge in order to guide you more effectively as you develop your potentialities.

As you grow from child to youth to adult, establishing a family life of your own and accepting larger social responsibilities, we will work with you to improve conditions for all children and youth.

SO MAY YOU grow in joy, in faith in God and in man, and in those qualities of vision and of the spirit that will sustain us all and give us new hope for the future.

Aware that these promises to you cannot be fully met in a world at war, we ask you to join us in a firm dedication to the building of a world society based on freedom, justice, and mutual respect.

Readings

BARUCH, DOROTHY W., *How to Discipline Your Children* (New York: Public Affairs Committee, 1949). An unusually helpful pamphlet based upon Dr. Baruch's book, *New Ways in Discipline.*

DUVALL, EVELYN MILLIS, *Family Living* (New York: The Macmillan Company, 1961). Unit II consists of three chapters dealing directly with parent-adolescence interaction, problems in communication between parents and youth, and what it means to be a family member.

ECKERT, RALPH G., *What You Should Know about Parenthood* (Chicago: Science Research Associates, 1953). A provocative review for young people interested in checking how they will rate as parents, and what will happen when they have children of their own.

JENKINS, GLADYS GARDNER, HELEN SHACTER, and WILLIAM W. BAUER, *These Are Your Children* (Chicago: Scott, Foresman and Company, 1949). An attractive manual in child development written for young people.

OSBORNE, ERNEST G., *Understanding Your Parents* (New York: Association Press, 1956). A teen-agers' guide to getting along with the folks at home, compact enough to slip into your pocket for ready reference.

SPOCK, BENJAMIN, *Baby and Child Care* (New York: Pocket Books, Inc., 1957 edition). Widely read and often referred to as the "baby bible." This is a "must" for your personal library if you ever expect to have a baby.

CHAPTER FIFTEEN

We give Thee thanks . . .

FAMILY LIFE AND RELIGIOUS LIVING

When do interfaith marriages work?

What kind of religion should you teach your children?

What is the place of religion in the modern family?

In what way are families and religion interdependent?

$\mathcal{N}$EITHER JOHN NOR I EVER GO TO CHURCH, SO I GUESS THIS chapter does not concern us." This may be the response of some readers; but they are wrong. For whether or not they think that they have anything directly to do with religion and the church they are inescapably involved. In the first place, all of us live in a society in which religious institutions and ideas are prominent and powerful. Sunday may not be devoted to religious purposes, but it is a religious holiday. So also are Christmas, Easter, and Thanksgiving. A large proportion of all marriage ceremonies are performed by clergy. Our ideas and ideals of family relationships reflect to a very considerable extent the influence of the church.[1] However, a family without church connections is not thereby to be regarded as irreligious. Every individual and every family has some kind of religion, good or bad, whether they know it or not. For religion, contrary to widespread misconceptions, is not the same as the church. In fact, some faiths, such as Mohammedanism and Confucianism, do not have church organizations as we understand them. In many societies there is no separate church, as religion is coterminus with the tribe or state. In our culture there is much that is genuinely religious quite outside the church, for religion is basically

---

[1] For the sake of brevity the term "church" will be used in this chapter to designate all types of religious agencies and groups, Jewish as well as Christian.

what a man believes in and lives by. Every individual and every family must have some kind of faith, however limited and inadequate. There-fore we all face such questions as: What kind of religion do we now have, and how sound and satisfactory is it? How deliberate shall be our pursuit of religious goals? Through what institutions and practices can our basic values be most effectively achieved? Fundamental in the an-swering of each of these questions is the query, "What do we as a couple start with?" We shall begin our discussion, then, with the prob-lem of interfaith marriages.

The Question of Interfaith Marriages

Most authorities in the field of marriage including Catholic, Protestant, and Jewish leaders are agreed that interfaith marriage is risky, if not un-desirable. But young people themselves are increasingly disregarding these warnings. An extensive study by John L. Thomas discovers an in-crease for the 132 parishes included in the East and Middle East of the United States.[2] Roughly 30 per cent of all marriages sanctioned by the Roman Catholic Church were interfaith, and his figures show the pro-portion to have increased since 1910.[3] Furthermore, these interfaith marriages were only about 60 per cent of all unions between Catholics and non-Catholics.[4] If these figures are correct, nearly half of all Catho-lics who marry in this country take non-Catholic mates.

Objections to Interfaith Marriage. The attitudes which the major re-ligious faiths have had historically toward interfaith marriages are briefly summarized in Barron's People Who Intermarry.[5] The main reasons for their opposition can be stated briefly as follows:

[2] "The Factor of Religion in the Selection of Marriage Mates," American So-ciological Review (August, 1951), pp. 487–491.

[3] Two studies in intermarriage in New Haven, Connecticut, find that marriages of Catholics and non-Catholics have slightly declined. Ruby J. R. Kennedy, "Single or Triple Melting-Pot? Intermarriage Trends in New Haven, 1870–1940," American Journal of Sociology (January, 1944), pp. 331–339, and A. B. Hollingshead, "Cul-tural Factors in the Selection of Marriage Mates," American Sociological Review (October, 1950), pp. 619–627.

[4] Other studies of Catholic intermarriage are those of C. S. Mihanovitch, Fam-ily Life (December, 1948), p. 6, which indicated 25 per cent, and Judson Landis' study of 4108 families of college students, where he found an interfaith marriage per-centage of 23 per cent, American Sociological Review (June, 1949), pp. 402 ff.

[5] Milton L. Barron, People Who Intermarry (Syracuse: Syracuse University Press, 1946), and "Research on Intermarriage: A Survey of Accomplishments and Prospects," American Journal of Sociology (November, 1951).

Catholic. Catholics regard their religion as the only true faith, the only form of Christianity which is both complete and without error. If a Catholic marries a non-Catholic, he is not to permit the ceremony to be performed by someone other than a Catholic priest. If he does, he is automatically dropped from the Church and lost to the "true faith." If the non-Catholic signs an agreement to bring up all children in the Catholic faith, the priest will perform the ceremony. Even then, the non-Catholic may fail to live up to his agreement. Or, by the very fact of not being himself a Catholic, he may weaken the faith of his children.

Protestant. Many Protestants regard the Catholic religion as being in serious theological error. Those of "sound faith" ought not to run the risk of becoming led astray by "false teaching," or of risking the exposure of their children to it.

Ideological objections are far more common. Many Protestants regard Catholics as being under the domination of an ecclesiastical dictatorship. Unless the Catholic is willing to give up his church, the non-Catholic must agree to bring up his children in a religion which he regards as a relentless foe of his democratic ideals. He feels that no parent has a right to sign away the rights of his children to grow up as free men and women in such arbitrary fashion.

Jewish. Orthodox Judaism regards the preservation of Jewish tradition and practices of utmost importance. Intermarriage threatens the purity and strength of the Jewish faith. Nehemiah, in the Bible, felt so strongly that he cursed, struck, and pulled the hair of Jews married to foreign women. Ezra agonized over this same situation, and finally led a movement to require all Jewish people to divorce foreigners to whom they were married. Many liberal Jews, however, feel quite differently.

All faiths fear what is fairly well proved, that people of mixed marriages are less loyal to any faith than those in which both are members of the same faith.[6]

Religious Difference and Marriage Success

Most people who marry, however, are not religious leaders, nor are they too much concerned about the effects of their marriage upon their church. They want to know, "What will union with a member of another faith do to my marriage?" Let us look at this problem!

The first essential is clearly to understand what an interfaith marriage is. We usually understand that a Catholic–non-Catholic, or a Jewish-

[6] See the results of a study conducted by Murray Leiffer reported in *Time* (January 31, 1949), p. 64.

Gentile marriage is interfaith (although the latter may be primarily intercultural). We know too, that the larger Protestant bodies are so similar that marriage across such lines rarely presents a serious problem. But the teachings and expectations of certain smaller groups, such as Jehovah's Witnesses, Mennonites, and Seventh-Day Adventists, are so much at variance with those of other Protestant groups that intermarriage can cause serious difficulties. Yet marriage to one of the same denomination may also be an interfaith marriage. If one is ultra-conservative and the other liberal, if one regards church as very important and the other as not important, serious clashes over religion may result.

How do such differences affect marriage success? On the whole, differences in religion tend to make success more difficult. All the studies made indicate that the greater the similarity of religious background, the greater the chances of success. The greater the differences, the greater the risks of failure.[7] (For supporting data see the chart, "Religion and Broken Homes.")

Yet mixed marriages can succeed. Many do. If your marriage is mixed, you may have to work harder to make a go of it. But it is by no means doomed to failure. Church affiliation is but one out of a number of factors which can make for failure or success. Far more important are such qualities as character, mental health, and the attitude which you both take toward your differences, religious or otherwise.

The major problem of interfaith marriage will probably emerge when children arrive. Then your church may step in, not only in the person of the priest or minister, but also in the form of Grandma, or even Uncle Jim. Usually the children follow the religion of the mother, regardless of signed agreements or other factors, unless one of the couple is especially strong in his convictions. But in the final analysis, the decision is, or should be, yours. We who write books can do little more than help you know what to expect. Here are some points which you will wish to examine with especial care.

    [7] E. W. Burgess and Leonard S. Cottrell, Jr., *Predicting Success or Failure in Marriage* (New York: Prentice-Hall, 1939), pp. 50–51, 122–126; L. M. Terman and associates, *Psychological Factors in Marital Happiness* (New York: McGraw-Hill, 1938), p. 109; Howard M. Bell, *Youth Tell Their Story* (Washington: American Council on Education, 1938), p. 21; H. Ashley Weeks, "Differential Divorce Rates by Occupation," *Social Forces* (March, 1943), p. 336; and Judson T. Landis, *op. cit.*, p. 404.

1 *How intense is the loyalty of each to his own religious group?* Mary was a Catholic and Jim was a Methodist, but neither of them cared anything about church nor had attended for some time. They were married by a justice of the peace, and after their marriage both continued to stay away from church, even as they had before. Their families made no attempt to interfere. In consequence their differences caused almost no problem.

On the other hand, Bill and Sally, who belonged to two different and extremely narrow sects, each regarded the teachings of his or her church as the only true religious faith, and felt that the other lived in darkness and sin. They had agreed beforehand that each was to go his separate way, but after marriage neither could bear to see the loved one going to hell. Therefore each made ardent efforts to convert the other, in which their families heartily joined. Bill and Sally never divorced or separated, but the constant tension which developed between them embittered the whole relationship and had an especially unfortunate effect upon their children.

RELIGION AND BROKEN HOMES

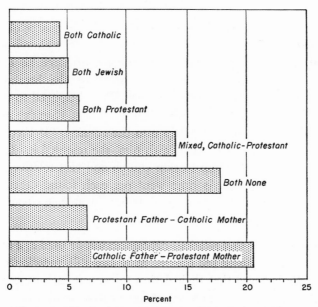

Percentage of Marriages of Mixed and Nonmixed Religious Faiths Ending in Divorce or Separation, 4108 Couples in Michigan, "Marriages of Mixed and Nonmixed Religious Faith" by Judson T. Landis, *American Sociological Review* (June, 1949), Table 1, p. 403.

2 *How many complicating factors are there, such as relatives and influential friends?* The church is not merely a religious body. Specifically it is Mama, Papa, and Uncle Bill. If they object to the faith of the married partner, it is natural that they should bring considerable pressure on behalf of their church, especially as the children are born. Remember that many parents give up their children with considerable reluctance and sometimes welcome any chance to keep a hold on the life of the young adult. Zealous friends and members of the clergy are often eager to push the claims of their church, even when it means bringing serious discord into the marriage.

3 *What aspects of religion does each feel most strongly about?* Some Christians regard dancing or attending movies on the Sabbath as a sin, whereas others openly encourage such activities. Among Jewish groups the conflict between those who observe Kosher and other orthodox regulations and those who disregard them may prove to be painful. Seeing the person to whom you are married freely indulge in activities which you have been brought up to regard as immoral is inevitably a strain on the whole relationship. Differences in theology indicated by such terms as "modernism" and "fundamentalism" may also cause difficulties.

Another phase of this issue concerns the whole matter of actively supporting the church. Fred believed strongly in the church and was an ardent worker in its activities. Before his marriage he had been president of the local Christian Endeavor. Later he became superintendent of the Sunday school. His wife, Ellen, belonged to the same church but was decidedly lukewarm in her interests. Sunday mornings she wanted to sleep, or take a trip into the country. If Fred insisted that she get up and go to church with him, she resented it. On a few occasions she persuaded him to skip church and visit relatives, and he felt guilty and disloyal. As time went on, each found other persons more sympathetic to their own interests, and wondered about the desirability of their marriage.

4 *Is there danger that religious differences will be used as a means by which one can dominate the other?* Sally and Bill, mentioned above, both honestly believed that their desires to convert each other were inspired solely by religious motives. A psychiatrist would have thought differently; he would have seen in their efforts subconscious attempts to dominate, with their religious ardor used as a smoke screen behind which to conceal their desire to control. So it often is, as we have suggested, with interfering family members.

5 *Are there other strong bonds to compensate for the religious difference?* Doris was a highly educated Catholic of the liberal group. Jacob was a reformed Jew. Both, however, regarded their respective religious groups primarily as social institutions designed to perform social functions. Both were vitally interested in good housing, the improvement of government, and all efforts for social welfare. The children, when they came, were given a social interpretation of the religious groups, and as they grew up were encouraged to choose their own affiliations. This breadth of attitude made possible not only a harmonious, but an enriched relationship which brought them close together. Their marriage was successful because both were actually of the same religion: the religion of humanity. When the fundamental values of each are similar, the religious label is of little importance.

6 *What compromises are both willing to make to solve the problem?* The church relationships of many people are nominal. They have no serious emotional attachments to any denomination or group. If this is true of both members of the couple and also of their families, a difference of denomination may represent little difficulty. They will probably solve the problem by belonging to no church at all. When a marriage partnership consists of one member who is very devout while the other has no strongly held religious convictions or antipathies, the problem is also not impossible. The indifferent one will just turn the whole matter over to the other. If the two have real and conflicting convictions, or if their families have, the problem can seldom be easily solved. Sometimes one will yield to the extent of agreeing to bring up the children in the faith of the other, as non-Catholics who are married by a Catholic priest are required to do. One member of the couple may adopt the faith of the other. Neither of these solutions is likely to prove happy. However sincere the individual making the change may be, there is an element of duress involved. "She" would not have changed had it not been necessary in order to get her husband. Religion is largely a matter of early emotional experiences, powerfully related to family loyalties. One cannot change these as he would a garment. After marriage both husband and wife find that the one who supposedly

changed is still what he was brought up to be and that it is impossible for him to be anything else.

Young people can hardly be expected to be more rational in religion than they are in other matters related to marriage. Emotional factors will pull them on, for weal or for woe. Those who are determined to cross faith lines, however, can increase the likelihood of success by frankly facing the situation and coming to some agreements *before the marriage.* These should involve specific and definite decisions on such questions as the following:

1 Who, if either, will change his church relationships? If this is done at all it should be done before the wedding.
2 If each retains his separate faith, where will they attend church, if at all?
3 In what faith, if any, will the children be brought up?
4 Are parents and relatives to be consulted? This is one of the most crucial and difficult problems, since parental approval is significantly related to later success of the marriage. Shall we keep our parents informed as we go along, or just keep quiet about the whole matter, marry, and let them howl about a *fait accompli?* The latter policy has in some instances proved to be the less difficult. It also has its risks.

Religion and Family Living

Although church groups have always been interested in families, in recent years this interest has increased remarkably. At first such interest was scattered and often negative. Clergy denounced and "viewed with alarm" the increase in divorce. Then here and there a minister began to take a more constructive attitude, and to do marriage counseling on a sounder basis. The increased interest of church groups became evident in the widespread adoption of "Mother's Day," which was in time expanded into National Family Week. In recent years this has become a national program in which churches of all three major faiths participate.

In recent years, denominational groups have established extensive programs. Departments of the Christian Family have been established, and an increasing literature developed. The Roman Catholic Church has an extensive program for training its members for marriage and family living, in the Cana and pre-Cana conferences. The Methodists have held national conferences on family life which have been attended by thousands. Jewish groups have given increasing attention to what has always been the center of their religious program: family life.

This rising concern has good basis in past religious traditions. Marriage, baptism, and the burial of the dead are religious rites which indicate the length and the depth of the concern of religion with families. Clergy have always counseled with, and given support to families as a regular part of their duties. The theology of religious faith has made extensive use of family terms, such as the Fatherhood of God and the Brotherhood of Man. Yes, the relationship between religion and family life has been central and prolonged. Why?

The Church Needs the Family. With few exceptions, people belong to and support churches because they have been taught to do so by their parents. Some parents contribute considerably to the religious education of their children. They read them Bible stories, or drill them in the catechism. In Judaism the main responsibility for the teaching of religion belongs to the family, not to the synagogue. A recent report states that in present-day Poland, every rabbi has been killed, yet the Jewish religion survives because it is being carried on by the families. Most Christians in America depend upon churches for the teaching of religion to their children. Yet it is the parents who largely support these churches, and develop loyalties in their children for them. Without such family support, no church could long continue without crippling losses. These facts are well understood. Less well understood is the relationship of family life to the central teachings of religion.

Families Lay the Basis for Religious Teaching. Religion has not only a knowledge, but an emotional or feeling aspect. The knowledges of religion can probably be taught better by specially trained teachers than by most parents. But for some teachings (including some of the knowledges) experience in family living seems essential. A church may teach that God is Love. But love can have meaning only for those who have already experienced it. Most people, especially children, are not likely to have had such experience outside their families. And how can a child understand about trust and faith in God, unless he has had experiences with people whom he could trust, and in whom he had faith? How many teachings of religion can be understood, only by those who have had a background of appropriate experiences in their own families!

So it is with religious loyalties. Religion will be important for most children only if they see that it is important to their parents. Parents may be able to give their children some *knowledge* about religion, merely by sending them to a church school where they will be taught by someone else. But religious attitudes and loyalties are usually learned only from parents who participate in and themselves support church activities.

What Shall We Teach Our Children? This question has in part already been answered. Our example teaches them much, whether we will or no. In the matter of direct instruction, those who belong to conservative groups have the simpler task. Their denomination usually has clear statements of its doctrines, often printed in a catechism. The task of the parent is to help the children memorize these statements. But for parents who hold "liberal" views, the task is often difficult. The impact of a scientific point of view makes them uncertain about religious doctrines. They see sincerely religious people who make messes of their lives and those of their children. They find it hard to see how religion has contributed materially to a solution of important social problems, such as war. They sense that there is something important in religion which their children should have. But what is this "something"? Because of their own uncertainties, they either do not try to teach their children anything about religion, or they are so "wobbly" and tentative in their teaching that nothing much results. Often they feel quite guilty about their failures. But what can they do? After all, you can hardly teach your children what you do not have yourself! The discussion which follows is intended to help those who are bewildered, as well as those who feel more confident.

What Is a Religious Family?

Many people define a religious family as a nice, ordinary, respectable family with a religious "plus." This "plus" usually includes beliefs (as in God, Christ, the Bible, or the Church), practices (church going, prayers, and Bible reading), and probably a rather high moral standard. This, however, is a family with religion, not a religious family. (See the diagram, p. 325, which illustrates the difference.) Religion at its best is not an addition to life, but a transformation of life. A religious family does not merely add a religious "plus." It is a family organized around religious ideals. This religious core relates all aspects of life

FAMILY AND RELIGION

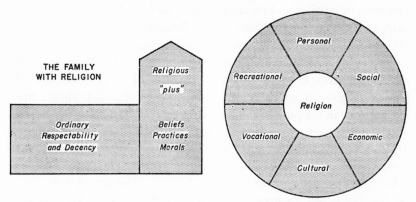

THE RELIGIOUS FAMILY

meaningfully to each other, and transfuses them with religious ideals. As a result, life is unified and takes on new meaning and basic worth. For the religious family, religion is not a set of often burdensome obligations. It gives to family life meaning and purpose, and is a source of wisdom, insight, and power.

Living Religion in the Family. The religious quality of a family is not to be judged by the fidelity with which parents teach their religious views to their children. Neither is it to be determined by the forms and ceremonies observed. Some will find prayers, especially at mealtime, to be a natural and helpful expression of religious faith. But whatever the form, we may expect considerable variation.

Prayer, for instance, has come down through the ages in a multitude of forms. For some it is formalized and structured, the very words being prescribed, yet for others it may be exceedingly spontaneous. A little girl shocked her formally religious parents by bursting out in her anxiety one evening with the prayer, "Oh, God, be with us, don't leave us now. If you do we're sunk." Surprising as this was to her parents who were accustomed to other ways of addressing the deity, the child's words had many of the elements which have caused prayer to persist so long as a satisfying form of religious expression.

Man's sense of his dependence upon forces outside of himself has led him from time to time to clarify his situation, analyze himself, unify his efforts, and solve his problems with capacities that emerge out of the dynamics of the prayerful attitude. Aside from supernatural implications, this approach is still sound, whether the rite be fixed or flexible. Similarly, other rites and practices of religion have their roots in human need and satisfaction and continue to have meaning for people to the extent to which they have been found effective.

But religion is not primarily a matter of beliefs, practices, or institutional relationships. It is primarily a matter of inner response. The type of religion to which a man can respond depends primarily upon the previous development of his own inner life. Crude, spiritually undeveloped persons will necessarily have a primitive and often tribal religion, regardless of what it is called. In reading of wars of religion or persecutions made in the name of religious faith, we have often thought, "How could religious people do such things?" The reason is that their religious faith was an expression of the kind of persons they were inside, and the label of "Christian" or whatever had little to do with their actions. We have often bewailed the distortion of Christian teachings by its avowed followers, but we need not be surprised. Exalted spiritual teachings can be understood only by those spiritually ready for them. If offered to others, they must inevitably be either rejected or distorted. Love can have meaning only for those who have experienced it. And for most, a sufficient experience can come only within the family circle. So it is with ideals of brotherhood, truth, and honor, even with the very concept of spirituality itself. Religion is like a skillful woodworker: he can make great and beautiful things only if he has the wood. The spiritual life can be built only if the materials for it already exist. The significance of the home for a truly spiritual religion is most important. So far as most people are concerned, only in the home can the inner attitudes develop which make a truly spiritual religion even possible.

In the development of religion within the family, the truly important consideration is the spirit which dominates all relationships. If religious teaching is to be effective, it must be inculcated into children as a normal result of the processes of living. In the final analysis the problem is not the teaching of religion in the family; it is rather to make the family religious.

The religious family derives its meaning and significance from purposes beyond itself. Many young people think of marriage in terms of their own personal satisfactions. When they think of an ideal situation they see a lovely house in the suburbs surrounded by shrubs; they think of a good social status, a suitable car, and a salary big enough to keep all these going without pinching. "We'll build a sweet little nest, somewhere in the West, and let the rest of the world go by," is a popular sentiment, but it is not religious. The truly religious person thinks of marriage rather in terms of establishing a cooperative unit of human relationships for the purpose of fulfilling religious objectives. This means, to begin with, that the family will be so conducted as best to satisfy the personality needs of its members. Husband and wife will give each other, and their children, that security of relationship which is a normal need of all.

The religious family will not, and cannot, remain isolated or complete within itself. Of necessity it will reach out into the community in wholesome and constructive activities. Religious parents will be active not only in personal social contacts, but in efforts to promote the well-being of the community. Children will take it for granted that their parents will participate in worth-while enterprises. One of the best descriptions of such religious family activities is to be found in the following testimony of Pearl Buck:

. . . I know my mother loved her children with all her heart, but certainly she never loved us with all her time. But we shared everything with her. She took us to her religious meetings and we went with her when she dispensed food and money to the poor and we helped her with her clinics and her housekeeping equally. We were pressed into every sort of service — not in her case for any obvious training of us, but simply because she had to have help. She was deeply involved in life and she involved us with her. We were early familiar with the sight of hunger and death and we knew because we had heard them the life problems of our surroundings. The result was that without knowing it I grew up hating sorrow and hardship but not afraid of either. I learned so early how to look on death that I cannot remember horror at a dead face. By the time I was grown a lot of the clutter of childhood was out of the way and without personal pain or even knowledge that I was learning I had learned what life is.

. . . The realities of life are not sad or dreary. Life is good to the very last drop, and evil and sorrow and grief are part of the whole. For the person whose home had been a part of the world the balance is never afterwards wrong. He will never be hopeless or despairing because he knows from the moment that he knows anything that there is evil and sorrow as there is also good and happiness, and he is not frightened as he would be if for all his childhood years he had been taught that real life was happiness and plenty and then found out that it is not. The anxiety with which so many of us face life and live life comes from the longing to get back into what we were taught as children, that happiness is the normal, the real atmosphere — that plenty and safety and security are to be expected. The truth is that nothing in life can be expected — the joy of living is to take what comes and fight against it or accept it — but live, and not try all the time to escape living and get away into some romantic refuge where everything ends happily.[8]

Community activities, if overdone, may indicate a basic dissatisfaction with the home and a desire to escape from its responsibilities. On the other hand, unless both parents get out to some extent (and this means the wife as well as the husband) they will not have much to contribute to the more intimate personal relationships of the family. Religious parents try to keep a sound balance between chasing around so much that family relationships are neglected, and sticking around so closely that they become dull and uninteresting, and constantly in the way. This balance is a natural consequence of recognizing that the meaning and significance of the family lies in values which exist outside and beyond itself.

The family, like the individual, finds its life in losing it in the large world. Just as the church steeple stands as a symbol of religion in the community, so the religious family stands out as a center of strength in every neighborhood. The family that is genuinely stable and secure within itself does more than spiritually nourish its own members. It finds itself called upon to share these strengths with neighbors and friends. Good families are the living cells of society: its sustaining pillars and its strength.

Readings

BLACK, ALGERNON D., *If I Marry Outside My Religion* (New York: Public Affairs Pamphlets, 1954). A clearly written summary of what the chief obstacles to mixed marriages are, the positions of the various religious bodies, and what can be expected as reactions from friends and families if you marry outside your own church.

BOSSARD, JAMES H. S., and ELEANOR S. BOLL, *One Marriage Two Faiths* (New York: The Ronald Press Company, 1957). Guidance on interfaith marriage written by a famous team of social research scientists out of firsthand case material.

BRAV, STANLEY R., ed., *Marriage and the Jewish Tradition* (New York: Philosophical Library, 1951). An impressive picture of modern Jewish

[8] Pearl S. Buck, "At Home in the World," *Marriage and Family Living*, February, 1942.

thought about marriage and family life written by more than a dozen outstanding Jewish social scientists and rabbis.

BRO, MARGUERITE HARMON, *When Children Ask* (New York: Harper & Brothers, 1956 edition). Helpful answers to children's most difficult questions about God, prayer, the church, death, resurrection, and Jesus and his teaching.

FAIRCHILD, ROY W., and JOHN CHARLES WYNN, *Families in the Church: A Protestant Survey* (New York: Association Press, 1961), A study of how American Protestant families live, think and respond to their churches.

PIKE, JAMES A., *If You Marry Outside Your Faith* (New York: Harper & Brothers, 1954). Counsel on mixed marriages by the renowned Bishop of the Episcopal Diocese of California.

THOMAS, JOHN L., *The American Catholic Family* (Englewood Cliffs, New Jersey: Prentice-Hall, Inc., 1956). A solid scientific study of how American Catholics are working out their marriage and family living.